W9-DFE-697

2012 STATE OF BLACK AMERICA®

★★★★★★★★★★★★★★★★★★★★★★★★★★★★★★★★★★★★★★

OCCUPY ᵗʰᵉ VOTE

★★★★★★★★★★★★★★★★★★★★★★★★★★★★★★★★★★★★★★

ⓣₒ EDUCATE, EMPLOY & EMPOWER

Contributors

Jacqueline Ayers

Lloyd C. Blankfein

Allie L. Braswell, Jr.

Gregory E. Carr, Ph.D., J.D.

Anna Maria Chávez

Garrick T. Davis

Amara C. Enyia, Ph.D., J.D.

Tatiana Garcia-Granados

Senator Kirsten Gillibrand

Chanelle P. Hardy, Esq.

Maria Rosario Jackson, Ph.D.

Haile Johnston

John Michael Lee

John Legend

Desireé Luckey

Darlene Marlin

James T. McLawhorn, Jr.

Marc H. Morial

Mayor Michael A. Nutter

Dr. Steve Perry

Kevin Powell

Tafaya Ransom

Nolan V. Rollins

Shari E. Runner

Congressman Robert C. "Bobby" Scott

Lee Shaw, Jr.

Hal Smith, Ed.D.

Steve Stoute

Madura Wijewardena

Valerie Rawlston Wilson, Ph.D.

Reverend Lennox Yearwood, Jr.

A
NATIONAL URBAN LEAGUE
PUBLICATION

R05012 60462

2012 STATE OF BLACK AMERICA

*Occupy the Vote to Educate,
Employ & Empower*

Editor-in-Chief

Chanelle P. Hardy, Esq.

Managing Editor

Hazeen Y. Ashby, Esq.

Managing Director

Amber C. Jaynes

Creative Director

Rhonda Spears Bell

Staff Editors

Jacqueline Ayers, Suzanne Bergeron,
Garrick T. Davis, Valerie Wilson and
Madura Wijewardena

Business Manager

Cara McKinley

_____

Design

Untuck Design

TABLE OF
CONTENTS

FROM THE PRESIDENT'S DESK

MARC H. MORIAL
PRESIDENT & CEO, NATIONAL URBAN LEAGUE

More than the economy, more than jobs, more than an excellent education for all children, the single issue that arguably stands to have the greatest impact on the future of Black America in 2012 is the vote. As Congress wrestles over measures to create jobs and grow the economy, a multi-state effort is underway to exclude those Americans most profoundly affected by the political process. More than half a century after the Voting Rights Act of 1965 was passed, protecting the Constitutional right to vote from infringement by poll taxes, literacy tests or other barriers, we continue fighting the very same battle. In 2011, claiming the threat of voter fraud,[1] 34 states attempted to pass legislation that would require a government-issued photo ID, shorten voting hours, curtail early voting, and/or impose absurd penalties limiting the registration process.[2] Despite the efforts of civil rights groups, social justice organizations and labor unions—including efforts that lead to a heartening victory in Ohio—these bills have become law in 14 states, with bills in 26 states still pending.[3]

This coordinated attack on the rights of citizens to participate in their government comes at a particularly perilous time for the poor and communities of color. With an African American unemployment rate still hovering above 13%, a Latino unemployment rate of nearly 11%, and the rate for white Americans still far above the level of full employment, the Washington, DC, obsession with slashing the federal budget is premature at best. The ongoing foreclosure crisis, staggering student loan debt and a failure to invest in education and training to prepare today's and tomorrow's workforce to thrive in an increasingly competitive global marketplace have stripped too many Americans of supports that are absent from the trickle-down economic framework.

The wealth gap and the system of privilege that has given advantage to the richest 1% of Americans at the expense of the other 99% made headlines this year with the genesis of the Occupy Wall Street movement. Hence, in the current environment, the most appropriate theme for this year's publication is *The State of Black America 2012: Occupy the Vote to Educate, Employ and Empower.* If we are to address the challenges facing those served by the National Urban League, we must start with the vote. We must fight voter suppression, we must educate citizens so that new laws won't catch them unaware on Election Day, and we must empower them to get to the polls.

This edition of *The State of Black America 2012* examines how increased civic participation by people of color will propel urban communities to educational and employment success, empowering those communities and in turn this nation. *The State of Black America 2012* begins with essays from Virginia Congressman, Robert C. "Bobby" Scott, and President of the Hip Hop Caucus, Reverend Lennox Yearwood, Jr. Congressman Scott discusses equal voting rights, while Reverend Yearwood explains how current voting rights legislation is a new form of Jim Crow laws aimed at keeping people of color from accessing their right to vote. These two are a must-read for those concerned about improving the well-being of both the African American community and the nation as a whole.

> We must fight voter suppression, we must educate citizens so that new laws won't catch them unaware on Election Day, and we must empower them to get to the polls.

A special education section, entitled *Should I Go to College?* features an interview with singer, songwriter, Grammy Award winner

and founder of the Show Me Campaign, John Legend; an essay from Dr. Steve Perry, founder of Capital Preparatory Magnet School and CNN Education Contributor, and several other notable contributions by educational advocates and scholars and the National Urban League's first-ever student essay contest winner from Howard University. These authors share their insights into how and why we should continue to promote college and technical programs attendance and completion even as tuition costs and unemployment rates for college graduates remain high. These pieces discuss the role of communities and public policies in providing students and families with the tools and information needed to make educational attainment an integral component of a sustainable career. It is our hope that this special section will remind communities of color they must continue to strive for equal education—through traditional or vocational means—if we wish to attain economic parity. However, we cannot win the fight to fund schools equally or make college tuition affordable for people of color without increased civic participation.

The State of Black America 2012 also features contributions from U.S. Senator Kirsten Gillibrand, Philadelphia Mayor Michael A. Nutter, Goldman Sachs CEO Lloyd C. Blankfein and Founder and CEO of Translation LLC, Steve Stoute. These authors discuss how career and technical education and investments in entrepreneurship drive job creation; how the fight against childhood obesity is critical to producing the next generation of healthy productive students and workers vis-à-vis the Fresh Food Movement; and how the National Urban League is partnering with the Goldman Sachs *10,000 Small Businesses Initiative* to create and sustain more black-owned businesses.

While a majority of the publication is focused upon steps to achieve the Urban League mission of economic equality, it also offers a glimmer of hope after the bleakness of a protracted recession—affiliate highlights celebrating the successes of the Urban League Movement in combating the rise of poverty in urban communities across the nation.

The Chicago Urban League is recognized for its focus upon educating teens to engender them with an entrepreneurial spirit. The Columbia (South Carolina) Urban League and Central Florida Urban League (Orlando) are featured for their work to aid African American and minority war heroes in accessing the resources they need to be economically self-sufficient in the face of disproportionate joblessness and homelessness. The Urban League of Greater New Orleans shares its entrepreneurial and rebuilding spirit as it works within the New Market Tax Credit paradigm to attract investment capital to low-income communities.

Although the state of Black America is not yet what we want it to be, in the 2012 elections, African Americans hold an important key to addressing the issues which plague our urban communities. It is my hope that this publication will inspire those that read it to Occupy the Vote to Educate, Employ and Empower all of America.

NOTES

[1] The Brennan Center for Justice at New York University School of Law, "The Truth about Voter Fraud," (*http://www.truthaboutfraud.org/case_studies_by_issue/*) (Accessed February 1, 2012)

[2] National Conference of State Legislators, "Voter ID Legislation 2012," (*http://www.ncsl.org/legislatures-elections/elections-campaigns/voter-id-2012-legislation.aspx*) (Accessed February 1, 2012)

[3] National Conference of State Legislators, "Voter ID Legislation 2012," (*http://www.ncsl.org/legislatures-elections/elections-campaigns/voter-id-2012-legislation.aspx*) (Accessed February 1, 2012)

INTRODUCTION TO THE 2012

EQUALITY INDEX

VALERIE RAWLSTON WILSON, PH.D.
NATIONAL URBAN LEAGUE POLICY INSTITUTE

The 2012 presidential campaign season is off to a running start and it is already clear that voters will be keenly focused on one thing—who will be the best candidate to restore traditional avenues into a strong middle class through widely accessible employment and educational opportunities. After a season of various "Occupy" protests across the country, Americans have expressed in no uncertain terms that they will no longer accept the growing income inequality that characterized the last decade. But as the 2012 Equality Index shows, the pursuit of equal opportunity has long been and continues to be a priority for Americans of color.

We begin with an overview of the 2012 Equality Indices of Black America and Hispanic America, focusing on those areas where the most change was observed relative to the 2011 Equality Index. We then discuss the status of the quest for equality in the areas of education and employment, two of the key ingredients for restoring America's middle class and the central theme of *The State of Black America 2012*.

INTERPRETING THE EQUALITY INDEX

The Equality Index measures the relative status of blacks, Latinos and whites in five areas of American society—economics, health, education, social justice, and civic engagement. For any given measure, the index is calculated as the ratio of the value for blacks (or Latinos) to that of whites.[1] To use median household income as an example, an index of 62% = $33,578/$54,168, where $33,578 is the median household income for blacks and $54,168 is the median household income for whites. Full equality is indicated by an index of 100%. Therefore, an Equality Index less than 100% suggests that blacks (or Latinos) are lagging behind whites, and an Equality Index greater than 100% suggests that blacks (or Latinos) are exceeding whites.

The overall Equality Index is a weighted average of indices calculated for each of the five sub-categories—economics, health, education, social justice and civic engagement. The indices for each of the five sub-categories are themselves weighted averages of indices calculated from individual variables (like the example of median household income used above) available from nationally representative data sources. The appropriate data sources and data years are indicated in the accompanying tables at the end of this chapter.

What's New in the 2012 Equality Index of Black America?

The 2012 Equality Index of Black America stands at 71.5% compared to a revised 2011 index of 71.4%. Revisions to the previous year's index are done for greater comparability across years and reflect data points that have been corrected, changed, removed from the current year's index or re-weighted so that less emphasis is placed on older data. In a ranking of the five broad categories included in the Equality Index, the most inequality between black and white Americans is in the area of economics (56.3%) followed by social justice (56.8%), health (76.5%), education (79.7%) and civic engagement (98.3%). Relative to last year's Equality Index, there was little change in 2012 because improvements in health (from 75% to 76.5%) and education (from 79% to 79.7%) were offset by a loss of ground in the other three areas—civic engagement (from 101.8% to 98.3%), social justice (from 58% to 56.8%) and economics (from 56.6% to 56.3%). A comparison of the revised 2011 and 2012 Equality Index is shown in Figure 1.

Civic engagement is typically the one area where Black America exceeds equality with White America. But in 2012, this index fell below 100% for only the second time in eight years. The decline in this year's civic engagement index was the result of a common trend in reduced voter registration and participation in non-presidential election years, but given the record numbers of registered voters and voter turnout for 2008, the contrast with 2010 was even more pronounced. As a result, the black-white voter registration index fell from 95% in 2011 to 92% in 2012 and the black-white voter participation index fell from 98% in 2011 to 90% in 2012.

The second largest decline was in the area of social justice. The decline here was driven primarily by increased occurrences of African Americans being stopped while driving as occurrences among whites decreased. The black-white stopped while driving index fell from 110% in 2011 to 95% in 2012.

The lost ground in civic engagement and social justice was partially offset by gains in health. Specifically, for African Americans, there were -23.4 fewer deaths per 100,000 people, but an additional 2.9 deaths for whites. This raised the black-white death rate index from 78% in 2011 to 80% in 2012. There was also some reduction in illicit drug and tobacco use by African Americans relative to whites, improving each of these indices by 10 percentage points and 5 percentage points, respectively. Finally, there was some progress in the number of children's AIDS cases for African Americans that raised the index for this variable from 7% in 2011 to 22% in 2012. Yet, despite this small step forward, African-American children remain far more vulnerable to contracting AIDS than white children.

The 2012 Equality Index of Black America stands at 71.5% compared to a revised 2011 index of 71.4%.

Long-term Trends in the Equality Index
Over the lifetime of the Equality Index of Black America, progress has been mixed at best. For example, the black-white index of median household income has remained stubbornly unchanged at around 61% since the Equality Index was introduced in 2005 while the indices

for the unemployment rate, the uninsured, the incarceration rate, and prisoners as a percent of arrests have increased. These increases represent areas of modest, but growing, equality. On the other hand, there has been a decline in the indices for the poverty rate, the homeownership rate, educational attainment (both high school and bachelor's degrees), and school enrollment rates (both preprimary and college), indicating areas of growing inequality. (See Figure 2)

The Equality Index of Hispanic America
The National Urban League introduced the Equality Index of Hispanic America[2] in 2010 as a way to expand the discussion of inequality in America to reflect both the shifting demographics of this country and many of the communities served by Urban League affiliates. The 2012 Equality Index of Hispanic America stands at 76.1% compared to a revised 2011 index of 76.7%. Like in Black America, a ranking of the five Equality Index categories reveals that economics (60.8%) and social justice (60.9%) are the areas of greatest inequality between Hispanic and (non-Hispanic) white Americans, followed by civic engagement (67.4%), education (75.8%), and health (104.4%). In 2012, Latinos lost ground, relative to their white counterparts, in the areas of civic engagement (from 71.7% to 67.4%) and social justice (from 63.5% to 60.9%), but experienced little or no change in the other three areas—health (from 104.8% to 104.4%), economics (unchanged at 60.8%) and education (from 75.1% to 75.8%). Figure 3 provides a comparison of the revised 2011 and 2012 Hispanic Equality Index.

Lost ground in civic engagement was due almost entirely to a disproportionate decline in Latino voter registration and voter participation relative to that of whites. Between 2008 and

Figure 1: *Change in Equality Index of Black America, 2011–2012*

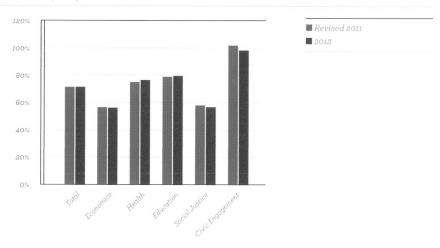

Figure 2: *2005/2012 Comparison of Selected Equality Index Variables*

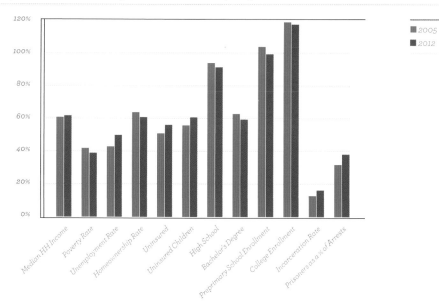

2010 election cycles, the share of registered Latino voters declined by -7.8 percentage points, compared to a decline of -5.3 percentage points in the share of registered white voters. These changes decreased the voter registration index from 81% in 2011 to 76% in 2012. The share of the Latino population that voted in the 2010 elections was -18.7 percentage points lower than in 2008, compared to -17.5 percentage points lower for whites, shifting the voter participation index from 75% in 2011 to 64% in 2012.

The social justice index declined as occurrences of being stopped while driving and rates of incarceration increased for Latinos, but decreased for whites. As a result, the stopped while driving index fell from 100% in 2011 to 92% in 2012 and the incarceration index fell from 40% in 2011 to 37% in 2012.

The Quest for Equality in Employment and Education

In the United States and around the world, education often serves as the pathway to economic empowerment and to a better life. However, the 2012 Equality Index suggests that there are clearly some obstructions along this path for African Americans and Latinos. For Black America, despite an education index of nearly 80%, the economic index hovers around 56%. For Hispanic America the story is similar—the education index is about 76% while the economic index is only 61%. More specifically, employment outcomes for blacks and Latinos are just a fraction of what their white counterparts enjoy. Moderate progress toward closing the persistent 2-to-1 unemployment rate gap between blacks and whites in this country was reversed during the Great Recession and as this year's index shows, just over half of the working-age black population was gainfully employed (measured by the employment-population ratio), compared to nearly 60% of working-age whites. For Latinos, the unemployment rate was 1.4 times that of whites, but the share of gainfully employed working-age Latinos was essentially the same as that of whites.

The education index tells a story of highs and lows in education-related outcomes for African Americans and Latinos in this country. Whereas African Americans rival or even exceed whites at most levels of school

Figure 3: Change in Equality Index of Hispanic America, 2011–2012

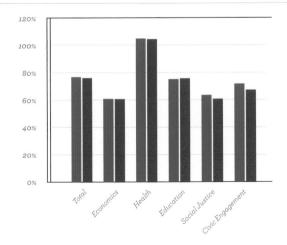

enrollment, there are some clear deficiencies in attainment and other areas that contribute to success within the educational arena and beyond. For example, only 40% of African-American college entrants actually complete a degree compared to 60% of white entrants. Almost half of all Latino college entrants complete a degree although their school enrollment rates tend to be lower and they have higher rates of high school dropout than both whites and blacks. Having a college degree greatly reduces the likelihood of unemployment and results in higher earnings over one's lifetime.

The 2012 Equality Index of Hispanic America stands at 76.1% compared to a revised 2011 index of 76.7%.

At the elementary to secondary school levels, African-American children are more than three times as likely as white children to live in poverty and nearly four times more likely to live in a home with no parent in the labor force. Furthermore, African-American public school students are more than two times as likely as white students to repeat a grade or be suspended and more than three and a half times as likely to be expelled. Rates of poverty among Latino children are similar to those of black children and they are 1.4 times more likely to repeat a grade and 1.2 times more

likely to be suspended, compared to whites. Each of these factors can be detrimental to a child's engagement in the educational process, detracting from their immediate and long-term success.

Conclusion

Based on this analysis of the 2012 Equality Index, it is clear that increased participation in the electoral process will be critical, not only in raising the numerical value of the Equality Indices of Black America and Hispanic America for 2013, but more importantly in raising the quality of life for African-American and Latino families. Each of the other areas of the Equality Index can be impacted when African-American and Latino voters choose to make their voices heard. So, will good paying jobs be created in urban communities? Will people continue to live longer and have access to health care? Will all children have an equal opportunity for a quality education? Will there be equal treatment under the law, regardless of an individual's race? Though the quest for equal opportunity will likely continue well beyond the 2012 elections, the answer to each of these questions begins with just one vote.

NOTES

[1] For negative outcomes like death rates or incarceration rates, the ratio is white-to-black so that the interpretation of the index (less than 100% suggests that blacks are doing worse relative to whites, and greater than 100% suggests that blacks are doing better than whites) is preserved.

[2] The Hispanic Equality Index is calculated similarly to the Equality Index of Black America, except that several data points used to calculate the black-white index were not available for Hispanics. To compensate for the unavailable data points, weights are redistributed among the available variables.

UNDERSTANDING THE

EQUALITY INDEX

MADURA WIJEWARDENA
NATIONAL URBAN LEAGUE POLICY INSTITUTE

WHY DOES THE NATIONAL URBAN LEAGUE PUBLISH AN EQUALITY INDEX?

Economic empowerment is the central theme of the National Urban League's mission. The Equality Index gives us a way to quantify progress toward this mission.

WHAT IS THE EQUALITY INDEX TRYING TO DO?

Imagine if we were to summarize how well African Americans and Hispanics are doing, compared to whites, in the areas of economics, health, education, social justice and civic engagement, and represent this with a pie.

The Equality Index measures the share of that pie which African Americans and Hispanics get. Whites are used as the benchmark because the history of race in America created advantages for whites that continue to affect access to opportunity.

2012 Equality Index of Black America is 71.5%. What does that mean?

That means that rather than having a whole pie (100%), which would mean full equality with whites in 2012, African Americans are missing almost 30% of the pie (Figure 1).

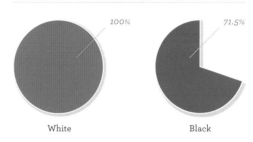

Figure 1: *2012 Equality Index is* **71.5%**

White   Black

How is the Equality Index calculated?

In keeping with the pie theme, the ingredients that go into baking the pie are economics, health, education, social justice and civic engagement. In each, we calculate how well African Americans and Hispanics are doing relative to whites and add them to get the Equality Index.

As with baking any pie, the ingredients are added in different amounts, based on the importance that we give to each (Figure 2).

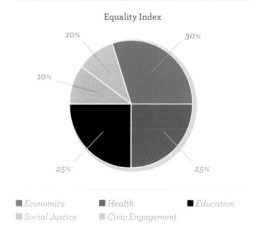

Figure 2: *Categories That Make Up the Equality Index*

Equality Index

- Economics
- Health
- Education
- Social Justice
- Civic Engagement

Is it possible to see how well African Americans and Hispanics are doing in each of the categories?

Yes. We show this in the tables included with the Equality Index.

Imagine each category is a mini-pie and interpret it in the same way as the Equality Index. So, an index of 56.3% for the economics category for African Americans in 2012 means that African Americans are missing close to half of the economics mini-pie.

Figure 3: *Equality Index for 2012*

CATEGORY	2012
Equality Index	**71.5%**
Economics	*56.3%*
Health	*76.5%*
Education	*79.7%*
Social Justice	*56.8%*
Civic Engagement	*98.3%*

Is it possible to see how well African Americans and Hispanics are doing over time?

Yes. The National Urban League has published the Equality Index and all the variables used to calculate it annually since 2005.

Figure 4: *Black-White Equality Index for 2006, 2009 & 2012*

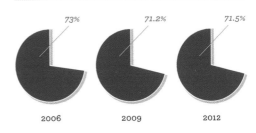

| 73% | 71.2% | 71.5% |
| 2006 | 2009 | 2012 |

Figure 5: *Black-White Equality Index for 2006, 2009 & 2012*

CATEGORY	2006	2009	2012
Equality Index	*73.0%*	*71.2%*	*71.5%*
Economics	*56.1%*	*57.4%*	*56.3%*
Health	*75.9%*	*76.8%*	*76.5%*
Education	*77.6%*	*77.0%*	*79.7%*
Social Justice	*74.2%*	*57.2%*	*56.8%*
Civic Engagement	*103.7*	*97.6%*	*98.3%*

It doesn't look like there's been much improvement in the Equality Index—what's the point?
Since the Equality Index is made up of a lot of different parts, improvements in one area are sometimes offset by losses in another area, leaving the overall index unchanged.

Change often happens slowly. The Equality Index offers solid evidence of just how slowly change happens, making it an important tool for driving policies needed in the ongoing fight against inequality.

Not all African Americans are doing poorly and not all whites are doing well. Why doesn't the Equality Index capture class differences?
The national data used to calculate the Equality Index is reported in averages for each of the racial groups. An average includes both people who are doing well and people who are not. An average is the easiest way to summarize a large amount of information, but can mask other important differences.

As the Equality Index continues to evolve, we are exploring ways to present some of the class differences that exist within racial groups, but are not captured by the average Equality Index numbers.

What should I do next?
Support the work of the National Urban League Policy Institute as we continue to advance policies such as *The National Urban League 8-Point Plan to Educate, Employ & Empower the Nation* (also published in this volume). This plan outlines the education and job-training steps necessary to put all of America back to work.

Read *The National Urban League 8-Point Plan to Educate, Employ & Empower the Nation* and stay up to speed with all the National Urban League is doing to close equality gaps and to fulfill our economic empowerment mission at *www.iamempowered.com*.

BLACK-WHITE

INDEX:

NATIONAL URBAN LEAGUE
2012 EQUALITY INDEX

GLOBAL INSIGHTS, INC.

Updated   History Revised   No New Data

2012 EQUALITY INDEX OF BLACK AMERICA	Source	Year	Black	White	Index	Diff. ('12-'11)
Total Equality Weighted Index					71.5%	0.000

ECONOMICS (30%)

Median Income (0.25)

	Source	Year	Black	White	Index	Diff.
Median Household Income (Real), Dollars	ACS	2010	33,578	54,168	62%	0.01
Median Male Earnings, Dollars	ACS	2010	37,392	51,397	73%	0.01
Median Female Earnings, Dollars	ACS	2010	32,299	39,326	82%	(0.01)

Poverty (0.15)

	Source	Year	Black	White	Index	Diff.
Population Living Below Poverty Line, %	ACS	2010	27.1	10.6	39%	0.00
Population Living Below 50% of Poverty Line, %	ACS	2010	12.7	4.8	38%	0.02
Population Living Below 125% of Poverty Line	ACS	2010	33.8	14.2	42%	0.00
Population Living Below Poverty Line (Under 18), %	CPS ASEC	2010	39.1	12.4	32%	(0.02)
Population Living Below Poverty Line (18–64), %	CPS ASEC	2010	23.3	9.9	42%	0.00
Population Living Below Poverty Line (65 and Older), %	CPS ASEC	2010	18.0	6.8	38%	0.04

Employment Issues (0.20)

	Source	Year	Black	White	Index	Diff.
Unemployment Rate, %	BLS	2011	15.8	7.9	50%	(0.04)
Unemployment Rate: Male, %	BLS	2011	17.8	8.3	47%	(0.06)
Unemployment Rate: Female, %	BLS	2011	14.1	7.5	53%	(0.03)
Unemployment Rate Persons Ages 16 to 19, %	BLS	2011	41.3	21.7	53%	(0.01)
Percent Not in Workforce: Ages 16 to 19, %	BLS	2011	75.1	63.2	84%	0.01
Percent Not in Workforce: Ages 16 and Older, %	BLS	2011	38.6	35.5	92%	(0.00)
Labor Force Participation Rate, %	BLS	2011	61.4	64.5	95%	(0.00)
LFPR 16 to 19, %	BLS	2011	24.9	36.8	68%	0.00
LFPR 20 to 24, %	BLS	2011	66.5	73.2	91%	0.01
LFPR Over 25: Less Than High School Grad., %	BLS	2011	37.9	47.8	79%	(0.02)
LFPR Over 25: High School Grad., No College, %	BLS	2011	62.2	59.8	104%	(0.00)
LFPR Over 25: Some College, No Degree, %	BLS	2011	70.8	66.2	107%	(0.00)
LFPR Over 25: Associate's Degree, %	BLS	2011	74.6	73.6	101%	(0.00)
LFPR Over 25: Some College or Associate Degree, %	BLS	2011	72.1	68.9	105%	(0.00)
LFPR Over 25: College Grad., %	BLS	2011	78.6	76.2	103%	(0.01)
Employment to Pop. Ratio, %	BLS	2011	51.7	59.4	87%	(0.01)

Housing & Wealth (0.34)

	Source	Year	Black	White	Index	Diff.
Home Ownership Rate, %	Census	2010	45.4	74.4	61%	(0.01)
Mortgage Application Denial Rate (Total), %	HMDA	2010	38.3	15.0	39%	(0.01)
Mortgage Application Denial Rate (Male), %	HMDA	2010	36.3	17.2	47%	(0.01)
Mortgage Application Denial Rate (Female), %	HMDA	2010	40.6	17.6	43%	(0.01)
Mortgage Application Denial Rate (Joint), %	HMDA	2010	36.5	12.3	34%	(0.02)
Home Improvement Loans Denials (Total), %	HMDA	2010	58.1	29.7	51%	(0.01)
Home Improvement Loans Denials (Male), %	HMDA	2010	59.1	36.8	62%	(0.00)
Home Improvement Loans Denials (Female), %	HMDA	2010	61.0	36.4	60%	0.01
Home Improvement Loans Denials (Joint), %	HMDA	2010	48.1	22.1	46%	0.00

Updated ▦ History Revised ☐ No New Data

2012 EQUALITY INDEX OF BLACK AMERICA	Source	Year	Black	White	Index	Diff. ('12-'11)
Percent of High-Priced Loans (More Than 3% Above Treasury)	HMDA	2010	6.1	3.4	56%	0.02
Median Home Value, 2000 Dollars	Census	2000	80,600	123,400	65%	0.00
Median Wealth, 2009 Dollars	EPI	2009	2,172	97,862	2%	0.00
Equity in Home, Dollars	Census	2004	54,000	92,000	59%	0.00
Percent Investing in 401(K), %	EBRI	2009	27.8	36.9	75%	0.02
Percent Investing in IRA, %	EBRI	2009	10.1	25.6	39%	0.04
U.S. Firms By Race (% Compared to Employment Share)	Census	2007	7.1	86.6	8%	0.02
Digital Divide (0.05)						
Households With Computer at Home, %	Census	2005	44.8	64.6	69%	0.00
Households With The Internet, %	NTIA	2010	57.8	74.9	77%	0.03
Adult Users With Broadband Access, %	NTIA	2010	55.5	71.8	77%	0.04
Transportation (0.01)						
Car Ownership, %	Census	2004	70.0	89.2	78%	0.00
Means of Transportation to Work: Drive Alone, %	ACS	2010	72.0	80.1	90%	(0.00)
Means of Transportation to Work: Public Transportation, %	ACS	2010	11.1	2.9	26%	(0.00)
Economic Weighted Index					56.3%	(0.003)

HEALTH (25%)						
Death Rates & Life Expectancy (0.45)						
Life Expectancy at Birth	CDC	2007	73.6	78.4	94%	0.00
Male	CDC	2007	70.0	75.9	92%	0.00
Female	CDC	2007	76.8	80.8	95%	0.00
Life Expectancy at 65 (Additional Expected Years)	CDC	2007	17.2	18.7	92%	0.00
Male at 65	CDC	2007	15.2	17.3	88%	0.00
Female at 65	CDC	2007	18.7	19.9	94%	0.00
Age-Adjusted Death Rates (Per 100,000): All Causes	CDC	2008	955.2	766.2	80%	0.02
Age-Adjusted Death Rates (Per 100,000): Male	CDC	2008	1,176.6	908.5	77%	0.02
Age-Adjusted Death Rates (Per 100,000): Female	CDC	2008	794.8	650.8	82%	0.02
Age-Adjusted Death Rates (Per 100,000): Heart Disease	CDC	2008	243.2	188.0	77%	0.01
Ischemic Heart Disease	CDC	2008	146.2	124.8	85%	0.02
Age-Adjusted Death Rates (Per 100,000): Stroke (Cerebrovascular)	CDC	2008	58.6	39.5	67%	0.01
Age-Adjusted Death Rates (Per 100,000): Cancer	CDC	2008	213.5	179.4	84%	0.01
Trachea, Bronchus, and Lung	CDC	2008	54.6	52.8	97%	0.02
Colon, Rectum, and Anus	CDC	2008	23.3	16.3	70%	0.00
Prostate (Male)	CDC	2008	47.0	21.0	45%	0.03
Breast (Female)	CDC	2008	31.9	22.5	71%	(0.01)
Age-Adjusted Death Rates (Per 100,000): Chronic Lower Respiratory	CDC	2008	31.1	48.7	157%	0.00
Age-Adjusted Death Rates (Per 100,000): Influenza and Pneumonia	CDC	2008	19.3	16.9	88%	0.01
Age-Adjusted Death Rates (Per 100,000): Chronic Liver Disease and Cirrhosis	CDC	2008	7.1	9.1	128%	0.10
Age-Adjusted Death Rates (Per 100,000): Diabetes	CDC	2008	41.3	19.1	46%	0.01

☐ Updated ▨ History Revised ☐ No New Data

2012 EQUALITY INDEX OF BLACK AMERICA	Source	Year	Black	White	Index	Diff. ('12-'11)
Age-Adjusted Death Rates (Per 100,000): HIV	CDC	2008	15.7	1.4	9%	0.00
Unintentional Injuries	CDC	2008	34.2	42.6	125%	0.10
Motor Vehicle-Related Injuries	CDC	2008	12.7	13.6	107%	0.04
Age-Adjusted Death Rates (Per 100,000): Suicide	CDC	2008	5.4	14.1	261%	(0.04)
Age-Adjusted Death Rates (Per 100,000): Suicide Males	CDC	2008	9.8	22.9	234%	(0.10)
Age-Adjusted Death Rates (Per 100,000): Suicide Males Ages 15–24	CDC	2007	10.3	18.2	177%	0.00
Age-Adjusted Death Rates (Per 100,000): Suicide Females	CDC	2008	1.7	6.0	353%	0.36
Age-Adjusted Death Rates (Per 100,000): Suicide Females Ages 15–24	CDC	2007	1.6	3.7	231%	0.00
Age-Adjusted Death Rates (Per 100,000): Homicide	CDC	2008	20.2	2.8	14%	0.01
Age-Adjusted Death Rates (Per 100,000): Homicide Male	CDC	2008	35.7	3.9	11%	0.01
Age-Adjusted Death Rates (Per 100,000): Homicide Males Ages 15–24	CDC	2007	85.3	4.9	6%	0.00
Age-Adjusted Death Rates (Per 100,000): Homicide Female	CDC	2008	5.6	1.8	32%	0.04
Age-Adjusted Death Rates (Per 100,000): Homicide Females Ages 15–24	CDC	2007	8.9	2.2	25%	0.00
Age-Adjusted Death Rates (Per 100,000) By Age Cohort: > 1 Male	CDC	2007	1,363.2	616.8	45%	0.00
Age-Adjusted Death Rates (Per 100,000) By Age Cohort: 1–4 Male	CDC	2007	45.3	28.1	62%	0.00
Age-Adjusted Death Rates (Per 100,000) By Age Cohort: 5–14 Male	CDC	2007	24.6	16.1	65%	0.00
Age-Adjusted Death Rates (Per 100,000) By Age Cohort: 15–24 Male	CDC	2007	168.1	104.6	62%	0.00
Age-Adjusted Death Rates (Per 100,000) By Age Cohort: 25–34 Male	CDC	2007	240.3	140.8	59%	0.00
Age-Adjusted Death Rates (Per 100,000) By Age Cohort: 35–44 Male	CDC	2007	378.9	228.4	60%	0.00
Age-Adjusted Death Rates (Per 100,000) By Age Cohort: 45–54 Male	CDC	2007	876.7	508.7	58%	0.00
Age-Adjusted Death Rates (Per 100,000) By Age Cohort: 55–64 Male	CDC	2007	1,870.8	1,057.5	57%	0.00
Age-Adjusted Death Rates (Per 100,000) By Age Cohort: 65–74 Male	CDC	2007	3,604.9	2,432.7	67%	0.00
Age-Adjusted Death Rates (Per 100,000) By Age Cohort: 75–84 Male	CDC	2007	7,169.0	6,152.7	86%	0.00
Age-Adjusted Death Rates (Per 100,000) By Age Cohort: 85+ Male	CDC	2007	12,964.7	14,588.3	113%	0.00
Age-Adjusted Death Rates (Per 100,000) By Age Cohort: >1 Female	CDC	2007	1,132.2	499.6	44%	0.00
Age-Adjusted Death Rates (Per 100,000) By Age Cohort: 1–4 Female	CDC	2007	39.0	22.7	58%	0.00
Age-Adjusted Death Rates (Per 100,000) By Age Cohort: 5–14 Female	CDC	2007	17.0	12.3	72%	0.00
Age-Adjusted Death Rates (Per 100,000) By Age Cohort: 15–24 Female	CDC	2007	48.9	42.7	87%	0.00
Age-Adjusted Death Rates (Per 100,000) By Age Cohort: 25–34 Female	CDC	2007	102.1	63.4	62%	0.00
Age-Adjusted Death Rates (Per 100,000) By Age Cohort: 35–44 Female	CDC	2007	229.1	134.4	59%	0.00
Age-Adjusted Death Rates (Per 100,000) By Age Cohort: 45–54 Female	CDC	2007	537.2	300.5	56%	0.00
Age-Adjusted Death Rates (Per 100,000) By Age Cohort: 55–64 Female	CDC	2007	1,047.4	651.3	62%	0.00
Age-Adjusted Death Rates (Per 100,000) By Age Cohort: 65–74 Female	CDC	2007	2,209.5	1,634.9	74%	0.00
Age-Adjusted Death Rates (Per 100,000) By Age Cohort: 75–84 Female	CDC	2007	4,902.9	4,385.4	89%	0.00
Age-Adjusted Death Rates (Per 100,000) By Age Cohort: 85+ Female	CDC	2007	11,997.4	12,856.7	107%	0.00
Physical Condition (0.10)						
Overweight: 18+ Years, % of Population	CDC	2010	33.9	36.3	107%	(0.02)
Overweight: Men 20 Years and Over, % of Population	CDC	2005-2008	33.8	40.2	119%	0.00
Overweight: Women 20 Years and Over, % of Population	CDC	2005-2008	27.0	26.5	98%	0.00
Obese, % of Population	CDC	2010	41.0	26.1	64%	(0.04)
Obese: Men 20 Years and Over, % of Population	CDC	2005-2008	37.2	32.4	87%	0.00

Updated   History Revised   No New Data

2012 EQUALITY INDEX OF BLACK AMERICA	Source	Year	Black	White	Index	Diff. ('12-'11)
Obese: Women 20 Years and Over, % of Population	CDC	2005-2008	50.5	33.2	66%	0.00
Diabetes: Physician Diagnosed in Ages 20+, % of Population	CDC	2005-2008	14.4	6.5	45%	(0.03)
AIDS Cases Per 100,000 Males Ages 13+	CDC	2009	78.0	9.8	13%	(0.00)
AIDS Cases Per 100,000 Females Ages 13+	CDC	2009	35.1	1.5	4%	(0.00)
Substance Abuse (0.10)						
Binge Alcohol (5 Drinks in 1 Day, 1X a Year)Ages 18+, % of Population	CDC	2009	14.3	27.5	192%	0.00
Use of Illicit Drugs in The Past Month Ages 12 +, % of Population	CDC	2009	9.6	8.8	92%	0.10
Tobacco: Both Cigarette & Cigar Ages 12+, % of Population	CDC	2009	26.5	29.6	112%	0.05
Mental Health (0.02)						
Students Who Consider Suicide: Male, %	CDC	2009	7.8	10.5	135%	0.15
Students Who Carry Out Intent and Require Medical Attention: Male, %	CDC	2007	2.5	0.9	36%	0.00
Students That Act on Suicidal Feeling: Male, %	CDC	2007	5.5	3.4	62%	0.00
Students Who Consider Suicide: Female, %	CDC	2009	18.1	16.1	89%	(0.10)
Students Who Carry Out Intent and Require Medical Attention: Female, %	CDC	2007	2.1	2.1	100%	0.00
Students That Act on Suicidal Feeling: Female, %	CDC	2007	9.9	7.7	78%	0.00
Access to Care (0.05)						
Private Insurance Payment for Health Care: Under 65 Years Old, % of Distribution	CDC	2008	39.0	57.7	68%	0.01
People Without Health Insurance, % of Population	Census: CPS ASEC	2010	20.8	11.7	56%	(0.01)
People 18 to 64 Without a Usual Source of Health Insurance, % of Adults	Census: CPS ASEC	2010	27.8	15.9	57%	(0.01)
People in Poverty Without a Usual Source of Health Insurance, % of Adults	Census: CPS ASEC	2010	39.5	39.4	100%	0.05
Population Under 65 Covered By Medicaid, % of Population	CDC	2009	29.1	10.4	36%	0.00
Elderly Health Care (0.03)						
Population Over 65 Covered By Medicaid, % of Population	CDC	2008	20.0	5.4	27%	0.00
Medicare Expenditures Per Beneficiary, Dollars	CDC	2007	16,891	15,460	92%	0.04
Pregnancy Issues (0.04)						
Prenatal Care Begins in 1st Trimester	CDC	2007	75.0	87.7	86%	0.00
Prenatal Care Begins in 3rd Trimester	CDC	2007	6.0	2.3	38%	0.00
Percent of Births to Mothers 18 and Under	CDC	2008	5.9	1.9	32%	(0.01)
Percent of Live Births to Unmarried Mothers	CDC	2008	72.3	28.7	40%	0.01
Infant Mortality Rates Among Mothers With Less Than 12 Years Education	CDC	2005	14.8	9.3	63%	0.00
Infant Mortality Rates Among Mothers With 12 Years Education	CDC	2005	14.2	7.1	50%	0.00
Infant Mortality Rates Among Mothers With 13 or More Years Education	CDC	2005	11.4	4.1	36%	0.00
Mothers Who Smoked Cigarettes During Pregnancy, %	CDC	2007	7.7	12.7	165%	0.00
Low Birth Weight, % of Live Births	CDC	2008	13.7	7.2	53%	0.00
Very Low Birth Weight, % of Live Births	CDC	2008	3.0	1.2	39%	0.02
Reproduction Issues (0.01)						
Abortions, Per 100 Live Births	CDC	2007	45.5	15.8	35%	0.00
Women Using Contraception, % of Population (Ages 15–44)	CDC	2006-08	54.5	64.7	84%	0.00

☐ Updated ▦ History Revised ☐ No New Data

2012 EQUALITY INDEX OF BLACK AMERICA	Source	Year	Black	White	Index	Diff. ('12-'11)
Delivery Issues (0.10)						
All Infant Deaths: Neonatal and Post, Per 1000 Live Births	CDC	2006	13.4	5.6	42%	0.00
Neonatal Deaths, Per 1000 Live Births	CDC	2006	9.0	3.6	40%	0.00
Postneonatal Deaths, Per 1000 Live Births	CDC	2006	4.4	1.9	43%	0.00
Maternal Mortality, Per 100,000 Live Births	CDC	2007	23.8	8.1	34%	0.00
Children's Health (0.10)						
Babies Breastfed, %	CDC	2007	58.1	76.2	76%	0.00
Children Without a Health Care Visit in Past 12 Months (Up to 6 Years Old), %	CDC	2008-09	6.4	4.1	64%	0.00
Vaccinations of Children Below Poverty: Combined Vacc. Series 4:3:1:3, % of Children 19-35 Months	CDC	2009	64.0	68.0	94%	0.00
Uninsured Children, %	Census: CPS ASEC	2010	11.0	6.9	63%	0.02
Overweight Boys 6–11 Years Old, % of Population	CDC	2005-2008	18.7	16.5	88%	0.05
Overweight Girls 6–11 Years Old, % of Population	CDC	2005-2008	21.3	14.5	68%	0.08
AIDS Cases Per 100,000 All Children Under 13	CDC	2009	0.1	0.0	22%	0.15
Health Weighted Index					76.5%	0.015

EDUCATION (25%)	Source	Year	Black	White	Index	Diff.
Quality (0.25)						
Teacher Quality (0.25 and 0.10)						
Middle Grades: Teacher Lacking at Least a College Minor in Subject Taught (High Vs. Low Minority Schools), %	ET	2000	49.0	40.0	85%	0.00
HS: Teacher Lacking An Undergraduate Major in Subject Taught (High Vs. Low Poverty Schools), %	ET	2008	21.9	10.9	88%	(0.03)
Per Student Funding (High Vs. Low Poverty Districts), Dollars	ET	2004	5,937	7,244	82%	0.00
Teachers With <3 Years Experience (High Vs. Low Poverty Schools), %	ET	2008	14.3	10.5	73%	0.26
Distribution of Underprepared Teachers (High Vs. Low Minority Schools), % (California Only)*	SRI	2008-09	5.0	1.0	20%	0.00
High poverty (minority) values are recorded in the black column, low poverty (minority) values are recorded in the white column						
Course Quality (0.15)						
College Completion, % of All Entrants	NCES	2002	40.1	60.2	67%	(0.02)
College Completion, % of Entrants With Strong HS Curriculum (Algebra II Plus Other Courses)	ET	1999	75.0	86.0	87%	0.00
HS Students: Enrolled in Chemistry, %	NCES	2005	63.6	67.1	95%	0.00
HS Students: Enrolled in Algebra 2, %	NCES	2005	69.2	71.2	97%	0.00
Students Taking: Precalculus, %	CB	2009	36.0	55.0	65%	0.00
Students Taking: Calculus, %	CB	2009	14.0	30.0	47%	0.00
Students Taking: Physics, %	CB	2009	44.0	54.0	81%	0.00
Students Taking: English Honors Course, %	CB	2009	31.0	43.0	72%	0.00

☐ Updated ☐ History Revised ☐ No New Data

2012 EQUALITY INDEX OF BLACK AMERICA	Source	Year	Black	White	Index	Diff. ('12-'11)
Attainment (0.30)						
Graduation Rates, 2-Year Institutions, %	NCES	2005	27.1	32.0	85%	0.04
Graduation Rates, 4-Year Institutions, %	NCES	2002	37.7	59.3	64%	(0.05)
NCAA Div. I College Freshmen Graduating Within 6 Years, %	NCAA	2002-'03	44.0	65.0	68%	0.00
Degrees Earned: Associate, % of Population Aged 18–24 Yrs	NCES	2008-09	2.2	3.0	74%	(0.03)
Degrees Earned: Bachelor's, % of Population Aged 18–29 Yrs	NCES	2008-09	2.1	3.8	54%	(0.03)
Degrees Earned: Master's, % of Population Aged 18–34 Yrs	NCES	2008-09	0.7	1.0	67%	0.01
Educational Attainment: at Least High School (25 Yrs. and Over), % of Population	Census	2010	84.2	92.1	91%	(0.00)
Educational Attainment: at Least Bachelor's (25 Yrs. and Over), % of Population	Census	2010	19.8	33.2	60%	0.01
Degree Holders, % Distribution, By Field						
Agriculture/Forestry	NCES	2001	0.7	1.2	56%	0.00
Art/Architecture	NCES	2001	3.3	2.9	114%	0.00
Business/Management	NCES	2001	19.5	18.1	108%	0.00
Communications	NCES	2001	3.2	2.4	135%	0.00
Computer and Information Sciences	NCES	2001	3.9	2.2	177%	0.00
Education	NCES	2001	15.3	15.3	100%	0.00
Engineering	NCES	2001	3.6	7.7	47%	0.00
English/Literature	NCES	2001	2.6	3.3	80%	0.00
Foreign Languages	NCES	2001	0.8	0.9	96%	0.00
Health Sciences	NCES	2001	5.4	4.5	120%	0.00
Liberal Arts/Humanities	NCES	2001	4.6	6.1	75%	0.00
Mathematics/Statistics	NCES	2001	2.4	1.4	169%	0.00
Natural Sciences	NCES	2001	6.0	5.6	106%	0.00
Philosophy/Religion/Theology	NCES	2001	0.9	1.3	70%	0.00
Pre-Professional	NCES	2001	1.6	1.1	146%	0.00
Psychology	NCES	2001	4.9	3.9	126%	0.00
Social Sciences/History	NCES	2001	8.1	4.9	165%	0.00
Other Fields	NCES	2001	13.1	17.2	76%	0.00
Scores (0.25)						
Preschool 10% of Total Scores (0.015)						
Children's School Readiness Skills (Ages 3–5), % With 3 or 4 Skills* *Recognizes all letters, counts to 20 or higher, writes name, reads or pretends to read	NCES	2005	44.1	46.8	94%	0.00
Elementary 40% of Total Scores (0.06)						
Average Scale Score in U.S. History, 8th Graders	NCES	2010	250	274	91%	0.02
Average Scale Score in U.S. History, 4th Graders	NCES	2010	198	224	88%	0.03
Average Scale Score in Math, 8th Graders	NCES	2011	262	293	89%	0.00
Average Scale Score in Math, 4th Graders	NCES	2011	224	249	90%	0.00
Average Scale Score in Reading, 8th Graders	NCES	2011	249	274	91%	0.01
Average Scale Score in Reading, 4th Graders	NCES	2011	205	231	89%	0.01
Average Scale Score in Science, 8th Graders	NCES	2005	124	160	78%	0.00

★ ★ ★ ★ ★ ★ ★ ★ ★ ★ ★ ★ ★ ★ ★ ★

Updated ▓ History Revised ☐ No New Data

2012 EQUALITY INDEX OF BLACK AMERICA	Source	Year	Black	White	Index	Diff. ('12-'11)
Average Scale Score in Science, 4th Graders	NCES	2005	129	162	80%	0.00
Writing Proficiency at or Above Basic, 8th Graders, % of Students	NCES	2007	81	93	87%	0.00
Writing Proficiency at or Above Basic, 4th Graders, % of Students	NCES	2002	77	90	85%	0.00
High School 50% of Total Scores (0.075)						
Writing Proficiency at or Above Basic, 12th Graders, % of Students	NCES	2007	69	86	80%	0.00
Average Scale Score in Science, 12th Graders	NCES	2005	120	156	77%	0.00
Average Scale Score in U.S. History, 12th Graders	NCES	2010	268	296	91%	(0.00)
Average Scale Score in Reading, 12th Graders	NCES	2009	269	296	91%	(0.00)
High School GPA's for Those Taking The SAT	CB	2009	3.00	3.40	88%	0.00
Sat Reasoning Test - Mean Scores	CB	2011	1,272	1,579	81%	(0.00)
Mathematics, Joint	CB	2011	427	535	80%	(0.00)
Mathematics, Male	CB	2011	435	552	79%	0.00
Mathematics, Female	CB	2011	422	520	81%	(0.00)
Critical Reading, Joint	CB	2011	428	528	81%	(0.00)
Critical Reading, Male	CB	2011	425	531	80%	(0.00)
Critical Reading, Female	CB	2011	430	526	82%	(0.00)
Writing, Joint	CB	2011	417	516	81%	(0.01)
Writing, Male	CB	2011	405	507	80%	(0.00)
Writing, Female	CB	2011	426	524	81%	(0.01)
ACT- Average Composite Score	ACT	2011	17.0	22.4	76%	0.00
Enrollment (0.10)						
School Enrollment: Ages 3-34, % of Population	Census	2009	58.5	56.8	103%	0.01
Preprimary School Enrollment	Census	2009	66.3	66.6	100%	0.04
3 and 4 Years Old	Census	2009	57.7	55.5	104%	0.06
5 and 6 Years Old	Census	2009	93.6	94.1	99%	0.01
7 to 13 Years Old	Census	2009	98.1	98.7	99%	(0.01)
14 and 15 Years Old	Census	2009	97.8	98.3	99%	0.00
16 and 17 Years Old	Census	2009	94.1	95.0	99%	0.01
18 and 19 Years Old	Census	2009	65.2	72.4	90%	0.05
20 and 21 Years Old	Census	2009	44.7	56.4	79%	0.07
22 to 24 Years Old	Census	2009	31.9	31.1	103%	0.20
25 to 29 Years Old	Census	2009	14.6	14.0	104%	(0.06)
30 to 34 Years Old	Census	2009	11.0	8.1	136%	(0.31)
35 and Over	Census	2009	3.7	1.9	196%	0.37
College Enrollment (Graduate or Undergraduate): Ages 14 and Over, % of Population	Census	2009	8.0	6.8	118%	0.11
14 to 17 Years Old	Census	2009	1.4	1.2	113%	(0.01)
18 to 19 Years Old	Census	2009	41.5	56.1	74%	0.09
20 to 21 Years Old	Census	2009	41.6	55.6	75%	0.08
22 to 24 Years Old	Census	2009	30.4	30.9	98%	0.17
25 to 29 Years Old	Census	2009	14.4	13.8	104%	0.02
30 to 34 Years Old	Census	2009	10.0	8.0	125%	(0.34)
35 Years Old and Over	Census	2009	3.4	1.8	186%	0.29

2012 EQUALITY INDEX OF BLACK AMERICA	Source	Year	Black	White	Index	Diff. ('12-'11)
College Enrollment Rate As a Percent of All 18- to 24-Year-Old High School Completers, %	NCES	2009	46.7	50.3	93%	0.11
Adult Education Participation, % of Adult Population	NCES	2004-05	46.0	46.0	100%	0.00
Student Status & Risk Factors (0.10)						
High School Dropouts: Status Dropouts, % (Not Completed HS and Not Enrolled, Regardless of When Dropped)	Census	2009	11.6	9.1	78%	(0.20)
Children in Poverty, %	Census	2010	39.1	12.4	32%	(0.02)
Children in All Families Below Poverty Level, %	Census	2010	39.1	11.7	30%	(0.02)
Children in Families Below Poverty Level (Female Householder, No Spouse Present), %	Census	2010	53.3	34.8	65%	(0.01)
Children With No Parent in The Labor Force, %	USDC	2000	20.3	5.5	27%	0.00
Children (Under 18) With a Disability, %	Census	2010	4.8	4.0	84%	0.03
Public School Students (K-12): Repeated Grade, %	NCES	2007	20.9	8.7	42%	(0.06)
Public School Students (K-12): Suspended, %	NCES	2003	19.6	8.8	45%	0.00
Public School Students (K-12): Expelled, %	NCES	2003	5.0	1.4	28%	0.00
Center-Based Child Care of Preschool Children, %	NCES	2005	66.5	59.1	89%	0.00
Parental Care Only of Preschool Children, %	NCES	2005	19.5	24.1	81%	0.00
Teacher Stability: Remained in Public School, High Vs. Low Minority Schools, %	NCES	2005	79.7	85.9	93%	0.00
Teacher Stability: Remained in Private School, High Vs. Low Minority Schools, %	NCES	2005	72.7	82.8	88%	0.00
Zero Days Missed in School Year, % of 10th Graders	NCES	2002	28.3	12.1	234%	0.00
3+ Days Late to School, % of 10th Graders	NCES	2002	36.4	44.4	122%	0.00
Never Cut Classes, % of 10th Graders	NCES	2002	68.9	70.3	98%	0.00
Home Literacy Activities (Age 3 to 5)						
Read to 3 or More Times a Week	NCES	2007	78.0	90.6	86%	0.00
Told a Story at Least Once a Month	NCES	2005	54.3	53.3	102%	0.00
Taught Words or Numbers Three or More Times a Week	NCES	2005	80.6	75.7	107%	0.00
Visited a Library at Least Once in Last Month	NCES	2007	24.6	40.8	60%	0.00
Education Weighted Index					**79.7%**	**0.007**

SOCIAL JUSTICE (10%)						
Equality Before The Law (0.70)						
Stopped While Driving, %	BJS	2008	8.8	8.4	95%	(0.14)
Speeding	BJS	2002	50.0	57.0	114%	0.00
Vehicle Defect	BJS	2002	10.3	8.7	84%	0.00
Roadside Check for Drinking Drivers	BJS	2002	1.1	1.3	118%	0.00
Record Check	BJS	2002	17.4	11.3	65%	0.00
Seatbelt Violation	BJS	2002	3.5	4.4	126%	0.00
Illegal Turn/Lane Change	BJS	2002	5.1	4.5	88%	0.00
Stop Sign/Light Violation	BJS	2002	5.9	6.5	110%	0.00
Other	BJS	2002	3.7	4.0	108%	0.00
Mean Incarceration Sentence (In Average Months)	BJS	2006	42	37	88%	0.00

★ ★ ★ ★ ★ ★ ★ ★ ★ ★ ★ ★ ★ ★ ★ ★

Updated ▓ History Revised ☐ No New Data

2012 EQUALITY INDEX OF BLACK AMERICA	Source	Year	Black	White	Index	Diff. ('12-'11)
Average Sentence for Incarceration (All Offenses): Male, Months	BJS	2006	45	40	89%	0.00
Average Sentence for Murder: Male, Months	BJS	2006	266	265	100%	0.00
Average Sentence for Sexual Assault	BJS	2006	125	115	92%	0.00
Average Sentence for Robbery	BJS	2006	101	89	88%	0.00
Average Sentence for Aggravated Assault	BJS	2006	48	42	88%	0.00
Average Sentence for Other Violent	BJS	2006	41	43	105%	0.00
Average Sentence for Burglary	BJS	2006	50	41	82%	0.00
Average Sentence for Larceny	BJS	2006	23	24	104%	0.00
Average Sentence for Fraud	BJS	2006	27	27	100%	0.00
Average Sentence for Drug Possession	BJS	2006	25	21	84%	0.00
Average Sentence for Drug Trafficking	BJS	2006	40	39	98%	0.00
Average Sentence for Weapon Offenses	BJS	2006	34	34	100%	0.00
Average Sentence for Other Offenses	BJS	2006	25	26	104%	0.00
Average Sentence for Incarceration (All Offenses): Female, Months	BJS	2006	25	26	104%	0.00
Average Sentence for Murder	BJS	2006	175	225	129%	0.00
Average Sentence for Sexual Assault	BJS	2006	32	72	225%	0.00
Average Sentence for Robbery	BJS	2006	54	61	113%	0.00
Average Sentence for Aggravated Assault	BJS	2006	29	30	103%	0.00
Average Sentence for Other Violent	BJS	2006	17	55	324%	0.00
Average Sentence for Burglary	BJS	2006	34	29	85%	0.00
Average Sentence for Larceny	BJS	2006	19	17	89%	0.00
Average Sentence for Fraud	BJS	2006	23	22	96%	0.00
Average Sentence for Drug Possession	BJS	2006	15	17	113%	0.00
Average Sentence for Drug Trafficking	BJS	2006	27	26	96%	0.00
Average Sentence for Weapon Offenses	BJS	2006	24	24	100%	0.00
Average Sentence for Other Offenses	BJS	2006	20	22	110%	0.00
Convicted Felons Sentenced to Probation, All Offenses,%	BJS	2006	25	29	86%	0.00
Probation Sentence for Murder, %	BJS	2006	3	4	75%	0.00
Probation Sentence for Sexual Assault, %	BJS	2006	16	16	100%	0.00
Probation Sentence for Robbery, %	BJS	2006	12	15	80%	0.00
Probation Sentence for Burglary, %	BJS	2006	20	25	80%	0.00
Probation Sentence for Fraud, %	BJS	2006	35	35	100%	0.00
Probation Sentence for Drug Offenses, %	BJS	2006	25	34	74%	0.00
Probation Sentence for Weapon Offenses, %	BJS	2006	25	23	109%	0.00
Incarceration Rate: Prisoners Per 100,000	BJS	2010	1,540	252	16%	(0.01)
Incarceration Rate: Prisoners Per 100,000 People: Male	BJS	2010	3,059	456	15%	(0.01)
Incarceration Rate: Prisoners Per 100,000 People: Female	BJS	2010	133	47	35%	0.00
Prisoners as a % of Arrests	FBI, BJS	2010	25.6	9.8	38%	0.02
Victimization & Mental Anguish (0.30)						
Homicide Rate Per 100,000	NACJD	2009	16.7	2.8	17%	0.01
Homicide Rate Per 100,000: Firearm	NACJD	2009	13.0	1.6	12%	0.01
Homicide Rate Per 100,000: Stabbings	NACJD	2009	1.5	0.5	30%	0.07

Updated ▨   History Revised ▨   No New Data ☐

2012 EQUALITY INDEX OF BLACK AMERICA	Source	Year	Black	White	Index	Diff. ('12-'11)
Homicide Rate Per 100,000: Personal Weapons	NACJD	2009	0.6	0.2	38%	(0.00)
Homicide Rate Per 100,000: Male	CDC	2007	39.7	3.7	9%	0.00
Homicide Rate Per 100,000: Female	CDC	2007	6.2	1.8	29%	0.00
Murder Victims, Rate Per 100,000	USDJ	2010	17.0	3.1	18%	0.02
Hate Crimes Victims, Rate Per 100,000	USDJ	2010	7.3	0.3	4%	0.00
Victims of Violent Crimes, Rate Per 100,000	BJS	2010	20.8	13.6	65%	0.06
Delinquency Cases, Year of Disposition, Rate Per 100,000	NCJJ	2008	3,022.2	1,394.5	46%	0.00
Prisoners Under Sentence of Death, Rate Per 100,000	BJS	2009	4.6	1.1	24%	0.00
High School Students Carrying Weapons on School Property	CDC	2009	5.3	5.6	106%	0.00
High School Students Carrying Weapons Anywhere	CDC	2009	14.4	18.6	129%	0.00
Firearm-Related Death Rates Per 100,000: Males, All Ages	CDC	2007	40.4	16.1	40%	0.00
Ages 1–14	CDC	2007	2.4	0.7	29%	0.00
Ages 15–24	CDC	2007	91.5	13.4	15%	0.00
Ages 25–44	CDC	2007	64.8	18.3	28%	0.00
Ages 25–34	CDC	2007	88.1	18.0	20%	0.00
Ages 35–44	CDC	2007	40.7	18.7	46%	0.00
Ages 45–64	CDC	2007	20.1	19.5	97%	0.00
Age 65 and Older	CDC	2007	11.4	27.3	241%	0.00
Firearm-Related Death Rates Per 100,000: Females, All Ages	CDC	2007	4.1	2.9	70%	0.00
Ages 1–14	CDC	2007	0.9	0.3	34%	0.00
Ages 15–24	CDC	2007	7.3	2.5	34%	0.00
Ages 25–44	CDC	2007	6.7	4.1	61%	0.00
Ages 25–34	CDC	2007	7.2	3.4	47%	0.00
Ages 35–44	CDC	2007	6.2	4.6	75%	0.00
Ages 45–64	CDC	2007	2.9	3.9	136%	0.00
Age 65 and Older	CDC	2007	1.3	2.2	172%	0.00
Social Justice Weighted Index					56.8%	(0.012)

CIVIC ENGAGEMENT (10%)						
Democratic Process (0.4)						
Registered Voters, % of Citizen Population	Census	2010	62.8	68.2	92%	(0.03)
Actually Voted, % of Citizen Population	Census	2010	43.5	48.6	90%	(0.08)
Community Participation (0.3)						
Percent of Population Volunteering for Military Reserves, %	USDD	2010	0.8	1.0	80%	(0.07)
Volunteerism, %	BLS	2010	19.4	27.8	70%	(0.02)
Civic and Political	BLS	2010	4.6	5.5	84%	(0.11)
Educational or Youth Service	BLS	2010	23.0	26.8	86%	(0.03)
Environmental or Animal Care	BLS	2010	0.5	2.7	19%	0.15
Hospital or Other Health	BLS	2010	5.9	8.1	73%	0.05
Public Safety	NCJJ	2010	0.3	1.4	21%	(0.09)
Religious	BLS	2010	45.4	32.6	139%	0.07

★ ★ ★ ★ ★ ★ ★ ★ ★ ★ ★ ★ ★ ★ ★ ★

Updated History Revised ☐ No New Data

2012 EQUALITY INDEX OF BLACK AMERICA	Source	Year	Black	White	Index	Diff. ('12-'11)
Social or Community Service	BLS	2010	13.7	13.6	101%	0.05
Unpaid Volunteering of Young Adults	NCES	2000	40.9	32.2	127%	0.00
Collective Bargaining (0.2)						
Members of Unions, % of Employed	BLS	2010	13.4	11.7	115%	0.00
Represented By Unions, % of Employed	BLS	2010	14.9	13.0	115%	0.00
Governmental Employment (0.1)						
Federal Executive Branch (Nonpostal) Employment, % of Adult Population	OPM	2008	1.2	0.8	145%	(0.02)
State and Local Government Employment, %	EEOC	2009	4.0	2.5	158%	(0.04)
Civic Engagement Weighted Index					98.3%	(0.034)

Source	Acronym
American Community Survey	ACS
U.S. Bureau of Justice Statistics	BJS
U.S. Bureau of Labor Statistics	BLS
College Board	CB
Centers for Disease Control and Prevention	CDC
U.S. Census Bureau	Census
Employee Benefit Research Institute	EBRI
U.S. Equal Employment Opportunity Commission	EEOC
Economic Policy Institute	EPI
The Education Trust	ET
Home Mortgage Disclosure Act	HMDA
Monitoring the Future	MTF
National Archive of Criminal Justice Data	NACJD
National Center for Education Statistics	NCES
National Center for Juvenile Justice	NCJJ
National Telecommunications and Information Administration	NTIA
Office of Personal Management	OPM
SRI International	SRI
Statistical Abstract of the United States	Stat. Ab.
State of Working America	SWA
U.S. Decennial Census	USDC
U.S. Department of Defense	USDD
Current Population Survey: Annual Social and Economic Supplement	CPS ASEC
U.S. Department of Justice	USDJ

HISPANIC-WHITE

INDEX:

NATIONAL URBAN LEAGUE
2012 EQUALITY INDEX

GLOBAL INSIGHTS, INC.

☐ Updated　▨ History Revised　☐ No New Data

2012 EQUALITY INDEX OF HISPANIC AMERICA	Source	Year	Hispanic	White	Index	Diff. ('12-'11)
Total Equality Weighted Index					**76.1%**	(0.006)

ECONOMICS (30%)

Median Income (0.25)

	Source	Year	Hispanic	White	Index	Diff.
Median Household Income (Real), Dollars	ACS	2010	40,165	54,168	74%	0.011
Median Male Earnings, Dollars	ACS	2010	30,798	51,397	60%	0.00
Median Female Earnings, Dollars	ACS	2010	27,035	39,326	69%	(0.01)

Poverty (0.15)

	Source	Year	Hispanic	White	Index	Diff.
Population Living Below Poverty Line, %	ACS	2010	24.8	10.6	43%	0.00
Population Living Below 50% of Poverty Line, %	ACS	2010	9.9	4.8	48%	0.01
Population Living Below 125% of Poverty Line	ACS	2010	32.9	14.2	43%	0.00
Population Living Below Poverty Line (Under 18), %	CPS ASEC	2010	35.0	12.4	35%	(0.01)
Population Living Below Poverty Line (18–64), %	CPS ASEC	2010	22.4	9.9	44%	0.01
Population Living Below Poverty Line (65 and Older), %	CPS ASEC	2010	18.0	6.8	38%	0.02

Employment Issues (0.20)

	Source	Year	Hispanic	White	Index	Diff.
Unemployment Rate, %	BLS	2011	11.5	7.9	69%	(0.01)
Unemployment Rate: Male, %	BLS	2011	11.2	8.3	74%	(0.01)
Unemployment Rate: Female, %	BLS	2011	11.8	7.5	64%	0.01
Unemployment Rate Persons Ages 16 to 19, %	BLS	2011	31.1	21.7	70%	(0.02)
Percent Not in Workforce: Ages 16 to 19, %	BLS	2011	71.7	63.2	88%	(0.02)
Percent Not in Workforce: Ages 16 and Older, %	BLS	2011	33.5	35.5	106%	(0.01)
Labor Force Participation Rate, %	BLS	2011	66.5	64.5	103%	(0.01)
LFPR 16 to 19, %	BLS	2011	28.3	36.8	77%	(0.05)
LFPR 20 to 24, %	BLS	2011	72.0	73.2	98%	0.01
LFPR Over 25: Less Than High School Grad, %	BLS	2011	61.0	47.8	128%	(0.02)
LFPR Over 25: High School Grad., No College, %	BLS	2011	72.7	59.8	122%	0.01
LFPR Over 25: Some College, No Degree, %	BLS	2011	76.5	66.2	116%	0.01
LFPR Over 25: Associate's Degree, %	BLS	2011	78.3	73.6	106%	0.01
LFPR Over 25: Some College or Associate Degree, %	BLS	2011	77.1	68.9	112%	0.01
LFPR Over 25: College Grad., %	BLS	2011	80.6	76.2	106%	(0.01)
Employment to Pop. Ratio, %	BLS	2011	58.9	59.4	99%	(0.00)

Housing & Wealth (0.34)

	Source	Year	Hispanic	White	Index	Diff.
Home Ownership Rate, %	Census	2010	47.5	74.4	64%	(0.01)
Mortgage Application Denial Rate (Total), %	HMDA	2010	26.5	15.0	56%	(0.02)
Mortgage Application Denial Rate (Male), %	HMDA	2010	26.7	17.2	65%	(0.01)
Mortgage Application Denial Rate (Female), %	HMDA	2010	28.2	17.6	62%	(0.02)
Mortgage Application Denial Rate (Joint), %	HMDA	2010	24.7	12.3	50%	(0.02)
Home Improvement Loans Denials (Total), %	HMDA	2010	54.9	29.7	54%	0.00
Home Improvement Loans Denials (Male), %	HMDA	2010	58.1	36.8	63%	0.02
Home Improvement Loans Denials (Female), %	HMDA	2010	60.1	36.4	61%	0.01
Home Improvement Loans Denials (Joint), %	HMDA	2010	43.8	22.1	50%	0.01

▧ Updated ▨ History Revised ☐ No New Data

2012 EQUALITY INDEX OF HISPANIC AMERICA	Source	Year	Hispanic	White	Index	Diff. ('12-'11)
Percent of High-Priced Loans (More Than 3% Above Treasury)	HMDA	2010	9.2	3.4	37%	(0.07)
Median Home Value, 2000 Dollars	Census	2000	105,600	123,400	86%	0.00
Median Wealth, 2002 Dollars	EPI	2009	7,932	97,862	8%	0.00
Equity in Home, Dollars	Census	2004	71,000	92,000	77%	0.00
Percent Investing in 401(K), %	EBRI	2005	19.0	36.9	51%	(0.00)
Percent Investing in IRA, %	EBRI	2005	8.5	25.6	33%	0.03
Digital Divide (0.05)						
Households With Computer at Home, %	Census	2005	39.1	64.6	61%	0.00
Households With The Internet, %	NTIA	2010	59.1	74.9	79%	0.07
Adult Users With Broadband Access, %	NTIA	2010	56.9	71.8	79%	0.09
Transportation (0.01)						
Car Ownership, %	Census	2004	78.2	89.2	88%	0.00
Means of Transportation to Work: Drive Alone, %	ACS	2010	67.6	80.1	84%	(0.00)
Means of Transportation to Work: Public Transportation, %	ACS	2010	7.9	2.9	37%	(0.01)

Economic Weighted Index   60.8%   (0.000)

HEALTH (25%)						
Death Rates & Life Expectancy (0.45)						
Life Expectancy at Birth	CDC	2007	81.1	78.4	103%	0.00
Male	CDC	2007	78.4	75.9	103%	-
Female	CDC	2007	83.7	80.8	104%	-
Age-Adjusted Death Rates (Per 100,000): All Causes	CDC	2008	532.2	766.2	144%	0.04
Age-Adjusted Death Rates (Per 100,000): Male	CDC	2008	630.7	908.5	144%	0.05
Age-Adjusted Death Rates (Per 100,000): Female	CDC	2008	445.7	650.8	146%	0.03
Age-Adjusted Death Rates (Per 100,000): Heart Disease	CDC	2008	126.3	188.0	149%	0.08
Ischemic Heart Disease	CDC	2008	90.0	124.8	139%	0.08
Age-Adjusted Death Rates (Per 100,000): Stroke(Cerebrovascular)	CDC	2008	30.9	39.5	128%	0.03
Age-Adjusted Death Rates (Per 100,000): Cancer	CDC	2008	114.6	179.4	157%	(0.00)
Trachea, Bronchus, and Lung	CDC	2008	20.5	52.8	258%	(0.00)
Colon, Rectum, and Anus	CDC	2008	11.9	16.3	137%	(0.02)
Prostate (Male)	CDC	2008	16.5	21.0	127%	0.04
Breast (Female)	CDC	2008	14.3	22.5	157%	(0.01)
Age-Adjusted Death Rates (Per 100,000): Chronic Lower Respiratory	CDC	2008	18.3	48.7	266%	('0.10)
Age-Adjusted Death Rates (Per 100,000): Influenza and Pneumonia	CDC	2008	14.0	16.9	121%	(0.03)
Age-Adjusted Death Rates (Per 100,000): Chronic Liver Disease and Cirrhosis	CDC	2008	13.7	9.1	66%	0.02
Age-Adjusted Death Rates (Per 100,000): Diabetes	CDC	2008	27.7	19.1	69%	0.00
Age-Adjusted Death Rates (Per 100,000): HIV	CDC	2008	3.6	1.4	39%	0.02
Unintentional Injuries	CDC	2008	27.9	42.6	153%	0.10
Motor Vehicle-Related Injuries	CDC	2008	11.4	13.6	119%	0.07

★ ★ ★ ★ ★ ★ ★ ★ ★ ★ ★ ★ ★ ★ ★

Updated ▦ History Revised ☐ No New Data

2012 EQUALITY INDEX OF HISPANIC AMERICA	Source	Year	Hispanic	White	Index	Diff. ('12-'11)
Age-Adjusted Death Rates (Per 100,000): Suicide	CDC	2008	5.6	14.1	252%	0.27
Age-Adjusted Death Rates (Per 100,000): Suicide Males	CDC	2008	9.3	22.9	246%	0.29
Age-Adjusted Death Rates (Per 100,000): Suicide Males Ages 15–24	CDC	2007	11.5	18.2	158%	0.00
Age-Adjusted Death Rates (Per 100,000): Suicide Females	CDC	2008	1.9	6.0	316%	0.16
Age-Adjusted Death Rates (Per 100,000): Suicide Females Ages 15–24	CDC	2007	2.2	3.7	168%	0.00
Age-Adjusted Death Rates (Per 100,000): Homicide	CDC	2008	6.6	2.8	42%	0.02
Age-Adjusted Death Rates (Per 100,000): Homicide male	CDC	2008	10.5	3.9	37%	0.04
Age-Adjusted Death Rates (Per 100,000): Homicide Males Ages 15–24	CDC	2007	30.0	4.9	16%	0.00
Age-Adjusted Death Rates (Per 100,000): Homicide female	CDC	2008	2.4	1.8	75%	(0.03)
Age-Adjusted Death Rates (Per 100,000): Homicide Females Ages 15–24	CDC	2007	3.5	2.2	63%	0.00
Age-Adjusted Death Rates (Per 100,000) By Age Cohort: >1 Male	CDC	2007	632.7	616.8	97%	0.00
Age-Adjusted Death Rates (Per 100,000) By Age Cohort: 1–4 Male	CDC	2007	28.0	28.1	100%	0.00
Age-Adjusted Death Rates (Per 100,000) By Age Cohort: 5–14 Male	CDC	2007	15.8	16.1	102%	0.00
Age-Adjusted Death Rates (Per 100,000) By Age Cohort: 15–24 Male	CDC	2007	115.3	104.6	91%	0.00
Age-Adjusted Death Rates (Per 100,000) By Age Cohort: 25–34 Male	CDC	2007	110.1	140.8	128%	0.00
Age-Adjusted Death Rates (Per 100,000) By Age Cohort: 35–44 Male	CDC	2007	166.3	228.4	137%	0.00
Age-Adjusted Death Rates (Per 100,000) By Age Cohort: 45–54 Male	CDC	2007	399.2	508.7	127%	0.00
Age-Adjusted Death Rates (Per 100,000) By Age Cohort: 55–64 Male	CDC	2007	831.4	1,057.5	127%	0.00
Age-Adjusted Death Rates (Per 100,000) By Age Cohort: 65–74 Male	CDC	2007	1,862.7	2,432.7	131%	0.00
Age-Adjusted Death Rates (Per 100,000) By Age Cohort: 75–84 Male	CDC	2007	4,364.8	6,152.7	141%	0.00
Age-Adjusted Death Rates (Per 100,000) By Age Cohort: 85+Male	CDC	2007	8,953.7	14,588.3	163%	0.00
Age-Adjusted Death Rates (Per 100,000) By Age Cohort: >1 Female	CDC	2007	539.9	499.6	93%	0.00
Age-Adjusted Death Rates (Per 100,000) By Age Cohort: 1–4 Female	CDC	2007	23.8	22.7	95%	0.00
Age-Adjusted Death Rates (Per 100,000) By Age Cohort: 5–14 Female	CDC	2007	12.3	12.3	100%	0.00
Age-Adjusted Death Rates (Per 100,000) By Age Cohort: 15–24 Female	CDC	2007	33.5	42.7	127%	0.00
Age-Adjusted Death Rates (Per 100,000) By Age Cohort: 25–34 Female	CDC	2007	43.4	63.4	146%	0.00
Age-Adjusted Death Rates (Per 100,000) By Age Cohort: 35–44 Female	CDC	2007	82.7	134.4	163%	0.00
Age-Adjusted Death Rates (Per 100,000) By Age Cohort: 45–54 Female	CDC	2007	204.0	300.5	147%	0.00
Age-Adjusted Death Rates (Per 100,000) By Age Cohort: 55–64 Female	CDC	2007	476.9	651.3	137%	0.00
Age-Adjusted Death Rates (Per 100,000) By Age Cohort: 65–74 Female	CDC	2007	1,162.1	1,634.9	141%	0.00
Age-Adjusted Death Rates (Per 100,000) By Age Cohort: 75–84 Female	CDC	2007	3,196.2	4,385.4	137%	0.00
Age-Adjusted Death Rates (Per 100,000) By Age Cohort: 85+Female	CDC	2007	8,318.9	12,856.7	155%	0.00
Physical Condition (0.10)						
Overweight: 18+ Years, % of Population	CDC	2010	38.1	36.3	95%	(0.03)
Overweight: Men 20 Years and Over, % of Population	CDC	2005-08	45.4	40.2	89%	0.00
Overweight: Women 20 Years and Over, % of Population	CDC	2005-08	30.9	26.5	86%	0.00
Obese, % of Population	CDC	2010	30.6	26.1	85%	(0.04)
Obese: Men 20 Years and Over, % of Population	CDC	2005-08	31.2	32.4	104%	0.00
Obese: Women 20 Years and Over, % of Population	CDC	2005-08	43.1	33.2	77%	0.00
Diabetes: physician Diagnosed in Ages 20+, % of Population	CDC	2005-08	11.8	6.5	55%	0.03
AIDS Cases Per 100,000 Males Ages 13+	CDC	2009	28.9	9.8	34%	(0.01)

2012 EQUALITY INDEX OF HISPANIC AMERICA	Source	Year	Hispanic	White	Index	Diff. ('12-'11)
AIDS Cases Per 100,000 Females Ages 13+	CDC	2009	7.9	1.5	19%	(0.01)
Substance Abuse (0.10)						
Binge Alcohol (5 Drinks in 1 Day, 1X a Year)Ages 18+, % of Population	CDC	2009	19.9	27.5	138%	0.00
Use of Illicit Drugs in the Past Month Ages 12 +, % of Population	CDC	2009	7.9	8.8	111%	(0.21)
Tobacco: Both Cigarette & Cigar Ages 12+, % of Population	CDC	2009	23.2	29.6	128%	(0.15)
Mental Health (0.02)						
Students Who Consider Suicide: Male, %	CDC	2009	10.7	10.5	98%	0.03
Students Who Carry Out Intent and Require Medical Attention: Male, %	CDC	2007	1.8	0.9	50%	0.00
Students That Act on Suicidal Feeling: Male, %	CDC	2007	6.3	3.4	54%	0.00
Students Who Consider Suicide: Female, %	CDC	2009	20.2	16.1	80%	(0.05)
Students Who Carry Out Intent and Require Medical Attention: Female, %	CDC	2007	3.9	2.1	54%	0.00
Students That Act on Suicidal Feeling: Female, %	CDC	2007	14.0	7.7	55%	0.00
Access to Care (0.05)						
Private Insurance Payment for Health Care: Under 65 Years Old, % of Distribution	CDC	2008	39.0	57.7	68%	(0.02)
People Without Health Insurance, % of Population	Census: CPS ASEC	2010	30.7	11.7	38%	0.01
People 18 to 64 Without a Usual Source of Health Insurance, % of Adults	Census: CPS ASEC	2010	41.4	15.9	38%	0.01
People in Poverty Without a Usual Source of Health Insurance, % of Adults	Census: CPS ASEC	2010	59.4	39.4	66%	0.01
Population Under 65 Covered By Medicaid, % of Population	CDC	2009	27.6	10.4	38%	0.00
Elderly Health Care (0.03)						
Population Over 65 Covered By Medicaid, % of Population	CDC	2008	21.1	5.4	26%	0.00
Medicare Expenditures Per Beneficiary, Dollars	CDC	2007	17,019	15,460	91%	(0.25)
Pregnancy Issues (0.04)						
Prenatal Care Begins in 1st Trimester	CDC	2007	72.4	87.7	83%	0.00
Prenatal Care Begins in 3rd Trimester	CDC	2007	6.2	2.3	37%	0.00
Percent of Births to Mothers 18 and Under	CDC	2008	5.3	1.9	36%	(0.02)
Percent of Live Births to Unmarried Mothers	CDC	2008	52.6	28.7	55%	0.00
Infant Mortality Rates Among Mothers With Less Than 12 Years Education	CDC	2005	5.2	9.3	179%	0.00
Infant Mortality Rates Among Mothers With 12 Years Education	CDC	2005	5.4	7.1	131%	0.00
Infant Mortality Rates Among Mothers With 13 or More Years Education	CDC	2005	4.6	4.1	89%	0.00
Mothers Who Smoked Cigarettes During Pregnancy, %	CDC	2007	2.4	12.7	529%	0.00
Low Birth Weight, % of Live Births	CDC	2008	7.0	7.2	104%	(0.01)
Very Low Birth Weight, % of Live Births	CDC	2008	1.2	1.2	98%	(0.00)
Reproduction Issues (0.01)						
Abortions, Per 100 Live Births	CDC	2007	21.3	15.8	74%	0.02
Women Using Contraception, % of Population (Ages 15–44)	CDC	2006-08	58.5	64.7	90%	0.00
Delivery Issues (0.10)						
All Infant Deaths: Neonatal and Post, Per 1000 Live Births	CDC	2006	5.4	5.6	104%	0.00
Neonatal Deaths, Per 1000 Live Births	CDC	2006	3.7	3.6	97%	0.00

Updated ■ History Revised ☐ No New Data

2012 EQUALITY INDEX OF HISPANIC AMERICA	Source	Year	Hispanic	White	Index	Diff. ('12-'11)
Post Neonatal Deaths, Per 1000 Live Births	CDC	2006	1.7	1.9	112%	0.00
Maternal Mortality, Per 100,000 Live Births	CDC	2007	7.2	8.1	113%	0.00
Children's Health (0.10)						
Babies Breastfed, %	CDC	2007	80.6	76.2	106%	0.00
Children Without a Health Care Visit in Past 12 Months (Up to 6 Years Old), %	CDC	2008-09	7.7	4.1	53%	0.00
Vaccinations of Children Below Poverty: Combined Vacc. Series 4: 3: 1: 3,% of Children 19–35 Months	CDC	2009	71.0	68.0	104%	0.00
Uninsured Children, %	Census: CPS ASEC	2010	16.3	6.9	42%	0.01
Overweight Boys 6–11 Years Old, % of Population	CDC	2005-08	28.4	16.5	58%	0.02
Overweight Girls 6–11 Years Old, % of Population	CDC	2005-08	21.2	14.5	68%	(0.05)
AIDS Cases Per 100,000 All Children Under 13	CDC	2009	0.030	0.022	73%	0.00
Health Weighted Index					**104.4%**	**(0.004)**

EDUCATION (25%)						
Quality (0.25)						
Teacher Quality (0.10)						
Middle Grades: Teacher Lacking at Least a College Minor in Subject Taught (High Vs. Low Minority Schools)*, %	ET	2000	49.0	40.0	85%	0.00
HS: Teacher Lacking An Undergraduate Major in Subject Taught (High Vs. Low Poverty Schools)*, %	ET	2008	21.9	10.9	88%	(0.03)
Per Student Funding (High Vs. Low Poverty Districts)*, Dollars	ET	2004	5,937	7,244	82%	0.00
Teachers With < 3 Years Experience (High Vs. Low Poverty Schools)* , %	ET	2008	14.3	10.5	73%	0.26
Distribution of Underprepared Teachers (High Vs. Low Minority Schools)*, %(California Only)	SRI	2008-09	5.0	1.0	20%	0.00

* High Poverty (Minority) Values Are Recorded in The Hispanic Column, Low Poverty (Minority) Values Are Recorded in The White Column

Course Quality (0.15)						
College Completion, % of All Entrants	NCES	2002	48.9	60.2	81%	0.01
College Completion, % of Entrants With Strong HS Curriculum (Algebra II Plus Other Courses)	ET	1999	79.0	86.0	92%	0.00
HS Students: Enrolled in Chemistry, %	NCES	2005	59.2	67.1	88%	0.00
HS Students: Enrolled in Algebra 2, %	NCES	2005	62.7	71.2	88%	0.00
Students Taking: Precalculus, %	CB	2009	45.3	55.0	82%	0.00
Students Taking: Calculus, %	CB	2009	19.3	30.0	64%	0.00
Students Taking: Physics, %	CB	2009	47.0	54.0	87%	0.00
Students Taking: English Honors Course, %	CB	2009	35.0	43.0	81%	0.00
Attainment (0.30)						
Graduation Rates, 2-Year Institutions, %	NCES	2005	32.8	32.0	103%	0.10
Graduation Rates, 4-Year Institutions, %	NCES	2002	46.2	59.3	78%	(0.01)
NCAA Div. I College Freshmen Graduating Within 6 Years, %	NCAA	2002-03	54.0	65.0	83%	0.00
Degrees Earned: Associate, % of Population Aged 18–24 Yrs	NCES	2008-09	1.6	3.0	55%	(0.07)
Degrees Earned: Bachelor's, % of Population Aged 18–29 Yrs	NCES	2008-09	1.3	3.8	33%	(0.03)

2012 EQUALITY INDEX OF HISPANIC AMERICA	Source	Year	Hispanic	White	Index	Diff. ('12-'11)
Degrees Earned: Master's, % of Population Aged 18–34 Yrs	NCES	2008-09	0.3	1.0	27%	(0.02)
Educational Attainment: at Least High School (25 Yrs. and Over), % of Population	Census	2010	62.9	92.1	68%	0.01
Educational Attainment: at Least Bachelor's (25 Yrs. and Over), % of Population	Census	2010	13.9	33.2	42%	0.02
Degree Holders, % Distribution, By Field						
Agriculture/Forestry	NCES	2001	1.1	1.2	96%	0.00
Art/Architecture	NCES	2001	4.8	2.9	166%	0.00
Business/Management	NCES	2001	19.5	18.1	108%	0.00
Communications	NCES	2001	3.3	2.4	140%	0.00
Computer and Information Sciences	NCES	2001	2.6	2.2	119%	0.00
Education	NCES	2001	10.7	15.3	70%	0.00
Engineering	NCES	2001	7.9	7.7	103%	0.00
English/Literature	NCES	2001	3.1	3.3	95%	0.00
Foreign Languages	NCES	2001	1.7	0.9	202%	0.00
Health Sciences	NCES	2001	4.4	4.5	98%	0.00
Liberal Arts/Humanities	NCES	2001	4.7	6.1	77%	0.00
Mathematics/Statistics	NCES	2001	2.4	1.4	167%	0.00
Natural Sciences	NCES	2001	4.9	5.6	88%	0.00
Philosophy/Religion/Theology	NCES	2001	1.8	1.3	132%	0.00
Pre-Professional	NCES	2001	2.0	1.1	182%	0.00
Psychology	NCES	2001	5.0	3.9	129%	0.00
Social Sciences/History	NCES	2001	4.7	4.9	95%	0.00
Other Fields	NCES	2001	15.4	17.2	89%	0.00
Scores (0.25)						
Preschool 10% of Total Scores (0.015)						
Children's School Readiness Skills (Ages 3–5), % With 3 or 4 Skills* *Recognizes All Letters, Counts to 20 or Higher, Writes Name, Reads or Pretends to Read	NCES	2005	26.0	46.8	55%	0.00
Elementary 40% of Total Scores (0.06)						
Average Scale Score in U.S. History, 8th Graders	NCES	2010	252	274	92%	0.01
Average Scale Score in U.S. History, 4th Graders	NCES	2010	198	224	88%	0.02
Average Scale Score in Math, 8th Graders	NCES	2011	270	293	92%	0.01
Average Scale Score in Math, 4th Graders	NCES	2011	229	249	92%	0.00
Average Scale Score in Reading, 8th Graders	NCES	2011	252	274	92%	0.01
Average Scale Score in Reading, 4th Graders	NCES	2011	206	231	89%	0.00
Average Scale Score in Science, 8th Graders	NCES	2005	129	160	81%	0.00
Average Scale Score in Science, 4th Graders	NCES	2005	133	162	82%	0.00
Writing Proficiency at or Above Basic, 8th Graders, % of Students	NCES	2007	80	93	86%	0.00
Writing Proficiency at or Above Basic, 4th Graders, % of Students	NCES	2002	77	90	85%	0.00
High School 50% of Total Scores (0.075)						
Writing Proficiency at or Above Basic, 12th Graders, % of Students	NCES	2007	71	86	83%	0.00
Average Scale Score in Science, 12th Graders	NCES	2005	128	156	82%	0.00

Updated　History Revised　☐ No New Data

2012 EQUALITY INDEX OF HISPANIC AMERICA	Source	Year	Hispanic	White	Index	Diff. ('12-'11)
Average Scale Score in U.S. History, 12th Graders	NCES	2010	275	296	93%	0.00
Average Scale Score in Reading, 12th Graders	NCES	2009	274	296	93%	(0.00)
High School GPA's for Those Taking The Sat	CB	2009	3.17	3.40	93%	0.00
Sat Reasoning Test: Mean Scores	CB	2011	1,358	1,579	86%	(0.00)
Mathematics, Joint	CB	2011	463	535	86%	0.00
Mathematics, Male	CB	2011	481	552	87%	0.00
Mathematics, Female	CB	2011	449	520	86%	0.00
Critical Reading, Joint	CB	2011	451	528	85%	(0.01)
Critical Reading, Male	CB	2011	456	531	86%	(0.01)
Critical Reading, Female	CB	2011	447	526	85%	(0.01)
Writing, Joint	CB	2011	444	516	86%	(0.01)
Writing, Male	CB	2011	439	507	87%	(0.01)
Writing, Female	CB	2011	448	524	85%	(0.01)
Act - Average Composite Score	ACT	2011	18.7	22.4	83%	0.00
Enrollment (0.10)						
School Enrollment: ages 3–34, % of Population	Census	2009	52.8	56.8	93%	0.02
Preprimary School Enrollment	Census	2009	54.2	66.6	81%	(0.01)
3 and 4 Years Old	Census	2009	41.9	55.5	75%	(0.02)
5 and 6 Years Old	Census	2009	93.7	94.1	100%	0.03
7 to 13 Years Old	Census	2009	97.3	98.7	99%	(0.00)
14 and 15 Years Old	Census	2009	97.9	98.3	100%	(0.00)
16 and 17 Years Old	Census	2009	92.6	95.0	97%	(0.00)
18 and 19 Years Old	Census	2009	57.1	72.4	79%	0.00
20 and 21 Years Old	Census	2009	37.2	56.4	66%	0.08
22 to 24 Years Old	Census	2009	20.4	31.1	66%	0.00
25 to 29 Years Old	Census	2009	9.5	14.0	68%	(0.01)
30 to 34 Years Old	Census	2009	5.6	8.1	69%	0.08
35 and Over	Census	2009	2.2	1.9	118%	(0.04)
College Enrollment (Graduate or Undergraduate): Ages 14 and Over, % of Population	Census	2009	5.4	6.8	79%	0.01
14 to 17 Years Old	Census	2009	1.4	1.2	117%	(0.23)
18 to 19 Years Old	Census	2009	32.7	56.1	58%	(0.04)
20 to 21 Years Old	Census	2009	34.4	55.6	62%	0.09
22 to 24 Years Old	Census	2009	19.3	30.9	62%	0.03
25 to 29 Years Old	Census	2009	9.2	13.8	67%	(0.00)
30 to 34 Years Old	Census	2009	5.3	8.0	66%	0.16
35 Years Old and Over	Census	2009	1.8	1.8	101%	(0.13)
College Enrollment Rate As a Percent of All 18- to 24-Year-Old High School Completers, %	NCES	2009	38.7	50.3	77%	0.02
Adult Education Participation, % of Adult Population	NCES	2004-05	38.0	46.0	83%	0.00

Updated ▉ History Revised ☐ No New Data

2012 EQUALITY INDEX OF HISPANIC AMERICA	Source	Year	Hispanic	White	Index	Diff. ('12-'11)
Student Status & Risk Factors (0.10)						
High School Dropouts: Status Dropouts, % (Not Completed HS and Not Enrolled, Regardless of When Dropped)	Census	2009	20.8	9.1	44%	0.04
Children in Poverty, %	Census	2010	35.0	12.4	35%	(0.01)
Children in All Families Below Poverty Level, %	Census	2010	34.6	11.7	34%	(0.01)
Children in Families Below Poverty Level (Female Householder, No Spouse Present), %	Census	2010	57.0	34.8	61%	(0.03)
Children (Under 18) With a Disability, %	Census	2010	3.5	4.0	114%	0.01
Public School Students (K-12): Repeated Grade, %	NCES	2007	11.8	8.7	74%	(0.04)
Public School Students (K-12): Suspended, %	NCES	2003	10.4	8.8	85%	0.00
Public School Students (K-12): Expelled, %	NCES	2003	1.4	1.4	100%	0.00
Center-Based Child Care of Preschool Children, %	NCES	2005	43.4	59.1	136%	0.00
Parental Care Only of Preschool Children, %	NCES	2005	38.0	24.1	158%	0.00
Teacher Stability: Remained in Public School, High Vs. Low Minority Schools, %	NCES	2005	79.7	85.9	93%	0.00
Teacher Stability: Remained in Private School, High Vs. Low Minority Schools, %	NCES	2005	72.7	82.8	88%	0.00
Zero Days Missed in School Year, % of 10th Graders	NCES	2002	16.5	12.1	137%	0.00
3+ Days Late to School, % of 10th Graders	NCES	2002	46.1	44.4	96%	0.00
Never Cut Classes, % of 10th Graders	NCES	2002	64.6	70.3	92%	0.00
Home Literacy Activities (Age 3 to 5)						
Read to 3 or More Times a Week	NCES	2007	67.6	90.6	75%	0.00
Told a Story at Least Once a Month	NCES	2005	49.8	53.3	93%	0.00
Taught Words or Numbers Three or More Times a Week	NCES	2005	74.3	75.7	98%	0.00
Visited a Library at Least Once in Last Month	NCES	2007	27.0	40.8	66%	0.00
Education Weighted Index					75.8%	0.007

SOCIAL JUSTICE (10%)						
Equality Before The Law (0.70)						
Stopped While Driving, %	BJS	2008	9.1	8.4	92%	(0.08)
Speeding	BJS	2002	44.4	57.0	128%	0.00
Vehicle Defect	BJS	2002	14.0	8.7	62%	0.00
Roadside Check for Drinking Drivers	BJS	2002	1.6	1.3	81%	0.00
Record Check	BJS	2002	7.8	11.3	145%	0.00
Seatbelt Violation	BJS	2002	5.5	4.4	80%	0.00
Illegal Turn/Lane Change	BJS	2002	5.7	4.5	79%	0.00
Stop Sign/Light Violation	BJS	2002	11.2	6.5	58%	0.00
Other	BJS	2002	6.2	4.0	65%	0.00
Incarceration Rate: Prisoners Per 100,000	BJS	2010	678	252	37%	(0.03)
Incarceration Rate: Prisoners Per 100,000 People: Male	BJS	2010	1,252	456	36%	(0.04)
Incarceration Rate: Prisoners Per 100,000 People: Female	BJS	2010	77	47	61%	(0.07)

Updated ▨ History Revised ☐ No New Data

2012 EQUALITY INDEX OF HISPANIC AMERICA	Source	Year	Hispanic	White	Index	Diff. ('12-'11)
Victimization & Mental Anguish (0.30)						
Homicide Rate Per 100,000: Male	CDC	2007	12.4	3.7	30%	0.00
Homicide Rate Per 100,000: Female	CDC	2007	2.5	1.8	72%	0.00
Hate Crimes Victims, Rate Per 100,000	USDJ	2010	1.5	0.3	20%	0.00
Victims of Violent Crimes, Rate Per 100,000	BJS	2010	15.6	13.6	87%	(0.00)
High School Students Carrying Weapons on School Property	CDC	2009	5.8	5.6	97%	0.00
High School Students Carrying Weapons Anywhere	CDC	2009	17.2	18.6	108%	0.00
Firearm-Related Death Rates Per 100,000: Males, All Ages	CDC	2007	13.4	16.1	120%	0.00
Ages 1–14	CDC	2007	0.8	0.7	86%	0.00
Ages 15–24	CDC	2007	30.7	13.4	44%	0.00
Ages 25–44	CDC	2007	17.7	18.3	104%	0.00
Ages 25–34	CDC	2007	21.8	18.0	82%	0.00
Ages 35–44	CDC	2007	12.6	18.7	148%	0.00
Ages 45–64	CDC	2007	9.7	19.5	202%	0.00
Age 65 and Older	CDC	2007	10.8	27.3	253%	0.00
Firearm-Related Death Rates Per 100,000: Females, All Ages	CDC	2007	1.5	2.9	187%	0.00
Ages 1–14	CDC	2007	0.3	0.3	111%	0.00
Ages 15–24	CDC	2007	2.8	2.5	87%	0.00
Ages 25–44	CDC	2007	2.3	4.1	176%	0.00
Ages 25–34	CDC	2007	2.5	3.4	136%	0.00
Ages 35–44	CDC	2007	2.1	4.6	222%	0.00
Ages 45–64	CDC	2007	1.5	3.9	262%	0.00
Age 65 and Older	CDC	2007	0.6	2.2	393%	0.00
Social Justice Weighted Index					60.9%	(0.026)

CIVIC ENGAGEMENT (10%)						
Democratic Process (0.4)						
Registered Voters, % of Citizen Population	Census	2010	51.6	68.2	76%	(0.05)
Actually Voted, % of Citizen Population	Census	2010	31.2	48.6	64%	(0.11)
Community Participation (0.3)						
Percent of Population Volunteering for Military Reserves, %	USDD	2010	0.4	1.0	40%	(0.06)
Volunteerism, %	BLS	2010	14.7	27.8	53%	0.01
Civic and Political	BLS	2010	3.1	5.5	56%	(0.05)
Educational or Youth Service	BLS	2010	35.7	26.8	133%	0.02
Environmental or Animal Care	BLS	2010	1.4	2.7	52%	0.16
Hospital or Other Health	BLS	2010	5.3	8.1	65%	(0.04)
Public Safety	BLS	2010	1.2	1.4	86%	0.32
Religious	BLS	2010	35.9	32.6	110%	0.02
Social or Community Service	BLS	2010	10.9	13.6	80%	0.03
Unpaid Volunteering of Young Adults	NCES	2000	30.7	32.2	95%	0.00

Updated ▨ History Revised ☐ No New Data

2012 EQUALITY INDEX OF HISPANIC AMERICA	Source	Year	Hispanic	White	Index	Diff. ('12-'11)
Collective Bargaining (0.2)						
Members of Unions, % of Employed	BLS	2010	10.0	11.7	85%	0.00
Represented By Unions, % of Employed	BLS	2010	11.1	13.0	85%	0.00
Governmental Employment (0.1)						
Federal Executive Branch (Nonpostal) Employment, % of Adult Population	OPM	2008	0.4	0.8	52%	(0.08)
State and Local Government Employment, %	EEOC	2009	1.8	2.5	73%	(0.02)
Civic Engagement Weighted Index					67.4%	(0.043)

Due to data availability, the 2012 Equality Index of Hispanic America does not include all the variables that were used to calculate the 2012 Equality Index of Black America. Therefore, weights were redistributed among the available variables and a comparable Black-White index was calculated solely to provide a consistent comparison between Blacks and Hispanics.

Source	Acronym
American Community Survey	ACS
U.S. Bureau of Justice Statistics	BJS
U.S. Bureau of Labor Statistics	BLS
College Board	CB
Centers for Disease Control and Prevention	CDC
U.S. Census Bureau	Census
Employee Benefit Research Institute	EBRI
U.S. Equal Employment Opportunity Commission	EEOC
Economic Policy Institute	EPI
The Education Trust	ET
Home Mortgage Disclosure Act	HMDA
Monitoring the Future	MTF
National Archive of Criminal Justice Data	NACJD
National Center for Education Statistics	NCES
National Center for Juvenile Justice	NCJJ
National Telecommunications and Information Administration	NTIA
Office of Personal Management	OPM
SRI International	SRI
Statistical Abstract of the United States	Stat. Ab.
State of Working America	SWA
U.S. Decennial Census	USDC
U.S. Department of Defense	USDD
Current Population Survey: Annual Social and Economic Supplement	CPS ASEC
U.S. Department of Justice	USDJ

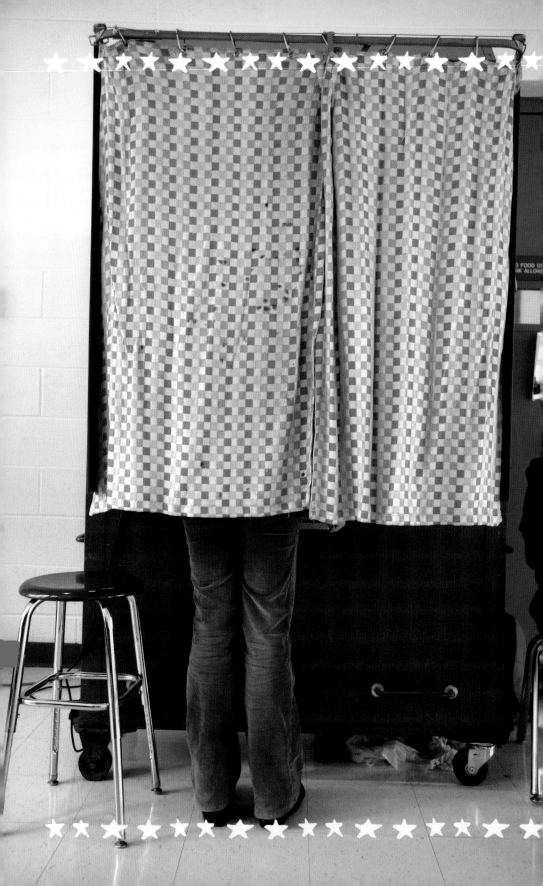

MINORITY VOTER PARTICIPATION:

REVIEWING PAST AND PRESENT BARRIERS TO THE POLLS

U.S. CONGRESSMAN ROBERT C. "BOBBY" SCOTT

In the over 46 years since its passage, the Voting Rights Act has guaranteed millions of minority citizens the right to vote. As the Supreme Court noted: "No right is more precious in a free country than that of having a voice in the election of those who make the laws under which, as good citizens, we must live. Other rights, even the most basic, are illusory if the right to vote is undermined."[1]

Poll taxes, literacy tests and other discriminatory schemes have been effective in undermining the effect of the minority vote. Since Emancipation and culminating in the 1960s, many brave Americans across the country fought to defeat these schemes despite great risks to life and limb. The March 7, 1965 events of "Bloody Sunday," in which my colleague from Georgia, Congressman John Lewis, suffered a fractured skull, aroused the conscience of the nation. As a result of such brave and relentless actions on the part of many, Congress passed the Voting Rights Act of 1965 and President Lyndon Johnson signed it into law.[2] →

The Voting Rights Act dismantled the schemes and barriers to voter participation. As a result, since 1965, the number of black elected officials across the country has increased from just 260[3] to over 10,500 today.[4] The number of Latinos who now hold public office has increased to 5,850[5], and the number of minority elected officials continues to rise among other minorities as well. These numbers demonstrate that the provisions in the Voting Rights Act are effective and also what we stand to lose if voting rights are not protected.

There are several important provisions in the Voting Rights Act, but I would like to highlight three areas that have proved essential to ensuring fairness and equal opportunity for minorities in the American political system. Section 5[6] protects voters by requiring that states with a documented history of discriminatory voting practices and low voter turnout submit planned changes in their election laws or procedures to federal officials or judges for prior approval ("preclearance"). Those states and areas that are covered by Section 5 were selected "the old fashion way: they earned it." It is important to note that preclearance does not punish states for the wrongdoings of the past. Instead, it prevents newly enacted voting practices that diminish the ability of citizens to elect their preferred candidates of choice. The real magic of Section 5 is that it is designed to stop an illegal scheme before it ever goes into effect. This prevents the perpetrators from benefitting from the scheme until such time as the victims can raise the money for the complex litigation necessary to overturn the scheme.

Sections 6[7], 7[8] and 8[9] contain the federal examiner and observer provisions of the Voting Rights Act, which allow federal employees to observe polling places and vote-counting activities. Federal observers have been deployed virtually every year from 1966 to the present. Because those involved in the election process know their actions are being observed by federal officials, they are discouraged from engaging in inappropriate behavior.

Section 203[10] provides important tools to ensure fundamental fairness in the voting process for language minority groups when English proficiency is limited. Section 203 works. When language assistance is available, voter participation goes up. We want to make sure that we are encouraging all eligible voters to participate.

Unfortunately, the existence of the Voting Rights Act does not deter some from becoming creative in their efforts to reduce voter participation. One current trend is to require certain oter identification with no or very limited exceptions. Currently, 31 states have laws on the books requiring all voters to show forms of identification before voting.[11] Fifteen of the states with these laws require photo identification, such as a driver's license;[12] in the other 16 states certain non-picture IDs are also acceptable.

While voter identification seems at first a good idea to deter voter fraud, this type of requirement has serious unintended consequences. The Brennan Center for Justice at the New York University School of Law conducted a nationwide study of voting age citizens in 2006 and found that African Americans are more than three times as likely as Caucasians to lack a government-issued photo ID, with one in four African Americans owning no such ID.[13] Moreover, no convincing evidence exists that says that in-person voter fraud, which is the only type of fraud that photo IDs could prevent, is a meaningful problem.[14]

★ ★ ★ ★ ★ ★ ★ ★ ★ ★ ★ ★ ★ ★ ★ ★

Fortunately, the Department of Justice has begun to address the voter ID problem. In late December 2011, the Department blocked South Carolina's voter ID law by denying preclearance under Section 5 of the Voting Rights Act. Hopefully, the Department will block similar voter ID laws in other states that are covered in part or whole by Section 5.

> Currently, 31 states have laws on the books requiring all voters to show forms of identification before voting.[11]

There is also a trend to limit opportunities for voter registration and early voting. Last year, at least five states enacted laws that reduced their early voting periods.[15] Additionally, several states introduced bills to end same-day voter registration and to restrict voter registration mobilization initiatives.[16]

Unfortunately, actions of this Congress haven't been particularly helpful to the effort to protect voting rights. There are, however, some in the Congress who seek to ensure that voting rights and opportunities are protected. For example, Congressional Black Caucus (CBC) Chairman Emanuel Cleaver recently announced that the CBC will launch a multi-city "voter-protection" tour kicking off the weekend of March 3 around the anniversary of "Bloody Sunday."

Clearly, the Voting Rights Act has been successful in protecting the right to vote. Yet,

as abolitionist Wendell Phillips noted, "[e]ternal vigilance is the price of liberty." Our voting rights protect our liberty. Thus, to preserve our democracy we must work to defeat the current efforts to roll back voting rights and protections. We must also remain ever vigilant to defeat such efforts when they arise in the future.

NOTES

[1] Wesberry v. Sanders, 376 U.S. 1, 17–18 (1964)

[2] 42 U.S.C. §§ 1973–1973(aa–6)

[3] Jack Nelson, "The Civil Rights Movement: A Press Perspective," American Bar Association: *Human Rights Magazine*, Fall 2001 (Volume 28, Number 4) (see at http://www.americanbar.org/publications/human_rights_magazine_home/irr_hr_fall01_nelson.html)

[4] Civic Engagement and Governance Institute, "Fact Sheet: National Roster of Black Elected Officials," Joint Center for Political and Economic Studies, November 2011 (see at http://www.jointcenter.org/sites/default/files/upload/research/files/National%20Roster%20of%20Black%20Elected%20Officials%20Fact%20Sheet.pdf)

[5] National Association of Latino Elected and Appointed Officials,"2011 Directory of Latino Elected Officials," January 26, 2011 (see at http://www.naleo.org/directory.html)

[6] 42 U.S.C. § 1973(c)

[7] 42 U.S.C. § 1973(d)

[8] 42 U.S.C. § 1973(e)

[9] 42 U.S.C. § 1973 (f)

[10] 42 U.S.C § 1973(aa)–(1a)

[11] Associated Press, "Iowa Secretary of State Unveils Voter Identification Proposal," *The Gazette*, January 26, 2012 (see at http://thegazette.com/2012/01/26/iowa-secretary-of-state-to-unveil-voter-identification-bill/)

[12] Ibid.

[13] Brennan Center for Justice at NYU School of Law, "Citizens Without Proof: A Survey of American's Possession of Documentary Proof of Citizenship and Photo Identification," Voting Rights And Election Series, 2006 at p. 3 (see at http://www.brennancenter.org/page/-/d/download_file_39242.pdf)

[14] American Civil Liberties Union. "Oppose Voter ID Legislation—Fact Sheet," American Civil Liberties Union, July 21, 2011 (see at http://www.aclu.org/voting-rights/oppose-voter-id-legislation-fact-sheet)

[15] Brennan Center for Justice at NYU School of Law, Wendy R. Weiser and Lawrence Norden, "Voting Law Changes in 2012," p. 3, (see at http://brennan.3cdn.net/9c0a034a4b3c68a2af_9hm6bj6d0.pdf)

[16] Ibid., pp. 19–33

THE RISE AND FALL AND RISE AGAIN

OF JIM CROW LAWS

REVEREND LENNOX YEARWOOD, JR.

There are many things of times past that we do not have much use for any longer. Typewriters, 35 millimeter film, VHS tapes, for example, are all things that we have replaced with newer technologies that better serve us. After all, is not progress the beauty of modern society? Innovation is constantly providing us with better tools to use in our daily lives. While phone booths to cell phones may be a light-hearted look at our transition from the 20th century to the 21st, unfortunately, unlike the disappearance of eight-track tapes, Jim Crow laws have come back with a vengeance in the 21st century. →

It is curious that our society has no problem leaving typewriters behind and adopting iPads, yet, we have a big problem when it comes to leaving inequality, discrimination and racism in the previous century.

I am sorry to report, that when it comes to the state of civil and human rights in this country, we are on the brink of regression. The voting rights of people of color are under attack. This is happening in the 21st century, over a half century after people died for the right to vote for African Americans. The outcry today is lackluster, however, mostly because people don't even know this is happening.

Over the past two years, a series of laws have been enacted in state legislatures that could prevent millions of people of color, students, ex-offenders, new Americans, and the elderly from casting ballots.

Jim Crow (a personification of the forces behind Jim Crow laws) of the 20th century was evil, but he was also not particularly sophisticated. When exposed by young people conducting non-violent civil disobedient protests, the country ultimately chose humanity over evil.

But today, James Crow, Jr., Esq., as I like to call him (again a personification of the forces behind discriminatory and racist policies of today), is much more sophisticated than his grandfather Jim Crow.

James Crow, Jr., Esq. knows that turning hoses and setting dogs on young protesters will doom his end goals. He also knows that discrimination by any other name is just as profitable for him. So, instead of outright attempting to deny access for people of color, poor people, young people and working-class people to the polls, he is successfully advocating for added barriers that happen to mostly affect these groups of people who tend to vote against his political and economic interests.

Over the past two years, a series of laws have been enacted in state legislatures that could prevent millions of people of color, students, ex-offenders, new Americans, and the elderly from casting ballots. Dozens of states have approved obstacles to voting. For example, Kansas and Alabama now require eligible voters to provide proof of citizenship before registering.[1] These five states—Florida, Georgia, Ohio, Tennessee and West Virginia have cut short their early voting periods.[2] Florida and Iowa prevented all ex-offenders from the polls, disenfranchising thousands of previously eligible voters.[3] And these six states—Alabama, Kansas, South Carolina, Tennessee, Texas and Wisconsin, now require voters to produce a government-issued ID before casting ballots.[4] A 2006 survey found that as many as 7 percent of U.S. citizens do not have ready access to documents to prove U.S. citizenship and 11 percent of U.S. citizens do not have government-issued photo identification.[5] African American citizens disproportionately lack photo identification—25 percent of African American voting age citizens do not have a current government issued photo ID, compared to 8 percent of white voting age citizens.[6]

It has become such a problem that the Department of Justice for the first time since 1994 had to exercise its powers under the Voting Rights Act to block a voter identification law enacted by a State.[7]

In a letter to the South Carolina government, Thomas E. Perez, the Assistant Attorney General for Civil Rights for the U.S. Department of Justice, said that allowing the new requirement to go into effect would have "significant racial disparities."[8]

He cited data supplied by the state as showing that there were "81,938 minority citizens who are already registered to vote and who lack"[9] such identification, and that these voters are nearly 20 percent more likely to be "effectively disenfranchised" by the change than white voters.[10]

This push for bringing back Jim Crow Laws did not start two years ago; there has been a segment of our country that has long tried to drive people of color away from the polls.

Paul Weyrich, a leading conservative activist who passed away one month after President Barack Obama was elected in 2008, told a gathering of evangelical leaders in 1980, "I don't want everybody to vote. As a matter of fact, our leverage in the elections quite candidly goes up as the voting populace goes down."[11] Following this line of thinking, since the 2010 election, conservative advocacy groups like the American Legislative Exchange Council (ALEC) founded by Weyrich have instituted various efforts to disrupt and suppress voting rights. In what

seems very much like a systematic campaign orchestrated by ALEC and based on model legislation promoted by ALEC, various states have taken steps to disrupt and suppress the right of U.S. citizens to vote. Recently, Senator Bill Nelson (D-FL) asked the U.S. Justice Department to investigate these new state voting laws and the role played by ALEC and others in enacting them.[12] In 2010, thirteen states approved changes to their election laws and another 24 states are weighing measures that have the effect of suppressing the ability of minority citizens to vote.[13]

To be clear, this has led to one of the most pervasive, and destructive political movements to keep millions of people of color, new Americans, students, ex-offenders and the elderly from casting ballots. There has never been in our lifetime, since we got rid of the poll tax and all the Jim Crow burdens on voting, such a drive to undercut the right of citizens to vote in this country.

The fact is that the real problem in American elections is not the myth of voter fraud, but how few people actually participate in the electoral process. Even in 2008, which saw the highest voter turnout in four decades, less than two-thirds of eligible voters went to the polls.[14]

This is what needs to be fixed to truly have a representative democracy in America. Modernizing our voting systems by instituting same day registration nationwide, meaning you could register and vote on the same day, would be *progress* towards equality in the 21st century. Or, automatically registering all Americans to vote when they turn 18, just like young men are automatically enrolled in the draft at 18, or we are all automatically enrolled in paying taxes when we start earning an income would be *progress* towards equality in the 21st century.

Modernizing our voting systems by instituting same day registration nationwide, meaning you could register and vote on the same day, would be *progress* towards equality in the 21st century.

As long as James Crow, Jr., Esq., through incredibly wealthy, non-transparent operations like ALEC, has us reacting to regressive policies attacking victories we won last century, they know we will not be able to fight for progress. We have been caught flat-footed, and it is time we go back on the attack. James Crow, Jr., Esq. is counting on us not calling the laws that are being passed in state legislatures for what they are—discriminatory. We must stand up, and remind America that even in the 21st century, discrimination by any other name is just as appalling as it was in the 20th century.

NOTES

[1] Ari Berman, "The GOP War on Voting," *Rolling Stone*, September 15, 2011 at *http://www.rollingstone.com/politics/news/the-gop-war-on-voting-20110830*

[2] Ibid.

[3] Ibid.

[4] Ibid.

[5] Brennan Center for Justice at NYU School of Law, "Citizens without Proof: A Survey of Americans' Possession of Documentary Proof of Citizenship and Photo Identification," Voting Rights & Elections Series, November 2006 at p. 2 and 3 at *http://www.brennancenter.org/page/-/d/download_file_39242.pdf*

[6] Ibid., at p. 3

[7] Charlie Savage, "Justice Department Cites Race in Halting Law Over Voter ID," *The New York Times*, December 23, 2011 at *http://www.nytimes.com/2011/12/24/us/justice-department-rejects-voter-id-law-in-south-carolina.html?_r=1*

[8] Thomas E. Perez (Assistant U.S. Attorney General) letter to C. Havird Jones, Jr. (Assistant Deputy Attorney General of the State of South Carolina) dated December 23, 2011 at p. 3 *http://media.charleston.net/2011/pdf/dojscvoteridletter_12232011.pdf*

[9] Ibid., at p. 3

[10] Ibid., at p. 2

[11] Ari Berman, "The GOP War on Voting," *Rolling Stone*, September 15, 2011 at *http://www.rollingstone.com/politics/news/the-gop-war-on-voting-20110830*

[12] Erika Bolstad and William Douglas, "Nelson Demands Probe of New Voting Laws," *The Miami Herald*, November 3, 2011 at *http://www.miamiherald.com/2011/11/03/2486146/nelson-demands-probe-of-new-voting.html*

[13] Ibid.

[14] U.S. Census Bureau, "Voting and Registration in the Election of November 2008," May 2010 at p. 2 at *http://www.census.gov/prod/2010pubs/p20-562.pdf*

THE 2012 N.U.L. 8-POINT EDUCATION AND EMPLOYMENT PLAN

EMPLOYMENT AND EDUCATION, EMPOWER THE NATION

NATIONAL URBAN LEAGUE POLICY INSTITUTE

In 2011, the National Urban League launched the 12-Point Jobs Plan to Put America Back to Work. In 2012, we are issuing a public call for immediate national action around the education and job-training steps necessary to achieve these goals. As a result of our long history of job training and education programs, the National Urban League understands the importance of equipping workers with a sound education. With the introduction of our 2012 Employment and Education Plan, we seek to raise this most urgent conversation to the top of our national news headlines. The time to act is now! →

Any serious discussion about the creation of jobs and economic opportunity must account for the basic shortcomings of our current national approach to education, from early education to adulthood, and beyond. These two concepts are closely rooted in their ultimate purpose, if not one and the same. Education, at its core, *is* economic readiness. Job training, by its very definition, *is* education in its most practical sense. The two cannot and must not be viewed separately. A broken national system of education will continue to yield a broken economy, built upon broken communities and broken lives.

This list of practical and actionable ideas is a recommended approach to solving America's crisis in education—one designed to spark serious discussion, while also serving as a policy playbook ready for action today. We view the following collection of ideas as the first step towards positive change, and a long-term education solution for America.

Although our traditional role has often been seen by many as a 'bridge' between the services available and the daily needs the underserved of our cities, we fully accept the growing challenge asked of a historic civil rights organization such as ours, to take the lead in forcing our country to confront those basic sources of economic hardship that we can and must change within our lifetime.

① Fair and Equitable School Funding for All
Nearly 60 years after the *Brown vs. Board of Education* decision, our nation's schools are inequitably funded and available funds are distributed unevenly.[1] If America is to achieve the vision of a globally competitive nation, no longer may we accept that the quality of a student's education is based primarily upon his or her zip code. We must have a laser-like focus on high academic outcomes for all students.

Federal and state funding must adequately fund high-quality *traditional and charter schools* by redesigning funding formulas to allow for effective intervention strategies and innovation in the classroom.

→ *Funding must be equitable so that educational outcomes do not depend on geography, race, national origin, language or school location.*

→ *States must compare and publicly report the amount of funding spent on all staff and instructional services to monitor and actively ensure the equity of investments within states and school districts as well as between schools.*

→ *A new national fund must be dedicated to low-performing middle and high schools to ensure that resources are made available according to the varying needs of students with a particular emphasis on school districts with concentrated student poverty.*

→ *Federal, State and Local Education policy must encourage, and incentivize longer school days, and a longer school year to allow for more time on task, as well as full inclusion of quality, extra activities such as sports, music, leadership development and the like.*

② Robust Early Childhood Education for Each Child
The availability of early learning opportunities for children is a significant predictor of the level of achievement students will achieve throughout their academic career. Early interventions for the youngest learners help to promote and ensure the economic health of our nation's future leaders.

→ *All states and districts must set a goal to provide universal access to high-quality preschool programs that prepare students for kindergarten.[2]*

→ *States should align their early learning systems with other education systems, so as to create a seamless education continuum from preschool to postsecondary education.*

→ *Childcare programs for ages 0–5 must fully integrate early learning principles and invest in strategies to support parents as their child's first teacher.[3]*

③ **Strengthening High Schools and Re-Engaging Students to Prevent Dropouts**

Too often the experiences of high school students do not prepare them adequately for postsecondary education and to enter the workforce. We must raise the high school graduation and college-completion rates of students of color to the level of white students by 2020 to add $310 billion to the U.S. economy.[4]

→ *High schools must provide academic supports for all students to overcome barriers to learning and teaching, integrate innovation and research-based methods to re-engage students especially for those students at risk for dropping out of school.*

→ *States must promote culturally relevant content knowledge and teaching that will prepare students to be more effective in a global economy.*

→ *High schools must include financial literacy education to prepare students to manage student and personal loans.*

→ *High schools must seek to engage community-based organizations such as Urban League*

affiliates in new and innovative ways, including in the development of high school improvement, wrap-around services and turnaround strategies.

④ **Robust STEM Focused Curriculum and Programs**

In order to fully prepare students for the fastest growing job sectors in America, all classrooms must adopt a robust STEM curriculum aligned with college and career-ready standards.[5] Students must be exposed to hands on learning outside of the classroom connecting students to STEM related careers.

→ *All classrooms must adopt a robust STEM curriculum aligned with college and career-ready standards and workplace expectations.*

→ *Schools, businesses and community-based organizations must work together to provide co-ops and lab experiences in the middle grades and STEM internships in high schools.*

→ *After-school and out of time programs, such as the National Urban League's Project Ready STEM program, a post-secondary success program for urban middle and high school students designed to provide them with the support and opportunities needed to succeed in STEM-related classwork, should be replicated and brought to scale through public and private partnerships.*

⑤ **Qualified, Effective and Diverse Teachers**

Low-income, low-performing students and students of color are far more likely than other students to have inexperienced, uncertified, poorly educated, and under-performing teachers.[6] In order to develop and support strong educators and school leaders, we must redefine the important role of teachers in contributing to our nation's current and future economic development by addressing the quality of the teaching profession as well as the effectiveness of existing and future teachers.

→ *States and school districts must elevate the teaching profession by providing competitive salaries based upon high quality performance.*

→ *Teachers must be provided mentorship and the necessary supports to succeed and have a defined career ladder that encourages innovation and improvement for those that have been in the classroom for many years.*

→ *Redefine the recruitment and training of teachers in teacher preparation programs while encouraging higher education programs to seek racial and gender diversity in recruitment efforts and prepare teachers to meet a wide range of student needs.*

→ *Qualified, effective teachers must be equally distributed and parents must be provided with transparent information about the preparation and certification of their child's teacher.*

⑥ **Strategic Workforce Development: Targeting Americans Most in Need**
The long overdue reauthorization of the Workforce Investment Act (WIA) has led to the reduction of investment in our nation's workforce, especially those programs that train unskilled and low-skilled adults and youth who have little attachment to the labor force, and older workers whose jobs will have been lost to the recent recession.[7] With long-term unemployment rates hovering above 40 percent since 2009, recent history shows that widespread GDP growth alone will not restore these job seekers to gainful employment. Strategic and effective workforce development therefore requires:

→ *Public/private investments and partnerships in our workforce development system targeted to low income communities.*

→ *Direct federal funding to national community-based intermediary organizations that have demonstrated expertise and effectiveness in workforce development.*

→ *Intensive services in basic education, pre-employment and skills training for high growth and emerging industry jobs of the 21st century.*

→ *Equal access to pre-apprenticeship programs that facilitate better access to unions and higher paying jobs.*

→ *Mandatory inclusion of Urban League affiliates, and other community based organizations on all local Workforce Investment Boards or any other local governing mechanism that may be established by WIA.*

→ *A reauthorized WIA must include conflict of interest provisions to prevent Workforce Investment Boards from functioning as direct service providers in competition with local community based providers.*

⑦ **New Job Training Models Coupled With Job Placement**
Job training programs must provide two services: 1) a full suite of skills that match the needs of employers, and 2) the assistance of successfully trained job seekers with job placement. To achieve this, job placement must be an integral part of any job training program

★ ★ ★ ★ ★ ★ ★ ★ ★ ★ ★ ★ ★ ★ ★ ★

and a national on-the-job training structure that is driven by employer needs and open to diverse organizations must be created. This requires:

→ *Partnerships of business, vocational education providers and community intermediaries addressing all the individual characteristics contributing to successful employment.*

→ *Reforming the old apprenticeship model to fit today's needs. Tax incentives for apprenticeships and community intermediaries to assist hard-to-reach workers must be included.*

→ *Wrap-around services addressing other causes of unemployment must be considered. An example is the crisis of those referred to as the 'long-term unemployed'. In their case, the lack of skills is often not the only impediment to getting a job.*

⑧ Improving and Integrating Current Data Systems

An effective youth-to-adulthood education, job training and job placement structure requires the collection of data that is necessary for efficient resource allocation.

→ *It is essential that this data be established based upon desired outcomes so that P-12 education, workforce development and higher education systems data are connected for a complete understanding of the impact of education on the outcomes (long and short-term) of students, workers and families.*

NOTES

[1] As reported in the National Urban League 2012 Equality Index, average per student funding in high poverty schools is $5,937 compared to $7,244 in low poverty schools.

[2] The 2012 National Urban League 2012 Equality Index reports that 44.1% of black children ages 3–5 have at least 3 of the requisite skills for school readiness compared to 26% of Latinos and 46.8% of white children in the same age group.

[3] According to the National Urban League 2012 Equality Index, 78% of black children are read to at home 3 or more times a week, versus 68% of Latinos and 91% of white children.

[4] As reported in the National Urban League 2012 Equality Index, 11.6% of all African Americans, 20.8% of all Latinos and 9.1% of all whites are high school dropouts. College graduation rates are 4-year institutions are 37.7% for African Americans, 46.2% for Latinos and 59.3% for whites.

[5] The 2012 National Urban League 2012 Equality Index reports that the average scale score in science for black 8th graders is 124, compared to 129 for Latinos and 160 for whites. For 12th graders the average science scores are 120 for blacks, 128 for Latinos and 156 for whites. According to the Alliance for Education report Education and the Economy: The Economic Benefits of Helping High School Dropouts Earn High School Diplomas and College Degrees, increasing the graduation rate would add $310 billion to the U.S. economy.

[6] According to the National Urban League 2012 Equality Index, 21.9% of high school teachers in high poverty schools do not have an undergraduate degree in the subject they teach compared to only 10.9% in low poverty high schools.

[7] As reported in the National Urban League 2012 Equality Index, only 19.8% of African Americans, age 25 and older, have a bachelor's degree compared to 13.9% of Latinos and 33.2% of whites. However, nearly one-third of all new jobs created between 2008–2018 will require at least a bachelor's degree.

A DREAM NOT DEFERRED

U.S. SENATOR KIRSTEN GILLIBRAND

What happens to a dream deferred?
Does it dry up like a raisin in the sun?
Or fester like a sore—and then run?
Does it stink like rotten meat?
Or crust and sugar over—
like a syrupy sweet? Maybe it just sags
like a heavy load.
Or does it explode?

In his iconic work "Harlem,"[1] the great Poet Laureate Langston Hughes eloquently articulated the danger that arises when the dreams of our young people are denied. These words still resonate with meaning today.

Everywhere I travel across New York State, too many families are struggling to find or keep a job as we recover from the worst economic downturn we have seen since the Great Depression. And when it comes to our youth, particularly at-risk youth in communities of color, there is an even greater jobs crisis. The numbers are startling. Nationwide, an estimated 31 percent of our African American youth, and 20 percent of our Latino youth are out of work—many without hope, or a concrete path towards a successful future.[2] →

Without immediate action from elected and community leaders, our youth are vulnerable to becoming a "lost generation." We know that long periods of unemployment early in a young person's work life can have lasting negative effects on their future. They will earn less, be less productive, acquire fewer skills and have fewer opportunities. Every day a young person goes without work, we risk losing a future teacher, a future entrepreneur, or a future community leader.

Research shows that unemployed teens are often more likely to drop out of school, engage in criminal behavior and have higher rates of teen pregnancy, all of which are leading indicators of a life of poverty and economic hardship.[3] In New York State, African American and Latino youth, two groups with the highest youth unemployment, are almost twice as likely to drop out of school among their peers and make up more than 80 percent of the city's detention centers.[4]

If we are going to out-educate, out-innovate and out-compete the global competition, we cannot leave any of our youth in any community behind.

The choice is clear. We must all come together to empower young people with the skills, education and experiences needed to ensure an equal opportunity to achieve the American Dream. One way we can act is by working to pass the *Urban Jobs Act of 2011* this Congress.

For the past year, I have been honored to work hand-in-hand in this effort with the National Urban League, my colleagues in the House of Representatives, such as Charles Rangel, Edolphus Towns and Gregory Meeks, my other colleagues in the New York Delegation, the Congressional Black Caucus and youth employment advocates from around the country.

This critically needed legislation would create an Urban Jobs Program to help connect at-risk young people to job opportunities. Our plan would provide grants to national nonprofit organizations with on-the-ground experience to offer our youth valuable services such as GED and post-secondary education programs, occupational skills, on-the-job training, and job placement services. There also may be holistic programs including health services, as well as interpersonal and basic living skills. The skills at-risk youth would acquire through this program are invaluable, both inside and outside the job market. When we provide a new level of support for an entire generation, we can help revitalize whole communities and cities.

During the summer of 2011, I had the opportunity to spend time at the headquarters of the New York Urban League with Congressman Charles Rangel, Assemblyman Keith Wright and many others to discuss the need for the Urban Jobs Act. There, I met an inspiring young woman named Melissa. Melissa told me that she is a single mom, with two children under the age of five, and yet despite her hardships, she was hopeful for her future because she knew that with some job training, her determination and dedication would make the difference.

Her heart was set on a dental assistance training program offered through the New York Urban League—where she had a part-time job. She lined up child care for her children so she could keep her job and start her training. She worked hard, and never missed a single day.

Today, Melissa is now working at the Westchester Medical Center with the help of the Urban League. And when she completes her exam for the Dental Assistant National Bar, which is the required test to become a State Certified Dental Assistant, she will have even more opportunities to keep advancing her career and her future.

Melissa had faith—faith in herself, faith in fundamental fairness and justice, faith that with just a little opportunity she would succeed. Wherever I travel across New York, I meet people just like Melissa. Eager, hardworking, full of what's possible, reaching for their greatest hopes and dreams. They are looking for an opportunity, a real chance to achieve their full God-given potential.

We owe it to Melissa and every other young person across this nation to fight for them in Washington. This is why President Obama and I are fighting so hard for justice and opportunity in our economy.

But if we are going to out-educate, out-innovate and out-compete the global competition, we cannot leave any of our youth in any community behind. We have to ensure our vulnerable youth get an education that will prepare them for the jobs of tomorrow. The fastest growing occupations of the last decade required expertise in the fields of science and technology, engineering and mathematics (S.T.E.M.), according to the Bureau of Labor and Statistics.

However, reports indicate that less than one-third of American students are proficient in math[5] and science[6]. Women and minorities are dramatically underrepresented—women make up only 24 percent of S.T.E.M. workers.[7] African Americans and Hispanics together receive less than five percent of all doctorates in mathematics, physics, chemistry, and computer science.

We simply have to do better. To boost S.T.E.M. education programs in America's elementary, middle and high schools, I have led the effort to pass the Engineering Education for Innovation (E2 for Innovation) Act, a targeted effort to increase the number of students who choose science and engineering careers, and to enhance America's competitiveness in the world economy. I have also proposed legislation to attract S.T.E.M. teachers to low-income schools.

There is no doubt that helping our youth compete in this difficult economy will have a lasting, positive impact throughout our communities. They are counting on us, and we simply cannot turn our back on them. While this challenge will not be solved overnight, it is a challenge that we must rise up together to meet head on because the price of an entire generation of young people being left behind is a moral and financial cost that is too great for our great nation to bear.

NOTES
[1] Hughes, Langston, op. cit.

[2] U.S. Bureau of Labor Statistics, "Employment and Unemployment Among Youth—Summer 2011," August 24, 2011 (see at *http://www. bls.gov/news.release/pdf/youth.pdf*)

[3] Andrew Sum, Joseph McLaughlin and Ishwar Khatiwada, "The 2006 Summer Job Market for the Nation's Teens: Who Got the Jobs and Who Didn't and Why We Should Care," Center for Labor Market Studies at Northeastern University, September 2006 (see at *http:// www.northeastern.edu/clms/wp-content/uploads/The_2006_ Summer_Job_Market.pdf*)

[4] Governor David Paterson's Task Force on Transforming Juvenile Justice, "Charting a New Course: A Blueprint for Transforming Juvenile Justice in New York State," December 2009 (see at *http:// www.vera.org/download?file=2944/Charting-a-new-course-A-blueprint-for-transforming-juvenile-justice-in-New-York-State.pdf*)

[5] National Center for Education Statistics, "Mathematics 2009, National Assessment of Educational Progress at Grades 4, 8 and 12" (see at *http://nationsreportcard.gov/math_2009/math_2009_report/*)

[6] National Center for Education Statistics, "Science 2009, National Assessment of Educational Progress at Grades 4, 8 and 12" (see at *http://nces.ed.gov/nationsreportcard/pdf/main2009/2011451.pdf*)

[7] David Beede, Tiffany Julian, Beethika Khan, Rebecca Lehrman, George McKittrick, David Langdon and Mark Doms, "Education Supports Racial and Ethnic Equality in STEM, U.S. Department of Commerce, Economics and Statistics Administration," September 2011 (see at *http://www.esa.doc.gov/sites/default/files/reports/ documents/educationsupportsracialandethnicequalityinstem_0.pdf*)

THE NATIONAL URBAN LEAGUE INTRODUCES NEW REPORT ON

THE STATE OF URBAN BUSINESS

NATIONAL URBAN LEAGUE POLICY INSTITUTE

In late 2011, the National Urban League (NUL) released *The State of Urban Business 2011: Metro Areas that Lead the Way*. With a focus on the top U.S. metro areas for black-owned businesses, this report is another step forward in the continuing enhancement and evolution of the National Urban League's agenda to fulfill its mission "to enable African Americans to secure economic self-reliance, parity, power and civil rights." In its focus upon closing the adverse "equality gaps" that disadvantage African Americans and other emerging ethnic communities in urban areas, the National Urban League has increasingly supported the growth and development of minority-owned businesses as an essential element of job creation and economic empowerment. →

Indeed, in assessing the status and development potential of African-American and other urban businesses, *The State of Urban Business 2011* recognizes the role of entrepreneurship in job creation.[1] Not only are entrepreneurs credited with creating more than two-thirds of net new jobs, but smaller firms, especially African-American and other minority businesses, are especially important for their support and hiring of underserved populations.[2,3]

With more than three-quarters (75.8%) of the U.S. population residing in urban areas, and an even larger (87.0%) percentage of African Americans residing in urban areas, it is important that African Americans have opportunities and support to establish and grow successful businesses.[4] Successful business growth for urban businesses can help alleviate the extraordinarily high levels of African-American unemployment, which have hovered at approximately twice the unemployment rates of whites through varied business cycles since the tracking of such data back to the 1960s.[5] Despite the well-documented lack of access to capital that continues to inhibit the growth and development of African-American-owned businesses, these businesses continue to play a notable role in providing jobs in our economy. The 2007 Survey of Business Owners from the most recent U.S. Economic Census showed that African-American-owned firms increased their hiring by 20.6%, to more than 909,552 jobs. Without these jobs, the ranks of unemployed African Americans may have risen almost two-thirds (62.8%) to as many as 2.3 million in 2007, the most recent year for which comprehensive data are available. Moreover, larger African-American-owned firms paid average salaries across all employees of $30,000 and more.

Top U.S. Metro Areas for Black-Owned Businesses

Featured in this inaugural edition of the State of Urban Business report is a ranking of some of the top metro areas for black-owned businesses in America. This analysis is different from others because it is based largely on the actual performance of businesses within these areas as opposed to solely on the economic or demographic characteristics of the metro areas. Beginning with a very specific definition of business success—the ability to generate a high level of revenue—NUL researchers made use of the Black Enterprise Magazine (BE) Top 100 List of the nation's highest grossing black-owned industrial/service companies to identify metro areas with multiple businesses that meet this criterion over the five year period of 2007–2011.[6]

Eleven metro areas made this initial cut and were ranked based on seven characteristics of black-owned businesses in each metro area as reported in the Census Bureau's 2007 Survey of Business Owners:

1. *Washington-Arlington-Alexandria, DC-VA-MD-WV*

2. *Los Angeles-Long Beach-Santa Ana, CA*

3. **Tie between** *Chicago-Joliet-Naperville, IL-IN-WI* **and** *Detroit-Warren-Livonia, MI*

4. **Tie between** *Atlanta-Sandy Springs-Marietta, GA* **and** *Charlotte-Gastonia-Rock Hill, NC-SC*

5. *St. Louis, MO-IL*

6. *Dallas-Fort Worth-Arlington, TX*

7. *Cleveland-Elyria-Mentor, OH*

8. *New York-Northern New Jersey-Long Island, NY-NJ-PA*

⑨ *Philadelphia-Camden-Wilmington, PA-NJ-DE-MD*

In addition to the ranking, the report also includes a profile of each of the featured metro areas that highlights programs and policies geared toward minority business development.

Key Findings on Dynamics of African American Business Ownership

In addition to the top metro area rankings, this report presents four key findings based on analysis of the U.S. Census Bureau's 2007 Survey of Business Owners (SBO) and the Kauffman Firm Survey (KFS). These data offer important information about the dynamics of business ownership among African Americans operating both new (in operation five years or less) and established businesses.

The analysis of SBO and KFS data reveal that:

① *The greatest weakness in African-American entrepreneurship is not in starting businesses, but rather in growing these businesses to a scale sufficient for sustained and significant revenue generation.*

② *For young firms (5 years), the ability to expand the customer base beyond individuals and to conduct a larger share of business with other businesses and the government is critical to firm growth and survival.*

③ *While the most challenging problems facing all businesses since 2008 have been slow or lost sales and unpredictability of business conditions, an "inability to obtain credit" remains more of an obstacle for African-American business owners than for any other group.*

④ *Black-owned firms are most likely to receive business training, mentoring or technical assistance from lower cost providers like the SBA or a non-profit association for small businesses.*

Recommendations for Growing and Strengthening Minority Business Ownership

Based on these findings, NUL offers the following recommendations for growing and strengthening black-owned as well as other minority-owned businesses:

① *Increase funding available for small business loans.*

② *Raise the set-aside cap for government small business contracts.*

③ *Unbundle federal contracts and clearly define" small business" to increase access to opportunities for small business.*

④ *Establish robust small or minority business set-aside or procurement goals at all levels of government (federal, state and local) and implement third party monitoring of these goals.*

⑤ *Encourage support for private sector supplier diversity programs.*

⑥ *Establish a permanent and focused minority and urban business technical assistance fund.*

⑦ *Permanently eliminate SBA loan guarantee fees.*

National Urban League Empowering Communities and Changing Lives through Entrepreneurship

In accordance with the key findings and recommendations of this report, *The State of*

Urban Business 2011 also highlights a number of NUL programs and initiatives that are helping to provide much needed technical assistance and financial support of urban businesses.

These include:

→ **The Entrepreneurship Center Program (ECP)**, *in its 6th year of operation with nine centers operating in Atlanta, GA, Chicago, IL, Cincinnati, OH, Cleveland, OH, Jacksonville, FL, Kansas City, MO, Los Angeles, CA, New Orleans, LA and Philadelphia, PA. Five of these nine locations are in cities that made our list of Top Metro Areas for Black-owned Businesses. The services offered by the ECP-assisted entrepreneurs in receiving $20.19 million in new bonding, new contracts and financing during 2010.*

→ **New Market Tax Credit Program (NMTC)/Strategic Alliance between Stonehenge Community Development and the National Urban League** *through which we have deployed $352.5 million of the allocations as of the 3rd quarter of 2011, closing 28 NMTC allocations in various states around the U.S. with investments ranging in size from $3 million to $25 million. This has led to the creation or saving of more than 8,000 jobs nationwide.*

→ **The Urban Empowerment Fund**, *a planned future endeavor of the National Urban League to fill a credit gap that has widened during the last two years, particularly in minority communities. The Urban Empowerment Fund will invest in new and expanding small businesses, non-profit organizations, community facilities and affordable housing development in underserved communities of color*

throughout the country. Through its lending activity, the Urban Empowerment Fund will help empower African Americans to attain economic self-sufficiency and to create sustainable, vibrant minority communities throughout the country.

Conclusion

The State of Urban Business 2011: Metro Areas that Lead the Way was the first installment in what shall become an annual resource that effectively unifies data analysis, practice, and policy to create an easily accessible reference guide for existing and potential small business owners, major corporations and government agencies seeking to expand supplier diversity, policy-makers, community based organizations, and consumers.

This year's focus on the top U.S. metro areas for black-owned businesses encompasses just one aspect of urban business. Forthcoming editions of the report will be centered around other topics of interest, including a more comprehensive analysis of the diversity of racial and ethnic groups doing business in urban areas, analysis of the top businesses with regards to supplier diversity, evaluation of federal, state and local government agency policies and progress toward meeting minority and women-owned business contracting goals, and examination of newly emerging business industries as well as industries with high-growth potential. Future editions of the report will also feature contributing or guest authors who have distinguished themselves in the field of entrepreneurship and business development to provide a fresh and up to date perspective on the State of Urban Business.

Finally, longer range plans for the State of Urban Business include the development of

an NUL survey and a corresponding award
for businesses that have positively impacted
employment and economic development in
urban communities.

*The State of Urban Business 2011: Metro Areas
that Lead the Way* is available in its entirety at
http://www.iamempowered.com/soub/2011

NOTES

[1] Most New Jobs in the United States Are Created by New Business
Entities. See Reynolds, Paul. 2007. "Entrepreneurship in the United
States: The Future is Now," *International Studies in Entrepreneurship*,
Volume 15, p. 1

[2] Headd, Brian. 2010. "An Analysis of Small Business and Jobs," *Small
Business Research Summary*, No. 359, Office of Advocacy

[3] Ibid.

[4] U.S. Census Bureau Data from the American FactFinder, DP-1: Profile
of General Population and Housing Characteristics: 2010 and DP05:
American Community Survey Demographics and Housing Estimates

[5] Table 588. Civilian Population—Employment Status by Sex, Race
and Ethnicity, U.S. Census Bureau, Statistical Abstract of the United
States: 2012

[6] We focus on industrial/service companies because this group included
the greatest diversity in terms of type of businesses. BE also publishes
a list of the top 100 auto dealerships, the top 60 financial services
firms, and the top 15 advertising agencies

CREATING
JOBS *AND*
OPPORTUNITIES
THROUGH MINORITY OWNED BUSINESSES

LLOYD C. BLANKFEIN

Small business owners across the United States have the power to unlock America's economic growth and job-creation potential. We have seen this borne out in recent census data—with black-owned small businesses increasing three times as fast as the national rate, and growing their revenues by 55 percent, as compared to 34 percent for all other businesses, between 2002 and 2007.[1] We have also seen this hold true through our own experience at Goldman Sachs, where we have partnered with community organizations, like the National Urban League, to provide small business owners around the world with the tools they need to grow and create new jobs. →

At Goldman Sachs, in our business and our philanthropic initiatives, we seek to drive economic growth and opportunity. In 2008, we launched *10,000 Women*, our first strategic philanthropic initiative aimed at providing women business owners in developing countries with business education and technical assistance. Our own research pointed to a strong correlation between women's education and broader economic growth, but called for a fresh approach to deliver this global model locally. That is why we pursued local partnerships—joining forces with more than 80 educational and non-profit partners in 22 countries, including Rwanda, Nigeria, Brazil, and China. In three short years, *10,000 Women* has reached more than 5,500 women—and counting—with 80% of surveyed graduates increasing their revenues within eighteen months of graduation and 66% adding new jobs.

We were encouraged by these results and wanted to see how we could replicate this model of providing both business education and technical assistance for small businesses in the United States. Leading business, academic and non-profit experts—like Warren Buffett, Marc H. Morial, and Dr. Michael Porter of Harvard Business School—reinforced the idea that small businesses needed a combination of business education, networking and capital to jumpstart their growth. They also pointed to community based organizations—specifically, community colleges and Community Development Financial Institutions (CDFIs)—as the ideal partners to deliver business education and capital. It quickly became clear that community-based economic development organizations, like the National Urban League, were best equipped to provide technical assistance and networking opportunities to high growth small businesses.

Since April 2010, Goldman Sachs *10,000 Small Businesses* has reached nearly 600 underserved business owners in the United States. These businesses represent a broad range of industries—from manufacturers, to IT businesses, to security and landscaping companies. They also represent the diversity and potential of American small business—with more than 40% being Black or Latino-owned businesses, as compared to the national average of 15%.[2]

Significantly, these businesses are following in the steps of our global cohort of *10,000 Women* participants—translating important knowledge from the program into immediate growth and job-creation. Jessica Johnson and Rhys Powell—profiled to the right—are just two examples of how Black-owned business owners are working with *10,000 Small Businesses* to affect real change in their local communities.

10,000 Small Businesses is a partnership-driven model and chief among our partners is The National Urban League (NUL). Goldman Sachs' roots with the NUL go back a long way. Paul Sachs, the grandson of our founder Marcus Goldman, was the National Urban League's first treasurer. Today, our partnership with the NUL remains strong. When Warren Buffet and I were forming a national Advisory Council for *10,000 Small Businesses*, Marc H. Morial was an obvious choice. As the President and CEO of the NUL, Marc has championed the economic empowerment of underserved communities nationally, expanding the organization's reach to nearly 100 local affiliates across 36 states, which provide services to more than 2 million people.

NUL's local chapters were also ideally positioned to work hand-in-hand with *10,000 Small Businesses'* community college and CDFI partners to source high potential small business applicants and deliver business clinics and

Jessica Johnson

Graduated September 2011

BUSINESS DESCRIPTION: Johnson Security Bureau is a third generation, family-owned and operated security agency located in the South Bronx.

CHALLENGE: When Jessica's father passed away in 2008, the family business was in financial jeopardy. Its revenues had dropped and the majority of its employees had left for better job prospects.

PROGRAM BENEFITS: Negotiations workshop provided practical advice on securing favorable contracts; one-on-one business advising helped her create a 5-year Business Growth Plan; networking opportunities with business owners and the people of Goldman Sachs helped identify new business opportunities.

RESULTS: Hired 50 new employees; won 12 new contracts, more than doubling her client base; doubled revenues over the previous year and on track to surpass $1 million by year end.

Rhys Powell

Graduated November 2011

BUSINESS DESCRIPTION: Red Rabbit is a Harlem-based business that provides alternative and healthy meals to students.

CHALLENGE: Rhys' business was going through a period of rapid growth, and needed to establish the processes and Business Growth Plan to ensure a smooth transition for the company.

PROGRAM BENEFITS: 5-year Business Growth Plan, created through the program, has charted key actions to manage continued growth; financial and negotiations coursework prepared Rhys to secure premium pricing for his goods; advising from 10,000 Small Businesses staff and fellow business owners encouraged Rhys to explore the creation of an Advisory Council.

RESULTS: Hired 30 new employees; nearly doubled revenues in 2010 and expects sales to double again in 2011, surpassing $2 million; won 6 new contracts totaling almost $1 million from different schools across New York City.

networking sessions to participating business owners. Take Nolan Rollins and Andrea Zopp, whose teams in New Orleans and Chicago have leveraged their NUL Entrepreneurship Centers and local relationships to provide value added services and to connect participating businesses to contracting and business-to-business opportunities.

Importantly, in its centennial year, the National Urban League launched its JOBS Rebuild America Agenda, which continues to prioritize minority-owned small business growth through wrap-around services and jobs fairs across the country. It is the range of services the NUL offers that is so important to minority owned businesses. It is the combination of direct technical assistance through initiatives like *10,000 Small Businesses* and NUL's broader entrepreneurship programming that is helping to strengthen small businesses across the U.S.

While we are still in the early stages of *10,000 Small Businesses*, we are committed to working closely with the National Urban League and other partners across the country to help give business owners the tools they need to grow their businesses and create new jobs. We believe that public-private partnerships— like *10,000 Small Businesses*—will play an important role in this work, and are proud to partner with some of the strongest community organizations in the country to help ensure that small businesses continue to be an engine of American growth and prosperity.

NOTES

[1] U.S. Census Bureau. Survey of Business Owners (SBO)—Black-Owned Firms: 2007. *http://www.census.gov/newsroom/releases/archives/business_ownership/cb11-24.html*

[2] Note: 15% is the combination of Black-owned businesses (~7%) and Latino-owned businesses (~8%). U.S. Census Bureau. Survey of Business owners (SBO)—Black Owned Firms: 2007. *http://www.census.gov/econ/sbo/get07sof.html?13*. Survey of Business Owners—Hispanic-Owned Firms: 2007. *http://www.census.gov/econ/sbo/get07sof.html?11*

AT RISK:

THE STATE OF THE BLACK MIDDLE CLASS

CHANELLE P. HARDY, ESQ., VALERIE R. WILSON, PH.D.,
MADURA WIJEWARDENA AND GARRICK T. DAVIS

NATIONAL URBAN LEAGUE POLICY INSTITUTE

Perhaps no American accomplishment of the late 20th Century has symbolized our success more than the opening of the primary paths to economic stability to significant numbers of Americans, including racial minorities, immigrants and the descendants of working class families.

The expanding collective prosperity of African Americans is particularly emblematic of this era, in that the civil rights gains of the last 50 years forced open the door of full-fledged American prosperity to all those who had been barred from its many comforts in decades past, either through economic, legislative, and racial apartheid, or some institutionalized combination of all the above.

In modern America, life, liberty, and the pursuit of happiness means widespread access to an education that affords one the ability to succeed in college, work and life, sustainable employment with benefits and a living wage, and safe, decent and affordable housing obtained on fair terms. →

The Great Recession has earned its title. It has been dreadfully effective in erasing those economic gains most frequently identified with the American Century—the ability of a gainfully employed family to reasonably house, educate, and fend for itself under ordinary circumstances without external assistance, either public or private. Indeed, the Great Recession has proven 'Great' in that its destructive power has surpassed anything remotely familiar to Americans today. Only the Great Depression of the 1930s comes close, and that national emergency forced us to respond with a wholesale urgency typically reserved only for the most dire of foreign threats.

Working Americans were the most immediate beneficiaries. The idea of an open ladder of economic ascendancy was made increasingly real. Over the ensuing decades, these individual beneficiaries came to be collectively identified in the loosest sense as the American 'middle class.'

This rather broad term borrowed from the science of economics, has developed a social connotation all its own. In many ways, it means something very different to each person who uses it. Yet, most people commonly understand the group this term seeks to describe. It is in this sense that those African Americans whose social and economic lives were validated, if not directly improved as a result of the hard-fought victories of the last 50 years in the areas of education, housing, the workplace and the ballot box, might readily self-identify themselves as the 'middle class'. These individuals and families do not view the middle class as a technical term. They see the middle class as an aspiration, if not their present actuality. They see its mere possibility as a validation of their hopes, their dreams, their daily toil, and in many ways, their lives.

It is for this reason that the middle class is commonly referred to as evidence of America's progress. It is also one reason why the health and ultimate survival of the black middle class is so singularly important. The black middle class serves as a very real measure of the viability of America as we would have it to be.

Of course, many of those directly served by the National Urban League would be more accurately described as 'working class', a title equally broad in its meaning and identification, but one commonly understood to be of a lower economic standing than the middle class. A sizeable number of those we serve are in fact, closer to, and in some instances well below the prevailing income level considered by the US Census Bureau and other economists as the 'poverty line'. Twenty-first century America has yet to develop an economic and political system that renders poverty and inequality obsolete. This very fact is what drives the mission of the National Urban League today, and has done so for its 101 year existence.

What makes this moment in our economic existence so alarming, is that the number of people we serve who aspire to reach the middle class, but live among the lower economic classes is exploding at rates that are as breathtaking as they are unnerving. In fact, the population that the National Urban League services, that solidly belongs to the middle class, is exploding. Our service population is more diverse than at any time in the past, encompassing a growing range of ethnicities and nationalities. This phenomena is indicative a new brand of need within America's cities. This indicates an extreme crisis.

The reason for this sudden and explosive growth in the number of Americans of all backgrounds, turning to the National Urban League for the most basic assistance is as clear as it is troubling.

The Great Recession is rapidly claiming the black middle class in America.

And the experience of black middle class is undeniably the experience of 21st century America. We share a common past. We are destined to share a common future.

This fact is irrefutable, and is at the heart of this essay. Taken in isolation, the negative economic statistics resulting from the Great Recession are clearly indicative of the severity of its impact in various areas. Month after month, the plummet in local housing values and sales of existing homes are compared to decades past with a detached sense of statistical marvel. Ever climbing unemployment figures are compared to the early 1980s, and often the Great Depression era with a similar statistical impartiality. The increasing cost of higher education is chronicled as an almost benign statistic, curiously observed with a level of collective detachment, as the price of college intersects with the number of new graduates—one measure headed to dizzying heights, the other cresting and earnestly spiraling downward.

What is seemingly lost in this parade of awful numbers is an assessment of their relative damage, and their personal toll. Exactly what is being lost in terms of America, and who is being hurt within these large and sometimes confusing figures?

Unfortunately, African Americans are disproportionately represented in each of these negative trends born of the Great Recession, relinquishing a generation of progress in a frighteningly brief span of time.

Consider the following:

Black Middle Class' 30 Years of Gains Are Lost
Our analysis of data from the U.S. Census Bureau and the U.S. Bureau of Labor Statistics will clearly establish that whether one looks at education, income or any other meaningful measure, almost all the economic gains that blacks have made in the last 30 years have been lost in the Great Recession that started in December, 2007 and in the anemic recovery that has followed since June, 2009. This means that the size of the black middle class is shrinking, the fruits that come from being in the black middle class are dwindling, and the ladders of opportunity for reaching the black middle class are disappearing.

What Do We Mean by "Middle Class"?

The introduction of this essay described a more popular notion of the middle class, but from a purely economic perspective, being a member of the middle class can be broadly defined as having an income that places one in the middle of the income distribution. This economic definition is used to guide our discussion of the state of the black middle class as we examine changes in median household income, homeownership rates and unemployment rates over the last two and three decades.

White and Black Middle Classes Are Not the Same

In using income alone to define "middle class", it becomes clear that being part of the white middle class is quite different from being part of the black middle class. This is largely because the income level at the middle of the income distribution, or the median household income, for whites is significantly higher than that of blacks since the average white household income is more than 1.5 times the average black household income:[1]

→ *Overall median household income in 2010 was $49,445*[2]

→ *White median household income in 2010 was $54,620[3]*

→ *Black median household income in 2010 was $32,106[4]*

Only one in three black households had income at or above the national median, while fewer than three in ten had income at or above the median for white households.[5]

Last 30 Years' Gains in Black Employment Vastly Diminished

The black unemployment rate saw a slow but steady decline after reaching a catastrophic peak of 21.2% in January 1983.[6] The most dramatic declines occurred during the economic expansion of the 1990s[7] when the average black unemployment rate went from 14.2% in 1992 down to 7.6% in 2000.[8] The Great Recession and the recovery has pushed the black unemployment rate back close to the levels in the early 1980s—the average black unemployment rate in 2011 was 15.8%.[9] This is almost a complete reversal of gains made over nearly 30 years.

Not only has the black unemployment rate risen in absolute terms, but progress made toward closing the black-white unemployment rate gap

has been lost as well. The gap between white and black unemployment rates narrowed from 11.1 percentage points in 1983 to 4.2 percentage points in 2007. In 2011, the gap had risen to 7.9 percentage points.[10]

Black Median Household Income Falling at Alarming Rates

As noted earlier, black median household income in 2010 was $32,106 and even through the economic expansions of the 1980s and the 1990s, it has persistently lagged behind that of white households. The extent of the gap between black and white median household incomes can be seen by the fact that the black median household income in 2010 was 30% less than what white median household income was in 1980 (using 2010 dollars).[11] Despite this gap, there were tremendous gains in median household incomes between 1992 and 2000—32% increase for blacks and 14% increase for whites.[12]

The Great Recession and the recovery have led to a dramatic widening of the gap between white and black middle income households. Although both blacks and whites suffered declining median household incomes during and since the recession, the decline for blacks

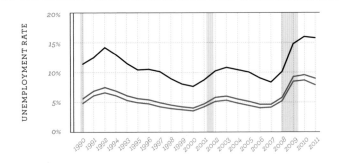

Figure 1: *Unemployment Rates: 1990–2011*

UNEMPLOYMENT RATE

20%
15%
10%
5%
0%

1990 1991 1992 1993 1994 1995 1996 1997 1998 1999 2000 2001 2002 2003 2004 2005 2006 2007 2008 2009 2010 2011

— White
— Black
— Overall

Source: Current Population Survey, U.S. Bureau of Labor Statistics

Note: Highlights cover recessions as decided by National Bureau of Economic Research

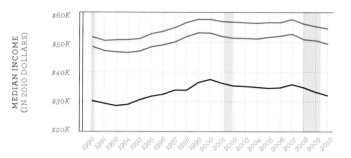

Figure 2: *Median Household Incomes: 1990 to 2010 (in 2010 dollars)*

Note: Highlights cover recessions as decided by National Bureau of Economic Research

---

has been considerably higher—between 2008 and 2010, white median household income fell by 2.9% while the black median household income fell by 7.7%.[13] The last time blacks suffered a decline in median household income of this magnitude (over two years) was between 1979 and 1981 when it fell by 8.3%.[14]

The decline in median household incomes is not a problem limited to workers with lower levels of skills such as high school dropouts or those with only a high school diploma. Black workers with a 2-year associate's degree, which has traditionally been a solid pathway to middle class status, have experienced large declines in

median household incomes between 1999 and 2010. In that time period, this group of black workers experienced a 15% decline in median household income compared to a 10% decline for similar white workers.[15]

All Gains in Black Home Ownership Are Lost

One of the hallmarks of black economic advancement over the last several decades was the slow but steady increase in home ownership. The height of this was from the start of the economic expansion in 2001 to the peak of the housing boom in 2004—in that period black home ownership grew by 1.3 percentage

---

Figure 3: *Percent Change in Median Household Income by Education and Race: 1999-2010*

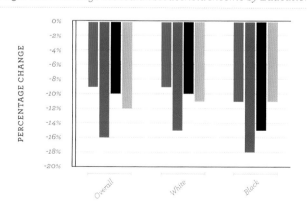

■ *Less than High School*
■ *High School*
■ *Associate's Degree*
▨ *Bachelor's Degree*

Source: Current Population Survey, U.S. Census Bureau

Figure 4: *Percentage Point Change in Home Ownership Rates From the Previous Year: 1995 to 2011*

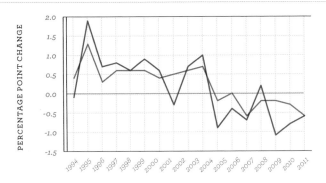

— White
— Black

Source: Current Population Survey/ Housing Vacancy Survey, U.S. Census Bureau

points and white home ownership grew by 1.7 percentage points.[16]

However, black home ownership has declined every year since 2004 (except for a slight increase in 2007 to 2008)—from 2004 to 2007, black home ownership declined a total of 2 percentage points compared to 0.8 percentage point decline for whites.[17] Since the recovery, black home ownership has been falling at just under twice the rate of white home ownership—from 2009 to 2011, black home ownership declined by 1.4 percentage points and white home ownership declined by 0.9 percentage points. This means that almost all the gains in black home ownership have been lost and

now we are at a point where there are real reversals in black home ownership.

Narrowing Pathways to Enter the Black Middle Class

Over the past 20 years or more, a postsecondary degree (either a 2-year associate's or a 4-year bachelor's degree) has become an increasingly crucial pathway for reaching middle class status. However, over the past 10 years, fewer workers without a postsecondary degree have been able to achieve middle income status. In 1999, 70% of the workers in the middle income quintile had no postsecondary degree, but by 2010, this had plummeted to 63%.[18]

Figure 5: *Educational Distribution of Middle Quintile*

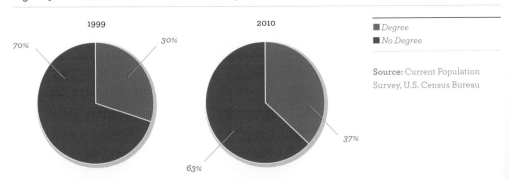

1999

2010

■ *Degree*
■ *No Degree*

Source: Current Population Survey, U.S. Census Bureau

70%

30%

63%

37%

Figure 6: Unemployment Rates for High School Graduates: 1992-2011

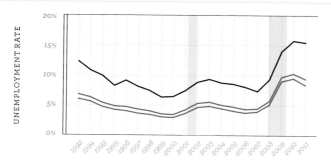

— White
— Black
— Overall

Source: Current Population Survey, U.S. Bureau of Labor Statistics

Note: Highlights cover recessions as decided by National Bureau of Economic Research

Unlike previous decades, when an associate's degree (or even a high school diploma) offered a solid pathway to middle class status, that pathway has narrowed considerably since at least 2000. This is primarily because workers with an associate's degree (or a high school diploma) have been buffeted by high unemployment since the Great Recession, a dramatic reversal of the gains made during the 1990s.

Until the jobless recovery of the 2000s and the Great Recession, black workers with a high school diploma or an associate's degree experienced the most dramatic declines in unemployment. Between 1992 and 2000, the unemployment rate for blacks with a high school diploma dropped by 5.9 percentage points (from 12.3% to 6.4%) and the rate for those with an associate's degree dropped by 4.9 percentage points (from 8.4% to 3.5%).[19] These dramatic improvements in unemployment rates of black workers were a central foundation of the great black middle class expansion.

The jobless recovery of the 2000s and the Great Recession have largely reversed these dramatic improvements. Today, a high school

degree or an associate's degree is by no means a guaranteed pathway to middle income status. The average unemployment rate for blacks with a high school degree in 2011 was 15.5% (3.2 percentage points higher than it was in 1992) and for those with an associate's degree, it was 12.1% (3.7 percentage points higher than it was in 1992).[20]

The Great Recession has spared few, if anyone in Black America. An especially troubling trend can be observed by looking at the fortunes of those with a 4-year college degree. The most significant impact of this trend has been on black college graduates who saw their unemployment rates skyrocket to an average of 7.1% in 2011.[21] This has led to an unprecedented widening of the gap between black and white college graduates—in 1992, the gap between the unemployment rates of black and white college graduates was 1.4 percentage points and in 2011 it had increased to 3.2 percentage points.[22]

Targeted Solutions Are Urgent

That which helped build the African American middle class is the same thing that built the middle class for all Americans. More families

Figure 7: *Unemployment Rates for Associate Degree Holders (2-Year Degree and Vocational Certificates): 1992–2011*

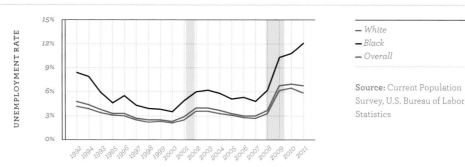

Note: Highlights cover recessions as decided by National Bureau of Economic Research

sending children to college through programs like the GI Bill and Pell Grants. FHA and VA loans allowed more families to buy homes and raise families in a safe, nurturing environment, while building an asset to pass on to their children. Diversity in the boardroom and on the manufacturing line has led to healthy meals on dinner tables and safe communities that add municipal revenues, not strain them. Yet, the very notion of that middle class is quietly slipping away. The data presented within these pages demonstrate, if nothing else, the lasting damage being wrought upon those Americans

whose economic well-being is synonymous with the possibilities offered to us all. In this sense, the viability of the black middle class is of relevance to all Americans.

The same deliberate, targeted, and sustained approach to community building responsible for its creation, is the same prescription for its ultimate survival. Programs such as targeted job training, Pell grants, small business lending, pre-and-post purchase housing counseling, and Medicare and Medicaid provide the foundation which makes middle class life possible. These

Figure 8: *Unemployment Rates for College Graduates (4-Year Degree): 1992–2011*

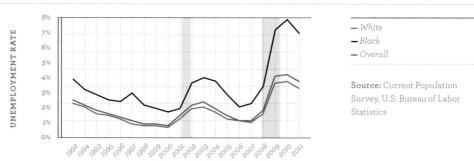

Note: Highlights cover recessions as decided by National Bureau of Economic Research

programs should not, and must not be sacrificed in a hyper-partisan debate designed to produce political winners and losers.

The current debate on deficit reduction is one that is both important and necessary. However, the American Dream did not come into existence by accident. We cannot stand by and watch it gradually and systematically be undone. The potential demise of the black middle class would be only the first step in this most undesirable of outcomes. The National Urban League believes there is still time. The time for action is now.

NOTES

1 White refers to white-not Hispanic except in the case of unemployment data where white includes both Hispanic and non-Hispanic.

2 U.S. Census Bureau, Current Population Survey—Annual Social and Economic Supplement, September 2011

3 Ibid.

4 Ibid.

5 Authors' analysis of the data from the Current Population Survey—Annual Social and Economic Supplement, September 2011

6 U.S. Bureau of Labor Statistics, Current Population Survey, Historical Tables

7 The Economic Cycle Dating Committee of the National Bureau of Economic Research dates the economic expansion of the 1990s from March 1991 to March 2001

8 U.S. Bureau of Labor Statistics, Current Population Survey, Historical Tables

9 U.S. Bureau of Labor Statistics, Current Population Survey, January 2012

10 Ibid.

11 Author's analysis of the data from the Current Population Survey—Annual Social and Economic Supplement, Historical Tables

12 Ibid.

13 Ibid.

14 Ibid.

15 Estimates based on NULPI analysis of 2010 Current Population Survey, Annual Social and Economic Supplement micro-data

16 U.S. Census Bureau, Current Population Survey/Housing Vacancy Survey (CPS/HVS), Historical Tables as at 1/13/2011

17 Ibid.

18 Author's analysis of the data from the Current Population Survey—Annual Social and Economic Supplement

19 U.S. Bureau of Labor Statistics, Current Population Survey, Historical Tables

20 U.S. Bureau of Labor Statistics, Current Population Survey, Historical Tables

21 U.S. Bureau of Labor Statistics, Current Population Survey, January 2012

22 U.S. Bureau of Labor Statistics, Current Population Survey, January 2012 and Historical Tables

TANNING OF AMERICA MAKES
GROWTH, PROSPERITY AND EMPOWERMENT EASIER

STEVE STOUTE

In his State of the Union address on January 24, 2012 President Obama again focused on entrepreneurship, especially the kind driven by exporting, as a vehicle for American growth and prosperity, reiterating his goal set in 2010 to double American exports in five years.[1]

America's greatest export is our culture. It is that culture that flows through iconic American products like Apple, Nike, Coca-Cola and Jay-Z's music. Our culture is the golden thread that meshes together the exceptional quality, ingenuity, creativity and value of these products that makes the American Dream accessible all across the globe. →

Millennials Have Changed the Face of America

Millennials are generally defined generally to be those born between 1977 and 1997—in 2012 they will be between 15 and 35 years old. There were about 85 million Millennials in 2010—over a quarter of the American population.[2]

Millennials have changed the face of America in many ways, making it more diverse. Non-white minorities made up 35% of the American population (July 2008–July 2009), up from 31% in 2000.[3] States and cities in America that are "majority minority" are rising—in 2010, 6 of the 10 largest cities were "majority minority"[4] and the primary cities in 58 metropolitan areas were "majority minority," up from 43% in 2000.[5] One in seven new marriages in 2008 was inter-racial or inter-ethnic![6]

This trend started by the Millennials is only intensifying. Between July of 2008 and July of 2009, 48.6% of the 4.3 million children born were non-white minorities—by contrast, about 40% of the children born 10 years ago were non-white minorities.[7] This is mostly driven by the increasing number of minority women who are in child-bearing ages (20–39 years old)[8]—these Millennial women are changing the face of America.

Tanning of America Makes Reaching Common Ground Easier

Along with the demographic complexion of America, the mental complexion of America has also changed—this is the phenomenon that I call "Tanning." This essentially means that cultural and demographic lines are becoming permanently blurred[9]—people are identifying themselves not so much through their race, but rather with a "mental complexion" based on common experiences and values that cut racial and socio-economic lines.[10]

No longer does our race or ethnicity define us culturally. Without these limitations and societal myopia, new and inspiring opportunities for redefining "community" are limitless and rich with possibility. At no other time in history has America had such an opportunity to change the landscape of cultural identity that includes embracing our differences in order to redefine and advance the common good of community. President Barack Obama's 2008 campaign was a groundbreaking success because a diverse coalition crossed barriers to create a new community defined by the same goal rather than lines of race, income, age, education or geography.

Leveraging Diversity Is Key to Business Success

Crossing lines of race and socio-economics is also critically important for success in business. Success in business depends on learning to speak with Millennial consumers using their language, codes, and visceral nuances that are continually and rapidly evolving. None of this is written in stone. Those who ignore this are suffering as a result.

Culturally curious entrepreneurs and executives have the most competitive edge in an economy forever changed by the Millennial mind-set. Cultural curiosity means embracing comfort in discomfort, developing a business identity that is ever evolving, progressive, and adaptable. It means being open-minded enough to contemplate bringing new concepts into the mainstream. Cultural curiosity means businesses becoming embedded in the culture.

Our Problems Are Not Insurmountable
The hurdles to face include the lack of
education, resources and opportunities that
are necessary to succeed in America. The
dropout rate for 16-24 year olds in 2009 was
5.2% for whites, 9.3% for blacks and 17.6% for
Hispanics—despite the high rates, these are
significantly better than in 1980 when dropout
rates were 11.4% for whites, 19.1% for blacks and
35.2% for Hispanics.[11] In 2007, black-owned
businesses were 7.1% of all businesses but
generated only 0.5% of all revenues.[12]

> People are identifying
> themselves not so
> much through their
> race, but rather with
> a "mental complexion"
> based on common
> experiences and values
> that cut racial and
> socio-economic lines.

Millennials are impacted tremendously by
the complete integration of technology into
their culture. This is especially true of blacks,
who are significantly higher adopters of
technology—78% of blacks and 48% of whites
used the internet to look for a job in 2009 and
2010,[13] 28% of blacks and 14% of whites used the
internet to get ideas about starting a business
in 2009,[14] 71% of blacks and 58% of whites used
online social networking in 2010[15] and 13% of
blacks and 5% of whites used Twitter in 2010.[16]

Creating Solutions Through Technology
and Education
Technology has made geography obsolete
since the immediacy of information morphs
attitudes and perceptions on a constant basis.
Neighborhoods are global and community
is kaleidoscopic. The traditional approach
to defining the marketplace by segregating
demographically is stiff, stagnant, and doesn't
reflect the evolution of America's mental
complexion. If culture defines the identity of a
community, then the marketplace is a mirror
that reflects that culture. The challenge today
is how businesses can adapt to a marketplace
that refuses to remain static.

Corporate philosophy needs to reach beyond
profits and see its ever-changing community
as an asset, not only a revenue stream.
Businesses need to position their brand as a
member of its community that provides not
only products but possibilities. Business and
enterprise have an unprecedented opportunity
to radically change the way we inspire and
innovate, the way we engage and encourage,
the way we teach and learn. For the first time
in American history, a college degree doesn't
guarantee a job, and yesterday's hustler
is today's entrepreneur. By sharing their
expertise, companies transform customers
into loyal members of the community who are
active and entrepreneurial.

This love of technology and social media
lends to a generation of highly connected,
mobile, culturally curious individuals who
are able to access resources that cultivate
their talents and create pathways to success.
But technology requires the education
system to evolve and businesses to adapt.
Companies, investors and governments need
to connect with Millennials and communicate

in ways that use technology as a gateway to opportunity and the fast lane to empowerment and independence.

The economy is hard on everyone, especially minorities who are forced to face limited opportunities due in part to the existence of institutionalized prejudices that continue to affect America. These days it is clear that a college degree is not a guaranteed path to success for blacks considering that the unemployment rate in December 2011 for black college graduates was 7.1% and for white college graduates it was 3.6%.[17]

One solution to this problem is to ensure that technology and other new mediums are used to maximize the experiences and opportunities that are available. Modern technology allows you to educate yourself; in a few clicks, you can be on the road to creating your own businesses online. Businesses are born and grown by empowering yourself with education, and not necessarily just the kind you get in the classroom.

Call To Action: Progress Through Policy Reforms

These hurdles are not insurmountable, but the existence of them should inspire innovation through public policies in order for society to reform and maximize the chances for blacks and other underserved communities. We must have the courage to follow through to see effective change. Here are some ideas on how we can make a difference through policy:

① *Create mentorship opportunities and other partnerships with businesses so that social consciousness and community support become an integral part of the branding process that all businesses use.*

② *Entrepreneurship must be incentivized on all fronts and people must be exposed to it at an early stage. For example, young people should be educated about the finances of student loans and the best way to manage them so that they can become entrepreneurs and launch businesses earlier in their careers.*

③ *Create new vocational tracks that provide fundamentals of businesses in a shorter period of time. Tying in businesses that offer "hands-on business expertise" into the education pipeline is critically important. A formal four-year college degree or a two-year associate's degree cannot be the only way forward and flexible vocational tracks will open doors to a larger segment of the population.*

④ *Allow students to intern at younger ages, as early as high school. This will provide an option in addition to afterschool programs and athletics that helps prepare students for applying to and attending college. The goal here is to ensure that career development is integrated into education at an early age and does not become something that you do later in high school or at college.*

⑤ *Include "professional etiquette" in high school/afterschool curriculums that guides students in resume building, attire, compliance issues, etc. The objective is to provide a full suite of skills necessary to compete for jobs and building businesses, and to realize that formal training is only one path to success.*

NOTES

1 President Barack Obama, Remarks by the President in State of the Union Address, U.S. Capitol, January 24, 2012

2 Author's estimates using U.S. Census Bureau, 2010 Census Summary File 1, 2010 at (see at http://factfinder2.census.gov/faces/tableservices/jsf/pages/productview.xhtml?pid=DEC_10_SF1_QTP1&prodType=table)

3 Conor Dougherty, "U.S. Nears Racial Milestone," Wall Street Journal, June 11, 2010 (see at http://online.wsj.com/article/SB10001424052748704312104575298512006681060.html)

4 Author's analysis of the data from the 2010 Decennial Census of the U.S. Census Bureau

5 William H. Frey, "Melting Pot Cities and Suburbs: Racial and Ethnic Change in Metro America in the 2000s," Brookings Institution Metropolitan Policy Program, May 2011 at p. 1

6 Jeffrey S. Passel, Wendy Wang and Paul Taylor, "Marrying Out," Pew Research Center, June 4, 2010 at p. ii

7 Ken Johnson and Daniel L. Lichter, "The Changing Faces of America's Children and Youth," Carsey Institute, Spring 2010 at p. 1 (see at http://carseyinstitute.unh.edu/news/Johnson-2009-Census.html)

8 Ibid.

9 Steve Stoute, "The Tanning of America: How Hip-Hop Created a Culture That Rewrote the Rules of the New Economy," 2011 at p. xvi–xvii

10 Ibid., p. xvii

11 National Center for Education Statistics, "Fast Facts: What Are the Dropout Rates of High School Students?," 2011 (see at http://nces.ed.gov/fastfacts/display.asp?id=16)

12 Author's calculations of data from U.S. Census Bureau, Survey of Business Owners 2007

13 Jon P. Gant, Nicol Turner-Lee, Ying Li and Joseph Miller, "National Minority Broadband Adoption: Comparative Trends in Adoption, Acceptance and Use," February 2010, Joint Center for Political and Economic Studies, p. 20

14 Ibid., p. 21

15 Emily Guskin, Paul Moore and Amy Mitchell, "African American Media: Evolving in the New Era," Pew Research Center's Project for Excellence in Journalism, March 14, 2011, p. 18 (see at http://stateofthemedia.org/2011/african-american/)

16 Aaron Smith and Lee Rainie, "8% of Americans Use Twitter," Pew Internet & American Life Project, December 9, 2010 (see at http://www.pewinternet.org/Reports/2010/Twitter-Update-2010/Findings.aspx)

17 U.S. Bureau of Labor Statistics, Current Population Survey, January 2012 and Historical Tables

THE ECONOMIC
WINDS OF CHANGE:
NEW MARKETS FOR AN OLD PROBLEM

NOLAN V. ROLLINS

For over 100 years the Urban League movement has been at the forefront of the nonprofit direct service model. Over the last century we have developed a unique expertise allowing us to identify the systematic barriers limiting opportunities for African Americans and other underserved populations in ongoing pursuit of the American Dream. However, identification alone does not accomplish the mission of the Urban League. We have proven equally adept at the development of programmatic initiatives that help to bring solutions to the challenges of those in need. The challenge of solution-oriented problem solving has required us to become experts in developing, identifying, qualifying, and partnering with the entities necessary to bring fundamental change to lives of our constituents. Such is the foundation of our 'Architects of Change' model for economic empowerment. Equally important is the Urban League's ability to implement policies in a manner consistent with the needs of emerging and underserved communities. →

The most reliable indicator of a society's values is its social agenda. Our American Story has witnessed numerous strides in social policy such as the Emancipation Proclamation, Women's Suffrage, Civil Rights, Equal Rights Amendments and Economic Inclusion of minorities to name a few. In each of these instances justice proved the tool used by insightful leadership in delivering innovative solutions to long-standing societal ills. The creation of impactful social policy first requires the ability to identify and define the problem to be addressed. Next, a sustainable solution must be developed with an implementation strategy built upon accountability and the measuring of overall impact. Finally, these policies must be understood by those closest to the communities, as well as those charged with their delivery.

One such innovation is the New Markets Tax Credit Program (NMTC). The NMTC Program was established by Congress to spur investment in low-income communities. The NMTC Program attracts investment capital to low-income communities by permitting investors to receive a tax credit against their Federal income tax return in exchange for making equity investments in specialized financial institutions called Community Development Entities (CDEs). Low-income communities are defined as those that the US Census Bureau identifies as having a poverty rate higher than 20%, or the median family income for the tract does not exceed 80% of the median family income for the state or area. "The credit totals 39 percent of the original investment amount and is claimed over a period of seven years (5% for each of the first three years, and 6% for each of the remaining four years). Since the NMTC Program's inception, the Community Development Financial Institutions (CDFI)

Fund has made 594 awards allocating a total of $29.5 billion in tax credit authority to CDEs through a competitive application process. This $29.5 billion includes $1 billion of special allocation authority to be used for the recovery and redevelopment of the Gulf Opportunity Zone."[1]

Helping Policy to find its Equilibrium in the Community

The ability to understand the impact of social policy is a competency necessary for all those trying to help lift communities up the economic and societal ladder. Strategic partnerships have proven useful in helping the Urban League deliver complex policy initiatives to those places most in need. The NMTC program is no exception. We have partnered with the Business Roundtable, an association of 150 CEOs representing the nation's largest corporations, the U.S. Department of Commerce through its Minority Business Development Agency, and Stonehenge Capital Company, a national finance company with expertise in private equity, tax credits and structured finance.

The ability to understand the impact of social policy is a competency necessary for all those trying to help lift communities up the economic and societal ladder.

★ ★ ★ ★ ★ ★ ★ ★ ★ ★ ★ ★ ★ ★ ★ ★

This partnership has yielded over $280 million in NMTC allocations used throughout the nation in communities most in need of an economic boost. These funds have supported minority businesses, built affordable housing, developed facilities for direct service organizations, and bolstered the inclusion of minority owned firms in development projects.[2] Urban League CEOs and their staff members have been critical to these and other projects, participating in increasing deal flow, due diligence on potential projects, community awareness and utilizing NMTC for League-centered development projects.

The Urban League of Greater New Orleans (ULGNO) brings NMTC to the 9th Ward
In 2005, the world watched while Hurricane Katrina breached faulty levees allowing flood-waters to drown the hopes, dreams and aspirations of a people who are inclined to love by their very nature. How do you restore hope to what seems like a hopeless situation? Civic leaders with the means and skills to implement social policy must also acknowledge this challenge as they promote changes that will help improve the lives of those they serve. The Urban League of Greater New Orleans (ULGNO) is doing this. We created the Urban Equity Development Corporation (UEDC)—a development entity incorporated to promote the need for economically viable communities throughout Louisiana. The UEDC is empowered to acquire, develop, sponsor, purchase and rehabilitate real property for ownership, sale or lease.

The creative use of the New Markets Tax Credit Program enabled the UEDC and the Urban League of Greater New Orleans to construct a child and family development center serving over 100 families in the 9th Ward, one of the city's hardest hit neighborhoods. The center includes computer access, food preparation areas, age and size appropriate learning environments, and stimulating indoor and outdoor play environments. This development is a symbol for the community. It tells the story of an organization that understands that community development requires both commitment and creativity. The partners assembled by ULGNO in building this beacon of hope in the 9th Ward include minorities at every level: the bank, general contractor, architect, engineer, and most importantly its owner/developer.

Policies alone do not guarantee their proper usage or intended results. Policies are only as good as their capacity to promote meaningful change in the lives of those who they are intended to serve. Modern day leadership demands that our leaders design innovative solutions using the tools provided to us. For over 100 years the Urban League has been adept at crafting complex policies into real change for those communities that need it most.

NOTES

[1] United States Congress. House of Representatives. "Community Renewal Tax Relief Act of 2000," Title I, Subtitle C: "New Markets Tax Credit." 106th Cong., 2nd sess. HR 5662. Washington: GPO, 2000. Print

[2] Stonehenge Capital Company: Community Development Banking. 2012. Stonehenge Capital Company, LLC. (see at *http://www. stonehengecapital.com/lines.cfm?page=overview&id=6*) (Accessed January 2012)

A CALL TO
ADVOCATE
FOR AMERICA'S MILITARY
VETERANS

ALLIE L. BRASWELL, JR., AND JAMES T. MCLAWHORN, JR.

When we were young men, our generation viewed joining the military as a pathway out of poverty. The military was deemed a great equalizer, and could serve as a vehicle toward prosperity. While serving on active duty we really did not understand the concept of a pension, and definitely did not have a grasp on what our benefits really meant. When we got out of the military, we participated in a one-week transition program, where we received a resume before we were sent on our way. Had we not had a strong support system when we returned home, we would not have navigated the transition well. Similarly today, many service members join the military to build a better future. Often, they come from single-parent families or families without a strong infrastructure. →

After two long, active theatres of military engagement, the long-awaited return of many hometown heroes has finally come. When these soldiers return to their local communities and complete their one-week transition program, to what will they come home? Given the recession, they may find it extremely difficult to find work. The family home they left might be gone due to foreclosure. The family they left may be even more broken because of the stressful effects of this economic downturn. In short, *repatriation back into civilian life* may be difficult without guidance and without proper information around the resources available to assist them as they attempt to transition.

Our Columbia (South Carolina) and Central Florida National Urban League affiliates have seen first-hand what members of the community and new veterans are experiencing. Some of the new veterans tell us that upon returning home, the last thing they want to think about is the Department of Veterans Affairs (VA). The veterans we meet tell us that they do not trust the government, do not trust the military and do not trust the VA.

These new veterans are not alone. According to the Vietnam Veterans of America (VVA) and Veterans of Modern Warfare (VMW)[1] there are 25 million veterans of the U.S. Armed Forces alive today and only 7.2 million of those veterans are enrolled in the VA system. Older veterans say the same thing, "No, I don't want to deal with the VA." Why is this? Because there is a stigma attached to the aid.

For instance, a veteran that we recently met has been home for two years, after serving two tours in Iraq. Upon arriving home, he began experiencing marital problems and his wife left him. This veteran's brother reports that he has since sat at home every night in the dark with a knife in his hand. While he receives medication from his local VA, he does not take it. Every month he dutifully goes to the VA to pick up his medicine, but he never takes it. He has not shared with the VA staff what he is experiencing. He is afraid that if he does, he will be diagnosed with Post Traumatic Stress Disorder (PTSD), and he will then lose access to his two children in a custody battle.

> Repatriation back into civilian life may be difficult without guidance and without proper information around the resources available to assist them as they attempt to transition.

This veteran's account is not a unique story. According to Congressional Testimony from the Hearing on Veteran Suicide Prevention,[2] delay in mental health treatment may lead to family break up, homelessness, criminal incarceration and even suicidal thoughts and action. The VVA and VMW report that approximately 300,000 veterans of the Iraq and Afghanistan wars—nearly 20% of the returning forces—are likely to suffer from either PTSD or major depression.[3] An additional 320,000 of the returning veterans from Iraq and Afghanistan may have experienced traumatic brain injuries during deployment. Additionally, Black war

★ ★ ★ ★ ★ ★ ★ ★ ★ ★ ★ ★ ★ ★ ★

veterans are more likely than White veterans to experience PTSD,[4] but are less likely to receive disability benefits for the disease.

The National Urban League has a long history of service to veterans dating back to World War I. Carrying on this tradition, Urban League affiliates in communities around the nation are doing their part to help veterans and their families get the help that they need. In Columbia, South Carolina, we are hosting workshops with church leaders through our Faith Based Community program to help them understand the symptoms of PTSD, and know how to help. In addition, we advocate and assist veterans and their families in interfacing with the VA system, including employment referrals and following up with the local U.S. Department of Labor Veterans Affairs' representative.

In Central Florida, about 20% to 30% of the population we touch are veterans. We spend a lot of time coordinating services for veterans who come through our door. If needed, we connect the veteran to a veterans' liaison person with the U.S. Department of Labor to perform a disability hearing or evaluation. Our counselors educate the veterans on their benefits and help with their workforce development efforts such as resume rewriting, skills training, and more. We also advocate on behalf of veterans by educating employers on the benefits of hiring veterans, while dispelling any myths about PTSD. We know that just because a vet has PTSD, it does not make him or her unemployable. In fact, we recently assisted a young marine diagnosed with PTSD. A company hired him and provided counseling through its employer assistance program. Today, that veteran is one of the company's most productive employees.

Based on our work and experience with veterans, we know that a community-based partnership can greatly expand the support system for veterans. Located in neighborhoods around the nation, community based organizations are trusted in their communities and can serve as indispensable partners to governmental agencies that serve veterans. We must be able to transition our veterans in a holistic manner and we suggest that one approach is to establish a Veterans' Repatriation Program (VRP). This program would have veteran advocate counselors who are trained and ready to work with veterans through the challenges they are facing, while getting them connected to the services they need and to the benefits they have earned, such as Post 9/11 GI bill benefits. A Veterans' Repatriation Program would include the following key components:

→ *Assessment of personal, family and medical needs of the veteran when he or she returns home;*

→ *A screening for qualifications;*

→ *An orientation period to schedule appointments, sign up for VA services;*

→ *Serve as the veteran's connection to the VA, other veterans' organizations and community mental health service providers;*

→ *Assisting veterans in understanding their educational benefits, registering them for their health benefits, and guiding them in pursuing their guaranteed VA loans; and*

→ *Navigating the new Post 9/11 GI bill benefits*

Our work is critical because our minority veterans are not faring well now that they have returned home. The recession, while incrementally improving, has dramatically affected urban communities, particularly minority communities, with high levels of unemployment. There is a 30.4% unemployment rate among veterans ages 18 to 24—the rate among African American veterans in this age group is 60.3% according to November 2011 Current Population Survey[5] estimates. Additionally, about 45% of homeless veterans are African American.

As we work with our war veterans, we continue to look for new ways in which we can assist our urban communities. Educating families and the church community about PTSD and helping veterans is essential, but it is also important to educate business owners in the community, including barbers, restaurants, gyms, convenience stores and nightclub owners as well.

Building a model through which to provide additional support for our war heroes can create a healthier, more stable transition. Strong support for veterans will mean stronger families, empowered communities, an increased tax base and a better economy. Therefore, helping veterans will result in increased education, business ownership, job creation and employment.

We must never forget the sacrifices our veterans have made for us. We owe it to them to advocate aggressively on their behalf. Therefore, we call on the nation to join us in aiding our returning war heroes. It is time to have this dialogue. We must transition our veterans in a holistic manner. If we do not, it will cost us as a society. If we do not act, families will continue to suffer and communities, especially our urban communities, will fall apart as an already strained social services system tries to bear the added pressure of higher unemployment and more crime as people struggle to find a means to survive.

NOTES

[1] Vietnam Veterans of America (VVA) and Veterans of Modern Warfare (VMW), "Veterans Fact Sheet" (see at *http://www. veteransnewsroom.com/files/press/VETERANS-Fact-Sheet-Veterans. pdf*) (Accessed on January 21, 2012)

[2] Congressional Testimony of Hearing on Veteran Suicide Prevention, December 2, 2011 (see at *http://www.va.gov/OCA/testimony/hvac/ sh/HVAC02DEC.asp*) (Accessed at January 21, 2012)

[3] Vietnam Veterans of America (VVA) and Veterans of Modern Warfare (VMW), "Veterans Fact Sheet" (see at *http://www. veteransnewsroom.com/files/press/VETERANS-Fact-Sheet-Veterans. pdf*) (Accessed on January 21, 2012)

[4] United States Department of Veteran Affairs, National Center for PTSD, "PTSD Among Ethnic Minority Veterans," Updated on December 20, 2011 (see at *http://www.ptsd.va.gov/professional/ pages/ptsd-minority-vets.asp*) (Accessed on January 21, 2012)

[5] Current Population Survey (CPS), Table 1, Employment Status of Persons by Veteran Status, Age, Race, Hispanic or Latino Ethnicity and Sex, Not Seasonally Adjusted, November 2011, pp. 19 & 20

A COMMON MARKET:
THE NEW BLACK FARMER

HAILE JOHNSTON AND TATIANA GARCIA-GRANADOS

Efforts to prepare the black community to compete and thrive in the 21st century workforce have rightfully focused on achieving educational equality and the development of appropriate job skills. The correlation between the attainment of a quality education and employment is well documented. Until recently, less focus has been placed on the health inequalities that exist in the black community, and how that impacts our ability to learn, earn, compete, live and thrive. Diet related maladies such as morbid obesity, diabetes, high blood pressure and heart disease have reached epidemic levels and are a limiting factor in our economic competitiveness, and perhaps more importantly, our quality of life. →

Simply put, the demand for healthy food in the black community is not being met by today's marketplace, and we are suffering because of it. Since the health challenges of our communities are largely related to our patterns of food consumption, there is a significant opportunity to reverse these trends by changing how and what we eat. What is good for our bodies can be good business within our neighborhoods too. Windows of opportunity for job and wealth creation exist through the reformation of the health and well-being of the black community. Positive by-products of this work include gains in personal productivity and savings in short and long-term healthcare costs.

Innovative programs geared toward building demand for healthful food through education have been introduced in minority and low-income communities throughout the country. On the supply side, many communities have begun to grow their own produce in formerly blighted lots that were left in the wake of population flight and poverty. Retail corner store initiatives are bringing a trickle of healthy food to some of these neighborhoods, and larger legislative efforts are subsidizing the construction of supermarkets in areas of the country identified as food deserts.[1] A food desert is defined as an area where a substantial number or share of residents have limited access to a supermarket or large grocery store where they can purchase healthy and affordable food(s).[2] While these movements represent steps in the right direction, there are still countless communities where healthy food is still not readily available to the most underserved. It is in these places where the greatest opportunities exist to strengthen our communities, improve the overall public health and expand economic opportunity by

connecting our people to quality affordable food. There is no one answer to solving our worsening health epidemic, but several interventions happening simultaneously can begin to shift the tide.

A food desert is an area where a substantial number of residents have limited access to a supermarket where they can purchase healthy and affordable food.

The following is a spotlight of a new approach to expanding food access by connecting urban and rural communities to each other.

In Philadelphia, a non-profit distribution organization called the Common Market rose out of one of the city's most blighted neighborhoods in an effort to reverse the community's growing negative health trends. What began with a question of how a predominately African-American community could impact its own health evolved into a multi-million dollar regional food distribution project serving many communities. The founders were frustrated by the fact that so much high-quality food was being grown near the city, yet it was only showing up at farmers' markets in affluent neighborhoods. Therefore, community residents Haile Johnston and

Tatiana Granados teamed up with partners from outside the community to envision new ways to bring healthy food into neighborhoods like theirs. Driven by the beliefs that access to healthy food is a fundamental human right, and that the people who grow our food should be paid and treated fairly, the Common Market connects producers and consumers through values-driven commerce. By aggregating food from more than 100 local farms, Common Market enables large-scale buyers to source food directly from the producers, cutting out the intermediaries present in our current food system. This efficient distribution model allows the farmers to receive more of the value of their product, while still providing affordable prices for consumers.

The Common Market is now the Philadelphia region's most significant distributor of local foods to schools and hospitals, providing "farm-to-school" logistics for nearly 100 educational institutions. By focusing on institutions that serve low-income and minority communities, the organization has been able to grow while making a positive impact on the most vulnerable members of our population - our children. Each week, participating schools receive cases of sustainably grown produce from farms within 150 miles of the city. These fruits and veggies are served in salad bars, as healthful snacks, or cooked as nutritious lunch offerings. Improving school food is an important way to improve health in our communities. Consider that:

→ *17 percent of U.S. children are overweight.[3]*

→ *Obesity rates among children have doubled in the last 10 years and tripled for adolescents.[4]*

→ *1 in 3 children born in the year 2000 will develop diabetes—make that 1 in 2 if the child is black or Hispanic.[5]*

→ *For the first time in 200 years, today's children are likely to have a shorter life expectancy than their parents.[6]*

Providing an efficient and affordable way for schools to access healthy food is a benefit to local farmers, a boon to local economies, and a way to make school meals, and the children who eat them healthier. Distributors like Common Market are the critical connectors that make these benefits possible.

Recent research shows that many Americans struggle with accessing healthy food, particularly those living in minority communities.[7] A multistate study found that only eight percent of African Americans live in a census tract with a supermarket, compared to 31 percent of whites. Not coincidentally, these communities suffer from the highest rates of diet-related diseases.[8] In Pennsylvania, the Fresh Food Financing Initiative has spawned new public and private investment in supermarkets in underserved urban and rural communities. Two independent operators in the Philadelphia area have become innovators in proving that the construction of super markets in low-income communities is a sound business decision. The addition of several The Fresh Grocer markets and Brown's ShopRite Super Stores has transformed food access in the communities they serve. Since these markets are developed in the most food-insecure communities; these operators have become natural partners of the Common Market's efforts. Connecting these communities to the freshest, highest quality, locally grown, sustainable and organic foods brings real food justice and equity to our region.

The introduction of supermarkets to Pennsylvania's food deserts through the Fresh Food Financing Initiative has been so successful that America is taking notice. Similar federal legislation has been approved launching the Healthy Food Financing Initiative—a partnership between the Departments of Treasury, Agriculture, and Health and Human Services. The introduction of healthy food retail investment has brought new jobs to communities suffering from years of economic blight. In a window of four short years, this legislation has helped in the development of 68 stores in underserved areas of Pennsylvania while creating or retaining 3,700 jobs and expanding healthy food access for more than 400,000 people.

In places where traditional supermarkets will not invest, and the corner stores do not serve the health needs of the community, non-traditional solutions are needed. Therefore, after establishing a presence in the institutional and retail sectors, the Common Market has begun focusing on the household consumption of healthy food through its "Farm-to-Faith" initiative. Common Market is now reaching out to churches, mosques and synagogues throughout the Philadelphia region to make the destination for spiritual healing, also the source for healthy food and the healing of the body. The historical connection between food, faith, and scripture makes the faith community the ideal partner for encouraging healthy eating behaviors. The Farm-to-Faith initiative will deliver cases of the highest-quality produce and eggs to a place of worship to be divided among program participants who also share in the work and cost. This is a real community building activity that will expand the access of healthy and affordable food in a place of trust, support and spiritual guidance.

A great by-product of connecting rural farmers to urban communities, is that Common Market has now created relationships of mutual value and respect between rural food producers and urban consumers. These are relationships based on economic interactions built around fairness. The maintenance of the farms' identity is a critical component in connecting the consumer to the farmer who produced the food, and the means by which it was grown. Additionally, where markets are close to minority and under-resourced farmers, distribution models like the Common Market can play a role in sustaining minority farmers. Black farmers are disappearing at alarming rates and need market support to insure their survival.[9] Therefore, creating market access for our most vulnerable farmers can help them to continue working their land while also improving the health and well-being of vulnerable communities. Moreover, consumers are enabled to make informed decisions about the food they purchase while fostering a connection to our land and agricultural heritage.

While the Common Market is just one example of a successful food distribution model, its origin within the urban black community makes it unique. It is a prime example of the leading role that we, as people of color, can take to build bridges of collaboration between vulnerable rural and urban populations. Through the connection of urban demand with rural farmers, we can improve the physical health of our urban communities and create economic opportunity on both sides of the food chain.

The Common Market is eager to help other communities replicate the success it has found in Philadelphia. For more information please see *www.CommonMarketPhila.org.*

NOTES

[1] See U.S. Department of Agriculture, Food Desert Locator (*http://www.ers.usda.gov/data/fooddesert/index.htm*) (Accessed February 2012)

[2] See U.S. Department of Agriculture, Food Desert Locator, About the Locator, (*http://www.ers.usda.gov/data/fooddesert/about.html#Defined*) (Accessed February 2012)

[3] CDC/NCHES, National Health and Nutrition Examination Survey 2005–2008

[4] National Center for Health Statistics. "Prevalence of Overweight Among Children and Adolescents: United States, 1999–2002" (*http://www.cdc.gov/nchs/products/pubs/pubd/hestats/overwght99.htm*) (Accessed February 2012)

[5] K.M. Venkat Narayan, James P. Boyle, Theodore J. Thompson, Stephen W. Sorensen, and David F. Williamson, "Lifetime Risk for Diabetes Melli tus in the United States," *Journal of the American Medical Association* 290, no. 14 (2003): 1884–1890

[6] S. Jay Olshanksy, Ph.D., Douglas J. Passaro, M.D., Ronald Hershow, M.D., Jennifer Layden, M.P.H., Bruce A. Carnes, Ph.D., Jacob Brody, M.D., Leonard Hayflick, Ph.D., Robert N.Butler M.D., David B. Allison, Ph.D. and David S. Ludwig, "A Potential Decline in Life Expectancy in the United States in the 21st Century," *The New England Journal of Medicine*, 2005: 352: 1138–1145

[7] Sarah Treuhaft, Allison Karpyn, "The Grocery Gap: Who Has Access to Healthy Food and Why it Matters," PolicyLink, (*http://www.policylink.org/atf/cf/%7B97C6D565-BB43-406D-A6D5-ECA3BBF35AF0%7D/FINALGroceryGap.pdf*) (Accessed February 2012)

[8] Kimberly Morland, Steve Wing, and Ana Diez Roux, "The Contextual Effect of the Local Food Environment on Residents' Diets: The Atherosclerosis Risk in Communities Study," *American Journal of Public Health*: November 2002, Vol. 92, No. 11, pp. 1761–1768. doi: 10.2105/AJPH.92.11.1761

[9] In 2007, fewer than 30,600 farmers in the nation were African-American, compared to the 233,000 black farmers counted in 1920. U.S. Department of Agriculture, 2007 Census of Agriculture: Black Farmers, 2007, (*http://www.agcensus.usda.gov/Publications/2007/Online_Highlights/Fact_Sheets/black.pdf*) (Accessed February 2012). Findings.aspx)

BLACK MEN *ARE* KILLING BLACK MEN.

THERE, I SAID IT.

MAYOR MICHAEL A. NUTTER

As I joined tens of thousands of my fellow Philadelphians to celebrate the anniversary of the birth of Dr. Martin Luther King, Jr. in January, a striking thought entered my mind.

In Dr. King's time the biggest threat to a black man was that a white man, wearing a hood, would snatch him up off the street and take him away to beat him, shoot him, lynch him or burn him. The black man was not safe to walk the streets in many of our nation's cities. Today, in 2012, black men are still being snatched from the streets, snatched from their families and their children by individuals wearing hoods. Only this time the hooded person is not white, but black. Of the 316 people who were murdered in Philadelphia last year nearly 75% of those killed were black men. Around 80% of those doing the killing?

Black men. →

Now, you might not expect me to talk about this issue. I'm a black man, proud of my race, my history and my heritage. However, as the Mayor of Philadelphia, the largest American city with an African American Mayor, I feel an obligation to step forward to talk about these issues. Furthermore, this is a problem in cities all throughout America and that's why mayors from across this country—Black, White, Hispanic, and Asian—stand united and are putting this issue on the national agenda. In America's big cities the majority of homicide victims are African American men, the majority of whom are killed by other African American men. This is a national epidemic, and there needs to be a national conversation on this topic.

If the Ku Klux Klan came to Philadelphia and killed almost 300 black men in one year, my city would be on lockdown. The U.S. Justice Department would be called upon. There would be a federal investigation. Congress would hold hearings. And yet, I don't hear a serious, rational, non-hysterical conversation from anyone addressing this epidemic.

This merits a national level conversation because we face a problem that affects us all. Yes, it obviously has a particular impact on the black community, but the repercussions are felt across all sections of society. In Philadelphia I spend one-third of my budget on the 'criminal justice complex', on catching, trying and locking up thousands of black men every year. These are dollars that I can't spend on schools, recreation centers, libraries, after-school activities or job training programs. It's just a waste.

But more importantly, this violence is tearing at the fabric of our communities, pulling us apart at the seams, poking holes in our humanity. This isn't a black problem or a white problem.

It affects us all. As Dr. King wrote from his Birmingham jail cell, we are all "tied together in a single garment of destiny. Whatever affects one directly, affects all indirectly." We are tied together by this violence, it changes us all, and therefore we all must be involved in the solution.

This is why in Philadelphia collaboration and partnership are at the core of everything we do to tackle the root causes and the symptoms of the violence in our city.

As one community leader put it, "We're turning the 'hood' back into a neighborhood." We're building a culture in which everyone feels affected by the problem and everyone can be part of the solution.

My Administration is working in close partnership with our District Attorney, Seth Williams, to crack down on anyone who carries an illegal gun in this city, putting them on notice that we will prosecute them to the fullest extent of the law, and that if we catch them with an illegal gun they're going to jail for up to five years. We're also working closely with our federal partners including the U.S. Attorney, ATFE, FBI, DEA and the U.S. Marshals to implement 'Operation Pressure Point', a multi-agency crack down on crime in targeted areas of the city which last year resulted in a 31% drop in homicides and 17% fewer shooting victims.

Let's be real. We all know that once the issue is in the hands of our law enforcement agencies, part of the battle has already been lost. We must be more focused on prevention than prosecution, on intervention rather than incarceration. This means targeting the highest-risk neighborhoods, engaging citizens and empowering them, because the community needs to be part of the solution.

That's what we have done through 'Philly Rising,' a new approach to city government that we're rolling out across Philadelphia. We go into high crime neighborhoods and ask the folks who actually live there, "What are the problems that need tackling in your community?" They identify the problems, we work with them to build capacity to address them, and through this, the community becomes the solution. In one North Philly neighborhood we experienced a 16% drop in crime during the first ten months of the program by clearing vacant lots, cleaning graffiti, and demolishing abandoned buildings. We partnered with Temple University to open a community computer center at a local elementary school that residents now use to apply for jobs, providing them with an alternative course of action to crime. As one community leader put it, "We're turning the 'hood' back into a neighborhood."

We're building a culture in which everyone feels affected by the problem and everyone can be part of the solution. We're working with our colleges and universities through 'PhillyGoes2College' to target students who are most at risk of not graduating from high school to ensure that not only do they graduate, but

that they also understand that a K-12 education is obsolete in a K-16 world, and therefore, college is essential. We're partnering with IBM to create 'Digital On-Ramps' that will help 175,000 youth and adults in Philadelphia over the next four years access the skills and training that they need to be competitive and reach their full potential. Different levels of government, corporations, foundations, educational institutions, and citizens, all working together to reduce both the opportunities for, and the incidences of violence in our communities.

This will be an uncomfortable conversation. There will be awkward moments. There will be those who feel unqualified to speak, and those who will seek to distort the discussion in service of much different motives. But we will speak out, we will address, we will tackle black-on-black violence in our communities and we will do it together because, again as Dr. King wrote, we are bound together "in an inescapable network of mutuality."

We will say what needs to be said but hasn't been; we will do what needs to be done but hasn't happened. Let the conversation begin.

INSPIRING INNOVATION:

THE CHICAGO URBAN LEAGUE YOUTH INVESTOR/ENTREPRENEURS PROJECT (YIEP)

SHARI E. RUNNER

For 10 years, the Youth Investor/Entrepreneurs Project has introduced hundreds of high school students to the intricate world of investing and enterprise development. The YIEP curriculum teaches financial literacy, but more specifically it is designed to spark innovation in young people by developing the critical thinking skills they need to understand the world and use their ideas to evaluate financial risks and opportunities. →

YIEP attracts students from all schools and backgrounds, but the program specifically targets African American teens. Participants commit to attending two-hour workshops every Saturday for 22 weeks, where they work in teams to develop business concepts and receive lectures from the program's director, Josh Mercer, as well as entrepreneurs, financial and banking experts, and career professionals. The program is equally split between the principles of investing and entrepreneurship.

YIEP students gain an understanding that the ability to create and control wealth is essential to stabilizing communities and ensuring access to economic opportunity. The black-white wealth gap has quadrupled since the mid-1980s from $20,000 to $95,000. Financial assets of white families grew from $22,000 to $100,000 but assets in Black households saw little increase, with an average median wealth of $5,000 in 2007.[1] Additionally, despite starting the highest number of businesses, African Americans trail other groups in total business revenues.[2] YIEP seeks to change this paradigm and improve economic outcomes in the African American community by producing a better educated pool of future investors and business leaders.

Today, young people must learn how to evaluate opportunity through a global lens with an eye toward technological advancement. Innovative projects are the ones that get noticed and funded. Therefore, YIEP aims to give our students access to the theoretical and practical knowledge that will allow them to succeed. And we are proud to report that our students are showing themselves to be quite apt protégés. They have consistently taken top honors at local and regional business plan competitions and 90 percent go on to attend college. They are an impressive group of young people capable of articulating opportunities in ways many adults cannot. Most importantly, they are developing problem solving skills and the ability to think outside of traditional boundaries.

> YIEP students gain an understanding that the ability to create and control wealth is essential to stabilizing communities and ensuring access to economic opportunity.

Their accomplishments can be exemplified by YIEP student, Hyaquino Hyacinthe, a 17 year old senior at Chicago's Kenwood Academy, who plans to attend college to study mechanical engineering with the goal of one day starting his own business. As a junior, he enjoyed his experience with the YIEP program so much that he enrolled for a second year. His commitment paid off as Hyaquino recently took first place in the business plan competition hosted by Northeastern Illinois University, advancing to the finals in Los Angeles in summer 2012.

When asked about his experience with YIEP, Hyaquino stated, "I always say, knowledge is the truth. Anytime you have a chance to receive something new, you should always do it. In the future, it will pay off. Education is power. Mr. Mercer teaches us that the best ideas come when you [are] younger. So if I get an idea for a business, I put it in writing."

★ ★ ★ ★ ★ ★ ★ ★ ★ ★ ★ ★ ★ ★ ★ ★ ★

YIEP is based on the principle that knowledge and most importantly access to knowledge is indeed truth. It is for this reason that our Chicago affiliate will continue to utilize our YIEP program to enrich and inspire our area youth to fully utilize their minds and engage in their communities while developing an entrepreneurial and financially savvy mindset. Our urban communities need these young entrepreneurs to advance not only business solutions, but also to craft those policies critical to alleviating societal ills. YIEP is just one of our creative approaches to empowering Chicago's teens.

NOTES

[1] Thomas M. Shapiro, Tatjana Meschede and Laura Sullivan, "The Racial Wealth Gap Increases Fourfold," The Institute on Assets and Social Policy, The Heller School for Social Policy and Management, Brandeis University, May 2010 (see at *http://iasp.brandeis.edu/pdfs/ Racial-Wealth-Gap-Brief.pdf*) (Accessed January 2012)

[2] Robert W. Fairlie and Alica M. Robb, "Race and Entrepreneurial Success: Black-, Asian-, and White-Owned Businesses in the United States," Executive Summary. Cambridge: MIT Press, October 2008 (see at *http://www.npc.umich.edu/publications/policy_briefs/ brief12/index.php*) (Accessed January 2012)

READY TO SUCCEED:

THE NATIONAL URBAN LEAGUE PROJECT READY: POST-SECONDARY SUCCESS PROGRAM

HAL SMITH, ED.D., JACQUELINE AYERS, AND DARLENE MARLIN

For more than 50 years, the National Urban League's Education & Youth Development divisions have worked to improve educational opportunities for African American students by developing innovative programs to support their academic achievement, encourage their civic involvement, and contribute to their intellectual, physical and emotional development. →

Our signature education program, *Project Ready*, is designed to help us reach the National Urban League's Education Empowerment Goal: that every American child is ready for college, work and life by 2025. *Project Ready* is designed to develop an individual student's knowledge and attitude towards, and capacity for, post-secondary success. Our model brings together research and promising practices in youth development, adolescent literacy, out-of-school time learning and student success, within the tradition and legacy of the Urban League Movement.

Project Ready currently enrolls 8th–12th grade students in historically underserved and under resourced communities across the country. Program participants receive academic support, social development and college exposure designed to more fully develop "readiness"— the information and perspective necessary for success, absent the need for remediation in college or career. Key strengths of *Project Ready* include:

→ *A focus on building the intellectual, leadership and social assets of a college and career-ready student population;*

→ *An inherent program flexibility that encourages local innovation and customization;*

→ *A clear and intentional focus on building and sustaining effective partnerships; and*

→ *The program's ability to serve an affiliate's larger goals of familial and communal empowerment.*

The *Project Ready* model explicitly integrates academic preparation for college and success after high school with positive youth development approaches. *Project Ready* students receive academic, social, cultural support and opportunities specifically designed to more fully develop the "career and college knowledge," necessary for collegiate and professional success beyond academic preparation. In addition to a specific focus on readiness, our approach emphasizes service learning, age-appropriate life skills such as time management and study skills, financial literacy, cultural and racial awareness, an appreciation for diversity and effective leadership.

Project Ready students receive academic, social, cultural support and opportunities specifically designed to more fully develop the "career and college knowledge," necessary for collegiate and professional success beyond academic preparation.

In order to achieve a successful integration of skill-building and social development, the *Project Ready* Post-Secondary Success Model is comprised of three key components: 1) Academic Support; 2) Social Development; and, 3) College & Career Awareness. More importantly, for each component, there is a set of explicit student outcomes and expected competencies that are guided by an Individual College Development Plan (ICDP).

2011 marked the end of the 6th year of *Project Ready* at 29 Urban League affiliate sites in 19 states. The more than 1700 students currently enrolled nationwide are each expected to make academic progress, benefit from cultural enrichment opportunities and develop the critical skills, attitudes and aptitudes necessary for post-secondary success.

The positive influence of the *Project Ready* program stays with our students long after their participation. For example, Tahji Jones, a senior at Brighton High School in Rochester, New York credits much of his academic and personal success to his participation in the Urban League of Rochester's *Project Ready* program. Through the program, he was given the opportunity to attend the National Urban League's Annual Youth Leadership Summit and the "Voices in Action: National Youth Summit," hosted by the U.S. Department of Education where he and other *Project Ready* students met with U.S. Secretary of Education Arne Duncan. He credits *Project Ready* with giving him purpose and helping to identify his goals for the future—

The Impact of *Project Ready*

CLEVELAND, OHIO

In order to develop career and college-ready literacy in participants, the Urban League of Greater Cleveland targeted students for their Project Ready Literacy project. Students spent 25 hours per month with a total of over 6500 contact hours developing a comprehensive and synergistic attention to reading, writing, speaking, listening and thinking. Improving reading comprehension beyond the basic level depends on the ability to master these skills, critically and completely. Utilizing the Ohio Achievement Assessment (OAA) as a tool to assess how much the student improved because of the intervention and support, Project Ready students started at 70.8% proficiency, but ended at 88%, easily surpassing the state standard for proficiency of 75%.

ROCHESTER, NEW YORK

The Urban League of Rochester's Project Ready program specifically targets high-achieving African American males, who alongside affiliate staff developed a service learning program focused on reducing childhood obesity in their community. They addressed the issue by being trained to become experts on healthy living, wellness and peer education. Students then used that knowledge and demonstrated leadership by launching a youth fitness clinic where participants visited a variety of stations. While at each station, an Urban League Project Ready Trainer taught them new skills and attitudes while informing their peers and young children how to maintain a healthy life style that would leave them better prepared to succeed and lead in school and in the larger community.

ELYRIA, OHIO

The Lorain County Urban League has a growing S.T.E.M. focus in its Project Ready program and has partnered with the NASA Glen Research Center in order to provide more robust S.T.E.M. content, a professional development workshop for local teachers at partner schools, and a series of experiments led by NASA subject matter experts. In addition, Project Ready participants in teams to plan and design an experiment at the Center utilizing simple objects, such as boxes, rubber bands, and empty plastic bottles. NASA scientist and engineers visited the partner school in order to provide more feedback on the experiments that students put together. Later Project Ready teams went to NASA to tour the facility and discuss their results with NASA engineers prior to the end of the program. Youth showed off their experiments and results at the Project Ready Family Night event. NASA and the Ohio Aerospace Institute also sponsored a Summer Airplane Camp exclusively for Project Ready youth.

to help ensure there are more African American male teachers in the classroom. Tahji is planning to major in education and has applied to 9 colleges. He has been accepted into Gannon University, but eagerly awaiting a response from his first choice, Harvard University.

Since the program's initial launch, there have been many success stories like Tahji's, leading the National Urban League to continue developing *Project Ready* through the inclusion of additional learning/developmental time, including a clear emphasis on summer learning to combat summer learning loss; an emphasis on service learning; the addition of innovative academic content and learning supports, including online resources; a clear literacy focus; a focus on science, technology, engineering, and math (STEM); a collaborative approach to planning, advising, content delivery and shared professional development; and building a rigorous data collection and evaluation approach. The National Urban League views these elements as foundational for improving educational and developmental outcomes for America's children and youth.

Therefore in 2011, we developed key enhancements to guide and encourage affiliate innovation in the program. The *Project Ready* 2.0 Curriculum Manual & User Guide, the Science, Technology, Engineering and Mathematics (S.T.E.M.) Manual and the Youth Development Framework and Guide were created as out of school time tools specifically designed to help affiliates reflect on their current programs, identify and codify effective approaches and activities, and suggest ways to develop programs that are aligned with the core foundation of the National Urban League's philosophy of high quality youth programming.

Additionally, to better gauge the program's impact, the NUL engaged the Academy for Educational Development (AED) to conduct an evaluation of *Project Ready* in order to assess the association between program participation and positive changes in knowledge and attitude of low-income urban students.

AED's *Project Ready* findings include:

→ *Project Ready programs provided participants with a wide variety of positive, structured academic and social development activities in nurturing environments while having a positive impact on their academic progress and interpersonal skill development.*

→ *The programs were implemented at in-school and out-of-school environments, demonstrating Project Ready's utility and adaptability and were reported to have engaged the students in interactive, hands-on learning experiences, and were characterized as successful.*

→ *Participating students, parents, program staff, and community stakeholders all expressed high levels of satisfaction with the program along with an expressed desire to continue the program in their communities.*

The National Urban League believes that providing children and youth with additional productive exposure to an array of learning and developmental opportunities, knowledgeable adults outside their families, and motivated peers can result in very different levels of student development and achievement. As a result of their participation in *Project Ready*, urban students are several steps closer to being ready to thrive and successfully compete in the 21st Century global marketplace.

★ ★ ★ ★ ★ ★ ★ ★ ★ ★ ★ ★ ★ ★ ★

PARTNERING TO
EMPOWER HEAL

A **SPECIAL COLLECTION** OF ARTICLES FROM OUR PARTNERS

HY KIDS

INTRODUCTION

healthy kids
out of school

BOY SCOUTS OF AMERICA

GIRL SCOUTS OF THE USA

NATIONAL COUNCIL OF LA RAZA

NATIONAL COUNCIL OF YOUTH SPORTS

NATIONAL 4-H COUNCIL

NATIONAL URBAN LEAGUE

POP WARNER

US YOUTH SOCCER

YMCA OF THE USA

Childhood obesity has more than tripled in the past three decades, according the Centers for Disease Control and Prevention. Obesity is more common among African-American and Mexican-American children than non-Hispanic white children. Given that tens of millions of young people participate in out-of-school time programs, a new public-private partnership, ChildObesity180, identified and convened after school providers as a promising opportunity for obesity prevention efforts.

Dedicated to educating and empowering the next generation of youth to lead happy, healthy lives, the National Urban League quickly committed to the effort. The new collaboration, Healthy Kids Out of School, is an alliance of nine national leaders that have united to adopt consistent nutrition and physical activity principles throughout their organizations. The founding partners organizations are the Boy Scouts of America, Girl Scouts of the USA, National Council of La Raza, National Council of Youth Sports, National 4-H Council, National Urban League, Pop Warner, US Youth Soccer, YMCA of the USA.

The partners agreed to a list of evidence-based recommendations that were specific enough to ignite change, yet flexible enough to be tailored for a variety of out-of-school-time programs with access to different resources, populations, cultures, and environments. These principles are:

1. *Drink Right: Choose water instead of sugar sweetened beverages.*

2. *Move More: Boost movement and physical activity in all programs.*

3. *Snack Smart: Fuel up on fruits and vegetables.*

For the first time, these organizations will provide clear, consistent messages to the youth participating in one or multiple out-of-school time activities. By adopting these principals, young people will be offered lifetime of lessons about healthy food choices and physical activity.

In the following two essays, two of the National Urban League's partners in this effort, the Girl Scouts of the USA and the Boy Scouts of America share more about their contribution to reverse the impact of childhood obesity.

HELPING GIRLS MAKE HEALTHY CHOICES

BY ANNA MARIA CHÁVEZ
GIRL SCOUTS OF THE U.S.A.

Over the last 30 years, according to the Centers for Disease Control, obesity rates have tripled among children ages 6 to 11 and doubled for those ages 12 to 19. Rates are higher for Hispanic children than for non-Hispanic whites, and higher still for African Americans. They are highest of all for African American girls: the CDC's 2010 figures indicate that 24% of African American girls are overweight.[1]

It's a dire situation. At Girl Scouts, our mission is to build girls of courage, confidence, and character, who make the world a better place. Obesity challenges that mission; our research and that of others tells us that being overweight puts girls at risk both physically and emotionally, and can negatively affect their ability to succeed as adults.

So we have a problem, one that affects not just African Americans but all of us. On the biological level, it's a simple problem: people become obese when they take in more calories than they burn. On every other level, particularly among girls, it's extremely complicated. In 2006, our Girl Scout Research Institute set out to examine the issue in a major research report, *The New Normal: What Girls Say about Healthy Living.*[2] The complete report is available for download at *www.girlscouts.org/research/publications/healthyliving.* I'd like to share with you a few key findings we've found helpful in shaping our own approach to helping girls lead healthier lives.

"Normal Healthy"

For most girls, being healthy has more to do with appearing "normal" and feeling accepted than with maintaining good diet and exercise habits. This fits in perfectly with practically everything we learn about girls; no matter what we start talking with them about, we end up talking about relationships. If a girl feels accepted by her peers (and her mother; our research shows that mothers are far and away the most influential role models for girls) and that she is normal by their standards, she's likely to be comfortable with her weight.

This has its good points and bad points. On the one hand, a girl who feels normal and accepted isn't going to be obsessing over her weight or depressed about it, or otherwise struggling with it emotionally. On the other hand, if her peers are overweight, and particularly if her mother is overweight, she may not be motivated to maintain a healthy weight herself.

Emotional Health is Key

By the same token, girls embrace a holistic view of health that reflects a clear connection between physical and emotional well-being. In the online survey for The New Normal, virtually all girls agreed with the statement, "Emotional health is as important as physical health." The vast majority (88%) of 11- to 17-year-old girls also agreed that "Feeling good about yourself is more important than how you look."

Not surprisingly, this ties directly into what we learned about girls' body image and their satisfaction with their weight. We divided the girls by actual weight status into three categories: underweight, normal weight, and at risk/overweight. In each category, we asked girls first which category they thought they belonged in, and then how satisfied they were with their current weight.

Results for the at risk/overweight group were eye-popping. Of the overweight girls who believed they were overweight, one percent said they were very satisfied with their weight, and thirty percent said they were very dissatisfied. Of the overweight girls who believed they were normal, 36 percent said they were very satisfied with their weight and none—zero percent—said they were very dissatisfied.

Awareness v. Behavior

In addition to perception issues, we uncovered some conscious choice issues. Although they demonstrate a good basic knowledge of healthy foods and eating behaviors, in practice many girls make poor choices with regard to diet and exercise. Factors contributing to the gap between awareness and behavior include the unavailability of healthy eating options, concerns that take precedence over health, such as fitting in and school performance, and peer pressure— not wanting to look "extreme" or weird.

Income

The strongest correlation for overweight exists between weight and income. For girls of all ages, the incidence of overweight is highest at the lowest income levels and plunges dramatically at the highest income level. The difference is so extreme that eight- to ten-year-old girls from the lowest income families (those making less than $35,000 in annual income) are three times more likely to be overweight than eight- to ten-year-old girls from families with annual incomes of over $100,000.

88% of 11- to 17-year-old girls agreed that "Feeling good about yourself is more important than how you look."

What Works?

As I said, it's complicated. The approach we take in Girl Scouts is to focus on the whole girl, rather than singling out one aspect of her life. Our national program, the Girl Scout Leadership Experience (GSLE), is based on a three-part development model: to teach a girl to know herself and trust her own values, to form healthy relationships with others, and to work together on goals for the common good. As they spend time in it, we find that the GSLE can help girls become better able to make healthy decisions—including decisions about nutrition and activity levels—in the face of difficult, stressful, confusing, or frightening situations.

And we find that one good result feeds another. As girls become more confident, they become more willing to take part in physical activities. (Our all-girl environment helps immeasurably with this; there are no boys to make them feel dorky or tell them they can't do things.) As they become more physically active they become even more self-confident, and they also begin to feel better. Healthy behavior becomes its own reward—which is the only way you can get it to stick. Nagging girls about their weight is no more a solution to obesity than truant officers are a solution to academic underperformance.

The success stories of our Girl Scouts—millions of them—tell us that Girl Scouting is not only helping girls enhance their learning experience and academic success, but also their chances of beating this pervasive, costly, and dangerous epidemic. However, to truly meet the needs of girls of every background and every community, which is what we try to do every day, we need help. We need parents, teachers, other youth-serving organizations, policy-makers—everyone—to recognize the significance of social and emotional wellness, and the need to address this issue holistically. For girls, emphasizing the positive emotional outcomes of healthy living makes all the difference.

NOTES

[1] National Center for Health Statistics. "Prevalence of Overweight Among Children and Adolescents: United States, 1999–2002" Downloaded from: *http://www.cdc.gov/nchs/products/pubs/pubd/hestats/overwght99.htm*

[2] Judy Schoenberg, Ed.M., Kimberlee Salmond, M.P.P., Paula Fleshman, M.S., "The New Normal? What Girls Say About Healthy Living.," New York, N.Y.: Girl Scouts of the USA, 2006. *http://www.girlscouts.org/research/publications/original/gs_study_summary.pdf* (Accessed January 2012)

HEALTHY BOYS STAND SCOUTSTRONG™

LEE SHAW, JR.
THE BOY SCOUTS OF AMERICA

Serving nearly 3 million young people between the ages of 6-21 has given the Boy Scouts of America (BSA) great insight on the critical issue of the health of our children. As an organization, BSA has promoted physical fitness since 1910. Physical Fitness has been at the core of our Aims and Purpose as identified in the Scout Oath:

On my honor I will do my best,
To do my duty
to God and my country
and to obey the Scout Law;
To help other people at all times;
To keep myself physically strong,
mentally awake,
and morally straight.

As you can see, addressing physical fitness is not new to Scouting. However today is a new day where, because of unhealthy habits, we may see the first generation that will be less healthy and have a shorter life expectancy than their parents.[1] The BSA understands the urgency in which we must operate. It is our obligation, to not only support change, but to take a leading role towards helping to educate and activate our young people in healthy living. Chief Scout Executive Bob Mazzuca is clear on how he sees the role of the BSA with respect to the health of America's youth. "We must aggressively create and promote programs that build healthier lifestyles for our younger generation. This means all young people—Scouts or not."

Physical Activity

The Boy Scouts have stressed physical activity and last year there were over a half million young people in the Scouting movement that took part in activities that were designed around being physically active for extended periods of time.

And we are continuing to seek new opportunities by collaborating with others, a Scout tradition. Realizing that there are many efforts to confront childhood obesity we have established alliances with many leading organizations that are widely recognized for improving wellness, fitness, and nutrition among youth. These organizations include The President's Council on Fitness, Sports and Nutrition (PCFSN), The First Lady's Let's Move initiative, and the National Urban League.

Recently, BSA launched a major health-related outreach program called SCOUTStrong™. Through the SCOUTStrong™ tagline FIT · FUEL · FUN, the BSA is embarking on an effort to re-define what it means to

be "Physically Strong" while emphasizing challenging and exciting outdoor activities like hiking, swimming and biking.

The BSA recently embarked on a new collaboration with the PCFSN called the SCOUTStrong™ Presidential Active Lifestyle Award, or SCOUTStrong™ PALA for short. PALA is one of many activity challenges offered by the PCFSN through their President's Challenge program. The PALA award is designed to motivate participants to be physically active on a regular basis by allowing them to participate in activities they enjoy.

> The Scouting program addresses the issue of child obesity head on by providing opportunities for outdoor experiences. The first step often includes getting unplugged and off the couch.

To earn the SCOUTStrong™ PALA Challenge Award, the participant is required to meet a daily activity goal of 30 minutes a day for adults and 60 minutes a day for kids under 18 for at least five days a week, six weeks total. Each week the participant will focus on a healthy eating goal. There are eight to choose from, and each week the participant should add a

new goal while continuing with their previous goals. Participants can take up to eight weeks to complete the program.

The best attribute of the SCOUTStrong™ PALA is that it stresses the health benefits of healthy eating and regular physical activity for anyone, at any fitness level.

Let's examine how one troop has become engaged in the SCOUTStrong™ PALA. Boy Scout Troop 123 in the Northern Lights Council of North Dakota recently saw 62 of its members and parents earn their SCOUTStrong™ PALA award. Youth and parents alike took part in this challenge to enhance and maintain their physical fitness. Their activities ranged from gardening to scuba diving to hiking in the North Dakota plains. Dr. Stephen McDonald, an active Troop Leader in Troop 123 was recently elected to President Barack Obama's Presidential Council on Fitness, Sports and Nutrition. Currently there are thousands of examples similar to these Scouts and parents throughout the country. We're quite proud to offer real solutions to the growing crisis of childhood obesity.

BSA is also optimistic about another collaboration. In 2010, as the National Urban League and the Boy Scouts of America each celebrated their centennial anniversary, a Memorandum of Understanding between our two organizations was signed. A pledge was made to support each other and empower communities and change lives in a variety of ways, including opportunities for physical fitness and solutions regarding health care.

The National Urban League serves thousands of young people who may be looking for an outdoor experience, as described by National Urban League CEO and President, Marc H. Morial. We believe Scouting can offer solutions to encourage physical fitness and active lifestyle in our local and national outdoor classrooms across America.

According to Barry Williams, the Director of the Baltimore County Department of Recreation & Parks, who also serves as the Board President of the Baltimore Area Council, Boy Scouts of America, "...[T]he Scouting program addresses the issue of child obesity head on by providing opportunities for outdoor experiences. The first step often includes getting unplugged and off the couch. It's amazing the fun our children can have by engaging in physical activities."

Nutrition

Nutrition is also another very important component in the overall health of our children. Scouting teaches how to make healthy eating choices by demonstrating ways to prepare meals following the nutritional guidelines set by the United States Department of Agriculture's (USDA) *ChooseMyPlate.gov* which illustrates the five food groups that are the building blocks for a healthy diet using a familiar image—a place setting for a meal. This life skill is at the very foundation of making healthy choices. Aspects of this info is available for ages 6 years old through 18 years of age because it's never too early to start.

As an organization that has been a child advocate for more than a century, we not only accept our responsibility in addressing childhood obesity, we embrace the opportunity to continue helping boys live SCOUTStrong™ to make a difference in a magnificent way!

NOTES

[1] S. Jay Olshanksy, Ph.D., Douglas J. Passaro, M.D., Ronald Hershow, M.D., Jennifer Layden, M.P.H., Bruce A. Carnes, Ph.D., Jacob Brody, M.D., Leonard Hayflick, Ph.D., Robert N. Butler M.D., David B. Allison, Ph.D. and David S. Ludwig, "A Potential Decline in Life Expectancy in the United States in the 21st Century," *The New England Journal of Medicine*, 2005: 352: 1138–1145

SHOULD I GO TO COLLEGE?

A **SPECIAL COLLECTION** OF ARTICLES & OP-EDs

INTRODUCTION: THE VALUE OF COLLEGE

CHANELLE P. HARDY, ESQ., NATIONAL URBAN LEAGUE POLICY INSTITUTE

It would not be entirely inaccurate to suggest that these are the best of times, as well as the worst of times for black students considering the benefits of a college education in 2012. On one hand, our colleges and universities provide access to a stunning array of diverse course offerings, study abroad programs and foreign language tracks, designed to position students to compete in a global marketplace. On the other, there is the recognition that these opportunities come at an ever-increasing cost. Students find themselves saddled with an increasing student debt load and no guarantee of employment as the unemployment rate—even for the college-educated—remains painfully high. Recent efforts by President Obama and Congress to relieve some of the financial strain confronting a growing generation of new college graduates, while laudable, offer only slim comfort. →

The Dilemma

Where yesterday's students approached college and college graduation with heady excitement—the opportunity to get out on one's own is only slightly outweighed by the opportunity to gain the skills necessary to position oneself for a thriving and prosperous future—today's graduates are gripped by anxiety. The confidence of the youth is tempered by the growing fear of the risky post-college job market that they have encountered since high school, and that they hear about from their older friends and colleagues. The tale of the business major working as a bartender, the pre-law graduate alternating between the job that pays the bills and the volunteer internship that provides needed career experience, is no longer the exception—it is becoming the rule. For black students in America, this can make for an especially unnerving dilemma, as we've long been taught to revere the very notion of a college education as a panacea of sorts; an economic point of arrival, and the beginning of a yellow-brick road to guaranteed prosperity. Perhaps part of the frustration being voiced by young graduates at countless political candidate forums and 'Occupy' rallies throughout the country is the sudden realization that much of what we've been taught to accept as an absolute and indisputable fact is being challenged at its very core.

The Question

Which brings us to a valid, if unsettling question on the part of today's high school student: "Should I Go to College?" After all, if college isn't the answer, what's the alternative?

Do we dare surrender the hard fought gains won by generations past—gains won as much for the benefit of future generations, as for their own? After all, borrowing from the recognized brilliance of Langston Hughes, the road to equal educational access protected by law "ain't been no crystal stair." Isn't it our collective duty to take full advantage? On the other hand, has the march of social progress bound us to an upward climb toward personal improvement that risks the unintended outcome of financially bankrupting us along the way?

The Facts

Let's consider a few facts that might help us to put this uniquely complicated question into proper perspective.

Figure 1: *Average Unemployment Rate By Education: 2011*

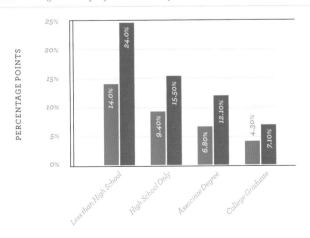

PERCENTAGE POINTS

- Less than High School: 14.0%, 24.0%
- High School Only: 9.40%, 15.50%
- Associate Degree: 6.80%, 12.10%
- College Graduate: 4.30%, 7.10%

■ *Overall*
■ *African Americans*

Source: U.S. Bureau of Labor Statistics, Current Population Survey, 2011

Figure 2: *Lifetime Earnings of African Americans by Level of Education*

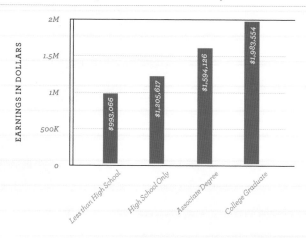

Source: U.S. Census Bureau, Education and Synthetic Work-Life Earnings Estimates: American Community Survey, September 2011

A college education is still a worthwhile investment when considered through a lens of income stability alone. Statistics show that in 2011, African Americans with only a high school degree had a rate of unemployment more than twice that of African Americans with a college degree.[1]

> On average, college graduates of almost any stripe experience labor market outcomes that are much better than those without a college education.

A college graduate is also likely to experience lifetime earnings substantially higher than those with lower levels of education. An African American college graduate is likely to experience twice the lifetime earnings of a high school dropout, and 65% more than those of a high school graduate. Additionally, an African American college graduate's lifetime earnings are 24% higher than those who hold an associate degree.[2]

Of course, all college degrees are not created equal, and this is undoubtedly true when one considers which undergraduate majors are statistically proven to confer higher average salaries. For example, median wage levels for undergraduates majoring in engineering and mathematics far outpace those of graduates majoring in the humanities and, unfortunately, education. However, the facts are clear and undeniable. On average, college graduates of almost any stripe experience labor market outcomes that are much better than those without a college education.

The Response

So the National Urban League has decided to pose this difficult question to a panel of

Figure 3: *Median Wage Levels for Undergraduate Majors*

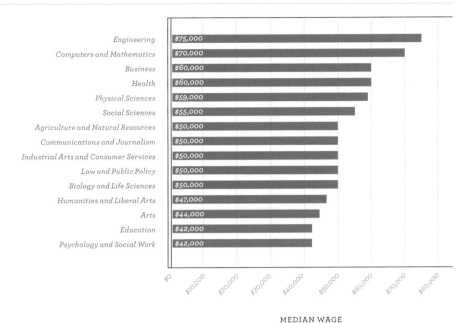

UNDERGRADUATE MAJORS

Engineering	$75,000
Computers and Mathematics	$70,000
Business	$60,000
Health	$60,000
Physical Sciences	$59,000
Social Sciences	$55,000
Agriculture and Natural Resources	$50,000
Communications and Journalism	$50,000
Industrial Arts and Consumer Services	$50,000
Law and Public Policy	$50,000
Biology and Life Sciences	$50,000
Humanities and Liberal Arts	$47,000
Arts	$44,000
Education	$42,000
Psychology and Social Work	$42,000

MEDIAN WAGE

Source: Georgetown University, Center on Education and the Workforce

education experts, policy-thinkers, authors, and leaders of government and industry. Their answers were as wide-ranging and thought-provoking as the question itself. We've shared their thoughts in a series of op-ed articles. And while there is no singularly correct answer to this question, the discussion is one that is well worth having, and that we are proud to begin right here, right now.

"Should I Go to College?"

NOTES

[1] U.S. Bureau of Labor Statistics, Current Population Survey 2011

[2] U.S. Census Bureau, Education and Synthetic Work-Life Earnings Estimates: American Community Survey, September 2011 at p.6

WHY A COLLEGE EDUCATION MATTERS

BY KEVIN POWELL

My mother raised me to go to college. From the time I could walk and talk, she constantly told me how important an education was, how it could greatly improve my life as compared to hers. That is because my mother is the product of the old American South, growing up in the era of "For Coloreds Only" and "For Whites Only" signs. Blatant racism and oppression worked together to limit her possibilities to an eighth grade education, and to picking South Carolina cotton. When my mother migrated North, to Jersey City, New Jersey, where I was born and raised, she found more employment opportunities, but because of the woeful neglect and absence of my father, and generations of poverty my family had known since slavery, my mother knew that she had to do something to break the vicious cycle of little to no possibilities beyond the meager earnings that awaited me.

So my mother taught me to read and write as early as age three. She also told me I could be something important in life, like a lawyer or a doctor, if I just did well in school. When I think back on it, I realize that my mother was a young woman in her 20s, at the height of the Civil Rights Movement. Even though she herself was never a participant, she caught the remarkable spirit of that historic period. Educational opportunities were often discussed during the movement. I believe that my mother heard those whispers and transferred them, along with the aspirations that had been snatched from her own impoverished life, to me.

By the time I was in the fifth grade, my mother could no longer help me with my schoolwork. I, an only child, became so angry with her. I think it was the first time I was ever ashamed of my mother. I regret feeling as such; because the hardcore truth is that my mother is one of the smartest human beings I've ever met; that rare person who could make something from nothing, in spite of the poverty, on any given day. That rare person who in spite of her own educational limitations, and the fact that she, herself, had never set foot on a college campus, knew that college would transform her son's life.

So literally from the beginning of high school I started to send away for college brochures. I read with amazement about far-off schools like Pepperdine University in California, and I often dreamed of what college would be like for me. By the time I was a senior in high school I was very skilled at the college application and SAT preparation process, and I simply brought home the admission and financial aid forms to my mother. I told her I had read through everything, and that she could simply sign by the X. She did each and every one of them, as a willing participant in her son's path to higher education.

I settled on Rutgers University, the state university of New Jersey, and my life was changed forever. It was there, in my first year, where I stumbled into the anti-apartheid movement, Reverend Jesse Jackson's first presidential campaign, and a kind of intellectual and cultural stimulation I had never experienced. I found myself thinking new thoughts, reading new kinds of books and, for the first time in my eighteen years, studying the great contributions of Black people to the world, in America, in the West Indies, and in Africa. My mind was expanding. My soul was churning. I was awakened and I am quite sure that college exposure is what made me the person I am today.

For it was at Rutgers that I evolved from a profoundly insecure young man who loved books, into the writer I had wanted to be since I was 11-years-old. First it was writing for the school's newspapers; eventually I broadened into poetry to express my thoughts about my life, about our planet. It was there at Rutgers that I went from a teenager utterly terrified of speaking in public to a most recognizable student leader and speaker on campus.

That is why when I encounter young people today I always ask how many are going to college. Depending on the school and area the number ranges from most, to barely any.

I come from a background of poverty, food stamps, government cheese, and tenement buildings where we were not really encouraged to pursue a college education. If not for my mother's vision, I doubt I would have known a college education could even be a reality for me.

That is why I feel so strongly about exposing our young people of color to higher education via college tours, interactive websites and, most importantly, by interacting with those of us who've attended college and can therefore share how important a college education has been in our lives.

I would share that a college education is one of the great equalizers in America. It is the single most important factor in my being able to move up from the class background of my mother and family to the Black professional I now am. I was the first person in my immediate family to attend college, and I took with me the very serious weight of what that meant. I was not only going to Rutgers University for myself, but for every single person in my family and community who would never have such an opportunity.

I would share with other first-generation college students that a college education represented a magical key in our hands, there to unlock any door that may be blocked by circumstance. All we have to do, with hard work, dedication and a dream of what we desire in life, is know that the only ceiling that will ever stop us from going up and forward with that college education is ourselves.

SACRIFICE IF YOU MUST—THE REWARD IS CLEAR

GREGORY E. CARR, PH.D., J.D.

The current challenges facing American higher education place students from Black, Brown and poor communities at a crossroads nearly sixty years since the landmark Brown v. Board of Education decision. Faced with the prospect of taking on mounting post-secondary educational debt but facing seemingly uncertain prospects of employment with only a high school diploma, many of these students ask themselves, "should I go to college?"

Last year's "Arab/North African Spring" reminded the world of the presence of a planet full of largely young people determined to put their best thinking to challenges of freedom, community and opportunity. This reality presents American universities in general and HBCUs in particular with opportunities to institutionalize visions of real world relevance in ways not heretofore fully imagined and/or articulated institutionally. Why college? Because the idea and reality of a college education symbolizes the "radical" idea of equipping the next generation of Americans with the necessary skills and awareness to solve human problems on national and international levels. If we do not do it, rest assured, others will, and the fading idea of "American Exceptionalism" will give way to the harsh reality of a debtor nation with an increasingly unprepared, unemployed and restive citizenry.

Faced with this prospect, the American academy has ushered in dramatic changes in the mission and demographic of the university. An already vicious and pronounced class divide is widening. Higher education is becoming less affordable for the poor and more affordable for middle and upper class students whose academic performance has frequently benefitted from enhanced K-12 opportunities. Ivy League institutions and others with great financial resources offer admission packages that cover all unmet financial need for entering students. Will those without the benefit of either considerable wealth or high-quality early education simply recede into the lengthening shadows of a new American Nadir?

The obvious answer to the question of whether or not to attend college is an unqualified 'yes'. After all, contemporary research confirms what we have known for some time: postsecondary education increases the possibility of entering the U.S. middle class. Georgetown University's Center on Education and the Workforce's 2011 study entitled Hard Times: College Majors, Unemployment and Earnings, reveals that those with a Bachelor's degree make 84% more money over the course of their lives than those possessing only a high school diploma. Further, according to the report, a new Bachelor's degree decreases the likelihood of unemployment by nearly 13% (from 22.9% unemployment for recent high school graduates to 8.9% unemployment for recent college graduates), and those who pursue technical and/or stable industry majors (e.g. computer sciences, education, healthcare, business and professional concentrations) have the most "recession proof" degrees. Finally, as the American economy improves, those with college degrees will be first in line to benefit through access to work, especially in their major fields.[1]

When we consider the stark realities of race and class (two categories inextricably intertwined in the American socio-economic order), the reality that intentionally forgoing college should not be an option is underscored. Higher high school dropout rates persist for African Americans (nearly ten percent) and Latinos (over eighteen percent) as compared to whites (nearly five percent). Only two percent of students from high-income families drop out of high school, compared with nearly nine percent of those from low-income households. These numbers led a recent commentator in Investor's Business Daily to muse that "the Education Gap, not the Income Gap, is our number one problem." [2]

An educated citizenry contributes to the economic health of the country, enabling the U.S. to compete in an interconnected and technologically advanced international job market. Simply put, an under-educated citizenry is the surest pathway to a steep—and perhaps permanent—American global decline.

Recognizing this reality, a tipping point in the national political will seems to be approaching, borne on rising popular discontent such as that symbolized in the "Occupy" movement and the continuing demand to improve public K-12 education for all students. Meanwhile, those asking themselves whether they should pursue a college degree must not delay. Seize opportunities to complete high school and to continue undeterred, from trade schools and community colleges to four-year colleges and universities and, if at all possible, graduate and professional degrees. Sacrifice if you must: the reward is clearly worth the investment.

Why college? Because higher education is the route to a life of fulfilled dreams and contributions. Particularly at Historically Black Colleges and Universities (HBCUs), opportunities for African American students to connect the social and cultural foundations that transformed American democracy in the Reconstruction, and Civil Rights/Black Power movement eras to new challenges abound. Universities are the source of the professional thinking class, and HBCUs have been the source of thinkers and leaders that have stood in deliberate opposition to legal, social and political arrangements that have worked to rob people of their highest aspirations.

As the American economy struggles to reinvent itself, students at HBCUs must take on a special role: they must pose different questions that will often reveal diverging and often conflicting answers, both in their classrooms and between their institutions and the nation. Students from the full spectrum of class, regional and national division must become broadly-aware and well-skilled, and some—even many—of them must enter teaching and service alongside or instead of corporate America.

Perhaps, then, the most central reason to choose to pursue a college education is to wed the potential of the creative human mind to the pursuit of a more just society for all, regardless of your field of study. This reason will connect to the faith of our Ancestors in the power of education, a faith that led directly to our greater and more abundant life.

NOTES
[1] For the full report, see: *http://www9.georgetown.edu/grad/gppi/ hpi/cew/pdfs/Unemployment.Final.update1.pdf*

[2] J.T. Young, "The Real Gap is in Education, Not in Income," *Investor's Weekly,* January 25, 2012

COMMUNITIES, SCHOOLS AND FAMILIES MAKE THE EDUCATION-CAREER CONNECTION

DESIREÉ LUCKEY

In these tumultuous times, it is easy to feel a sense of panic about the state of the economy and job market. Even as a college student, there is uncertainty about paying for school, finding a job, and knowing what moves to make to maximize the return on my degree.

While the prospects seem daunting now, it is important to promote college attendance and completion, and to provide families with the resources that they need to make the connection between college or technical training and the workforce. Community-based organizations and schools each play a critical role in making these resources available to families. As I complete my final semester as an undergraduate at Howard University, the influence of the Peoria (Tri-County) Urban League, the bevy of resources available to me at Howard University, and the institution's commitment to global citizenship have all adequately prepared me to compete in the global economy.

College attendance and completion offer lasting academic, personal and social benefits. Academically, higher education allows you to continue developing critical thinking skills beyond those developed in high school. Personally, college allows young people to define who they are in a more structured environment, while gaining exposure to the real world and adult decision-making. Socially, college gives students the opportunity to grow and learn from people of various backgrounds that they may not have met otherwise. Dialogue in classrooms, group projects, extracurricular activities, and events give students the chance to build relationships and to grow together.

There are also career benefits to college attendance and completion. Emphasis on the completion of higher education is essential because it is not enough just to start. As most people know, one can earn more money over a lifetime with a college degree than without one.[1] Higher education also gives individuals an advantage when it comes to job opportunities.[2] Though economies around the world are struggling right now, when they stabilize, people with more education will be in a better position than those with less education to compete for the higher-paying new positions.

Community-based organizations are critical in providing information to help families maneuver through the educational and career system. As a high school student, I was exposed to a wealth of opportunities through my participation in Tomorrow's Scientists, Technicians, and Managers (TSTM) at the Peoria (Tri-County) Urban League. From tutoring to community service to college trips, community-based organizations that support local students and their endeavors allow families to learn more about the opportunities available in their community and beyond. The more that people learn about college, technical and vocational programs, scholarships, and job opportunities locally, the stronger a community can become.

The national aspect of an organization such as the Urban League allows access to resources on a much broader level, which is important. But, the fundamental grounding in the community is what sustains growth and progress locally. Many of my peers who participated in TSTM are excelling academically, making positive contributions to the community, and are prepared to compete in a global workforce. Even for parents, community-based organizations are important because they provide adults a chance to exchange ideas and helpful information, network, and expose each other to new experiences and opportunities that foster growth. With the presence of concerned adult figures, students also see positive role models who exemplify where their hard work in school can take them career-wise.

Schools are also important to the dissemination of information regarding the connection between college or technical training and careers. Many schools suffer from lackluster academic advising, but this is one of the most critical steps in transitioning students from the umbrella of structured education to the real world. While in high school, it is important to promote communication between academic advisors, students and parents to facilitate an effective exchange of information. Once a student gets to college, the focus should shift to the larger picture—participation in a global economy.

Howard University's focus on global citizenship directs its efforts in assisting students to learn more about the world around them. One of the best ways that students can prepare to excel in a global economy is to travel outside of the United States. Howard University offers several summer study abroad programs that are much more affordable than those offered by many outside organizations, and students take these journeys with professors from their institution. As a member of the College of Arts and Sciences Honors Association, I received honors program funding along with the Lucy E. Moten Fellowship for study abroad. Studying in Australia was one of the most influential experiences in my life. It expanded my horizons by helping me to see the global influence of America and the importance of understanding the world in which we live.

In addition to providing opportunities outside the classroom, many of the courses at Howard are taught with an interdisciplinary focus. This year alone, the list of interdisciplinary courses offered ranged from "Music, Culture, and Black Protest" to "Argument and Activism in Art" to "Legacies of the Civil War". With exposure to multiple methodologies, theories, and perspectives, Howard University has created an academic environment that fosters in depth exploration of diverse topics. This multifaceted way of learning is great preparation for a world in which one may have to work with people who have ideologies that are different from their own. Hearing ideas presented from various points of view prepares us to be leaders who can function effectively in a global economy.

Globalization has made college attendance and completion an essential part of participation in a global society. While times are hard, it is important for families, schools, and community-based organizations to emphasize the importance of attaining higher education. The growth that college students experience academically, personally and socially is invaluable. Beyond just training for a job, Howard University has provided phenomenal opportunities and encouragement for its students to compete globally as citizens and leaders.

NOTES
[1] U.S. Census Bureau, Education and Synthetic Work-Life Earnings Estimates: American Community Survey, September 2011 at p. 6

[2] U.S. Bureau of Labor Statistics, Current Population Survey 2011

COLLEGE READINESS AND COMPLETION FOR YOUNG MEN OF COLOR

TAFAYA RANSOM & JOHN MICHAEL LEE

Developing the full extent of the nation's human capital is arguably more imperative now than ever before given the growing knowledge-based economy that demands workers with postsecondary degrees and the nation's shifting demographics.

Figure 1 shows that by 2050 there will be no single racial/ethnic majority in the United States, while Figure 2 shows that this will happen as early as 2019 among students enrolled in the nation's K-12 system. These projections suggest that the nation's economic competitiveness

Figure 1: *Projections of the Population by Race and Hispanic Origin for the United States: 2010 to 2050*

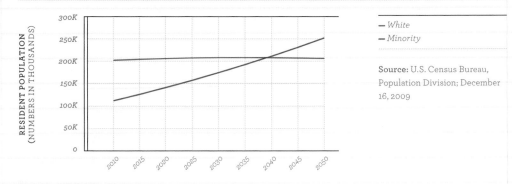

Source: U.S. Census Bureau, Population Division; December 16, 2009

will be ever more reliant upon groups that have traditionally been underrepresented in higher education. In fact, 46% of the 13.3 million additional degrees needed to reach President Obama's goal of leading the world in degree attainment by 2020 will have to come from African Americans, Hispanics, Native Americans and Asian Americans[1]. Thus, the persistent under-participation of any group in higher education is increasingly unsustainable.

The good news is that irrespective of race/ethnicity or socioeconomic status, the vast majority of high school students want to attend college. Among 2004 high school seniors, 84% of students planned to enroll in a two- or four-year college, including 91% of Asian Americans, 85% of African Americans, 85% of Whites, 81% of Hispanics, and 73% of Native Americans.[2]

Yet despite comparable college aspirations, racial disparities are prominent along the path to enter college and throughout college, with African Americans, Hispanics and Native Americans consistently underrepresented among college students and graduates. These disparities are exacerbated when gender is factored in, as young men of color fair worse than their female peers on most measures of postsecondary access and success.

Figure 2: *Percentage and Projections Distribution of the Race/Ethnicity of Public School Students Enrolled in Kindergarten Through 12th grade, Actual 1994-2007, Projection 2008-2019*

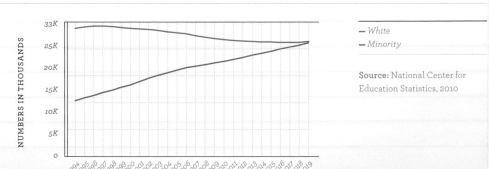

Source: National Center for Education Statistics, 2010

Higher Education Outcomes for Men of Color

Although the share of Americans participating in higher education has increased considerably in recent decades, consistently smaller shares of men than women participate. At the undergraduate level, young men of color are significantly outnumbered, with females accounting for 64 percent of African American enrollment, 58 percent of Hispanic enrollment, 54 percent of Asian American enrollment, and 60 percent of Native American enrollment (Figure 3).[3] Also, within communities of color, females earn more degrees than males across all levels of higher education—68 percent of African American degrees, 62 percent of Hispanic degrees, 56 percent of Asian American degrees, and 63 percent of

Educational Experiences of Young Men of Color suggest that minority men disproportionately experience the negative impacts of these influences. In high school, young men of color are underrepresented in rigorous curricular tracks, overrepresented in special education, overrepresented among grade repeaters, and receive less support and encouragement from their teachers and counselors. While attending college, men of color are working, juggling family obligations, frequently enrolled part-time and lack information on how to access support services. All of these factors have the potential to derail students' postsecondary education goals.

Capturing the Voices of Young Men of Color

As part of the initiative on the *Educational*

Figure 3: Female Percentage of Undergraduate Fall Enrollment in Degree-Granting Institutions by Race/Ethnicity

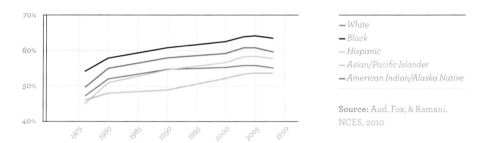

— White
— Black
— Hispanic
— Asian/Pacific Islander
— American Indian/Alaska Native

Source: Aud, Fox, & Ramani, NCES, 2010

Native American degrees are awarded to women. Figure 4 shows the gender disparities in bachelor's degree attainment during the 2007–08 academic year.[4]

Research has linked students' failure to enroll in and/or complete college to numerous explanatory factors, ranging from affordability and lack of support to family obligations and non-rigorous high school curricula. Findings from the College Board's initiative on the

Experiences of Young Men of Color, the College Board Advocacy & Policy Center partnered with the Business Innovation Factory (BIF) to explore the higher education experiences of young men of color more directly. The College Board and BIF engaged 92 African American, Asian American, Hispanic, and Native American college students from 39 institutions across the country to understand how they get ready, get in and get through college and the

Figure 4 : Percentage Distribution of Bachelor's Degree Awards by Race/Ethnicity & Sex: 2007–08

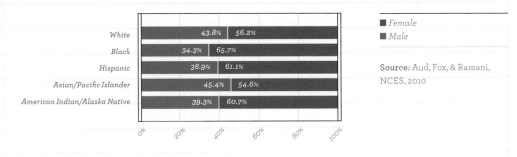

■ *Female*
■ *Male*

Source: Aud, Fox, & Ramani,
NCES, 2010

challenges they encounter along the way. Three themes resonated throughout this study:

- **Pressures of life:** Not only are these young men responsible for their academics, but sometimes they are also heads of households, parents and caregivers; have to work to pay for school; experience racial prejudice and are stereotyped along narrow definitions of people of color.

- **Paths to completion:** Young men of color do not always fit neatly into the education pipeline. That is, students take "non-traditional" routes to degree attainment, for example, dropping out of high school and then later receiving a GED (General Education Development) credential.

- **Webs of support:** There is an underestimation of how difficult it is for these students to locate, access and successfully utilize existing resources—especially non-academic resources—on college and university campuses.

The students who participated in the study also reported being overwhelmed by a number of challenges including: having the sole or dominant responsibility of supporting their

families, making ends meet financially, dealing with stereotypes, and overcoming difficult home or community situations. Notably, the insights these young men provided seemed to corroborate the research findings initially reported. Ultimately, the weight of the evidence speaks to the urgent need to advance the national dialogue and address significant educational roadblocks that stop men of color from reaching their full potential.

Recommendations

It is clear that no "easy" button can be pressed to solve the challenges facing young men of color on the path to degree attainment. Implementing solutions for these students must involve federal and state governments, local school districts, two-year and four-year colleges and universities, and community organizations at every level. Additionally, more research is needed across all racial/ethnic groups to identify the best policies, programs and practices that support students from high school to college completion. The following summary of recommendations is offered toward changing the discourse and the results for men of color in the United States.[5]

Recommendation ①: *Policymakers must make improving outcomes for young men of color a national priority.*

Policymakers can play a leading role in developing solutions, by creating policy initiatives and providing monetary incentives to encourage improving outcomes for young men of color at all levels. Examples of existing policy initiatives include the White House initiative on Educational Excellence for Hispanics and the University System of Georgia's African American Male Initiative.

Recommendation ②: *Increase community, business and school partnerships to provide mentoring and support to young men of color.*

Most of the work in solving the challenges facing young men of color will take place at the grassroots level. It will not be possible without the support and active participation of businesses and community based-organizations, such as Urban League affiliates across the country. Some of the solutions that businesses can implement include providing incentives/rewards for children of employees who do well in school, releasing parents to attend teacher conferences, and providing mentors for students in both K–12 and higher education. Community-based organizations must also work with businesses and communities to increase community involvement and to improve school and community collaboration. One excellent example of successful collaborations between businesses and community-based organizations is New York's Harlem Children's Zone (HCZ), led by Geoffrey Canada, which is one of the most extensive community-school collaborations in the history of the United States.

Recommendation ③: *Reform education to ensure that all students, including young men of color, are college and career ready when they graduate from high school.*

While the support of government, businesses and communities is needed to solve the challenges facing young men of color, schools, teacher, counselors and parents play vital roles in supporting these young men. Schools must find ways to re-design and re-invent themselves to serve a more diverse set of students. Schools such as Eagle Academy for Young Men in New York and Urban Prep Academy in Chicago are both great examples of schools that serve primarily low-income minority males, yet have found success in not only graduating these young men from high school but also ensuring that these young men are enrolling and succeeding in colleges and universities across the country.

Recommendation ④: *Improve teacher education programs and provide professional development that includes cultural- and gender-responsive training.*

It is important that teachers receive professional development on successful strategies that will allow them to provide culturally-sensitive approaches to ensuring positive outcomes for young men of color. It is also imperative that schools create a college-going-culture for all students.

Recommendation ⑤: *Create culturally appropriate persistence and retention programs that provide wrap-around services to increase college completion for men of color.*

Higher education is not exempt from its role in ensuring the success of young men of color in obtaining degrees. Institutions must make monumental efforts to improve campus racial climates—from the classroom to the student center. These efforts must permeate the entire university and include administrators, deans, staff and faculty. They should include providing more culturally-appropriate retention and support programming, implementing culturally-sensitive approaches to supporting mental health, and developing systems to monitor young men of color and provide them with ongoing support. Further, higher education must provide more institutional financial aid, access to internships and on-campus employment opportunities for men of color to help them meet the financial challenges they face.

Recommendation ⑥: *Produce more research and conduct more studies that strengthen the understanding of the challenges faced by males of color and provide evidence-based solutions to these challenges.*

One of the main findings of the research is there is simply not enough research available that concerns men of color, especially Asian American /Pacific Islanders and American Indians and Alaskan natives. Only slightly more information exists for Latinos. Though African American men have received greater attention in this area than other groups, much of the research that has been done is not evidenced-based and has not proven to be effective in solving the problems for African American males. There is a need for more data that can be disaggregated by race/ethnicity, gender, country of origin/ citizenship status, first language and best language; these data may disentangle part of the web of mysteries that still exist regarding men of color.

A Call to Action

Forty years ago, high school graduates and dropouts constituted the lion's share of the nation's workforce. In the decades to come, they will be decidedly left behind. In order to meet the challenges of the new, global economy the United States must find ways to improve the educational outcomes of groups that have traditionally been unsuccessful in higher education. As we have demonstrated, improving college readiness and completion for young men of color will be critical to ensuring the nation's competitiveness.

The research findings summarized in this essay provide a framework for understanding the educational crisis facing young men of color. The recommendations outlined are offered as an impetus for policymakers, businesses, communities, schools, postsecondary institutions, and researchers to recognize the urgency of the crisis and take action toward addressing it. We believe the evidence suggests that the barriers faced by men of color on the path to degree attainment can be overcome. However, as the strategies noted in the recommendations indicate, implementing effective and scalable solutions to move this agenda forward will require resources, commitment and political will and monumental effort on a variety of fronts. While we acknowledge the inherent challenge in failing to take on this challenge, we will have detrimental consequences not just for young men of color, but for the nation as a whole, if we do not.

REFERENCES

Aud, S., M. Fox, et al. (2010). "Status and Trends in the Education of Racial and Ethnic Groups," Washington, DC

Bitsoi, L. L. (2007). "Native Leaders in the New Millennium: An Examination of Success Factors of Native American Males at Harvard College," University of Pennsylvania

Chen, X., Wu, J., & Tasoff, S. (2010). "Postsecondary Expectations and Plans for the High School Senior Class of 2003–2004," Washington, DC.

Davis, J. E. and W. J. Jordan (1994). "The Effects of School Context, Structure, and Experiences on African American Males in Middle and High School." *Journal of Negro Education* 63(4): 570–587

Fries-Britt, S. L. and B. Turner (2002). "Uneven Stories: The Experiences of Successful Black Collegians at a Historically Black and A Traditionally White Campus." *The Review of Higher Education* 25(3)

Harper, S. R. (2004). "The Measure of a Man: Conceptualizations of Masculinity Among High-Achieving African American Male College Students." *Berkeley Journal of Sociology* 48(1): 89–107

Harper, S. R. (2005). "Leading the Way: Inside the Experiences of High-Achieving African-American Male Students." *About Campus* 10(1): 8–15

Lee, J. M., Edwards, K., Menson, R. & A. Rawls (2011). The College Completion Agenda 2011 Progress Report. New York, The College Board

Lee, J.M. & Ransom, T. (2011). "The Educational Experience of Young Men of Color: A Review of Research, Pathways and Progress." New York, The College Board

Moore, J. and J. Jackson (2006). "African American Males in Education: Endangered or Ignored?" *The Teachers College Record* 108(2): 201–205

Moore, J. L., M. S. Henfield, et al. (2008). "African American Males in Special Education: Their Attitudes and Perceptions Toward High School Counselors and School Counseling Services." *American Behavioral Scientist* 51(7): 907–927

Noguera, P. A. (1997). "Reconsidering the "Crisis" of the Black Male in America." Social Justice 24

Palmer, R. T., R. J. Davis, et al. (2009). "Exploring Challenges that Threaten to Impede the Academic Success of Academically Underprepared Black Males at an HBCU." *Journal of College Student Development* 50

Patton, J. O. (1988). "Black Men: Missing in Higher Education. Working Paper No. 10." Report: ED297043. 56 pp. Feb 1988

Saenz, V. B. and L. Ponjuan (2009). "The Vanishing Latino Male in Higher Education." *Journal of Hispanic Higher Education* 8

Santiago, D., & Callan, P. (2010). "Ensuring America's Future: Benchmarking Latino College Completion to Meet"

National Goals: 2010 to 2020. Washington, DC: Exelencia in Education

Strayhorn, T. L. (2008). "The Invisible Man: Factors Affecting the Retention of Low-Income African American Males." *NASAP Journal* 11(1): 66–87

Teranishi, R. (2002). "The Myth of the Super Minority: Misconceptions about Asian Americans." College Board Review (195): 16–21

Um, K. (2003). "A Dream Denied: Educational Experiences of Southeast Asian American Youth: Issues and Recommendations," Washington, DC, Southeast Asia Resource Action Center

Whiting, G. (2009). "Gifted Black Males: Understanding and Decreasing Barriers to Achievement and Identity," Roeper Review 31(4): 224–233

NOTES

[1] See Santiago & Callan (2010) for more information on degree production needed to meet President Obama's 2020 college completion goals

[2] See Chen, Wu, & Tasoff (2010) for more information on high school students' college aspirations

[3] See Aud, Fox, & Ramani (2010) for more information on undergraduate enrollment by race and gender

[4] See Aud, Fox, & Ramani (2010) for more information on degrees earned by sex and race/ethnicity

[5] See Lee & Ransom (2011) for more detailed recommendations for improving educational outcomes of young men of color

REAL REFORM IS GETTING KIDS ONE STEP CLOSER TO QUALITY SCHOOLS

DR. STEVE PERRY

Today's education reforms should come with a disclaimer: *No adults were harmed during the implementation of these policies.* This limits attempts to reform our schools to those strategies that can be implemented without adults losing their jobs. So we're left with these five-year plans that start with slapping a new theme on the same old school and instituting a 'strict' uniform policy.

Many of America's public school systems run like a 1970's factory. Innovation and quality are forfeited for efficiency. Adults in public school factories speak in industrial terms like *working conditions and workers' rights*. In American public school factories the product, an educated child, has taken a back seat to the producers, the employees, and the result is a recession.

Look, America knows how to run great schools as well as anyone. We know that the 187-day school year and 6 ½ hours school day are outdated. We know 45-minute classes have no foundation in brain research. We know that it must be mandatory for teachers to stay after school at least an hour every day instead of the 10 minutes most teacher contracts currently support. These conditions were negotiated to make adults' jobs comfortable. It's working. While anywhere from 30-60% of African American students drop out, over 95% of tenured teachers will stay.

We know that school choice is essential to ensuring kids are in the right school. Arts schools for those interested in the arts, science schools for our next George Washington Carver, traditional schools for the ones who want to stay close to home and private schools for those who may choose to board or study religion. This process works for selecting colleges and must be applied to all levels of school, yet at the primary, middle and high school levels school choice is billed as a threat to educators' employment and is often opposed by their unions.

The National Urban League signed on to a 2010 education white paper with six other civil rights organizations including the NAACP. The paper called for equal access to quality education. One strategy for achieving equality was the "Right to Transfer" for students in low performing schools. Less than a year later a New York Chapter of the NAACP went against this proposal and mostly minority parents by joining a lawsuit with the teacher's union to close schools of choice opened to replace failed schools where persistent disparities existed between the public schools and the charter schools sharing the same facilities. Minority parents and those from all cultures who support all children's rights to a quality education must hold anyone who impedes access to the right to choose great schools accountable, especially if these folks are minorities.

A false sense of confidence has emerged in America's schools. Many believe that education's problems are confined to the "hood". In a 2009 article, *The New York Times* supported this notion. It reported that the graduation rate in the nations largest urban districts was 53% while the nearby suburbs graduated over 70%.

The juxtaposition of failed urban schools with suburban schools slows the engines of school reform because likely reformers feel like their kids are safe from the dangers of urban education. The problem with this view of the education problem is that it is false and therefore problematic. The real problem with America's schools is not where they're located or what the students look like. The problem with America's schools is that our schools are too focused on adults.

When compared internationally, American public schools lose. Not just the urban schools, *homie*. When we control for wealth and Whiteness, and compare our Whitest and wealthiest schools to similarly grouped schools internationally, America's students STILL finish near the bottom.[2]

Let me be the first to own that our school, The Capital Preparatory Magnet School in Hartford, CT, would get whooped in an international comparison. My best kids would be simply overrun by the world's best. Even though we've been named by US News & World Reports for years as among America's Best High Schools, we, like the rest of America's best would get stomped like a roach at a rodeo by the stunningly effective international competitors.

In June 2011, Education Secretary, Arne Duncan, testified before the Senate subcommittee on immigration in support of the Dream Act that:

Today, even in tough economic times, our country has 3 million unfilled jobs. By 2018, we'll need to fill 2.6 million job openings in the fields of science, technology, and engineering, and mathematics.[3]

The reason that these jobs are unfilled amidst the worst recession of our lives is because America's schools haven't educated students who can fill them...but other countries have.

Mr. Duncan refers to these foreign born students as, "some of the country's best and brightest." He's right. The passage of the Dream Act would allow foreign-born students to stay in the US. The passing of the Act represents a Pyrrhic victory. While the high tech jobs will be filled, millions of American born students will remain undereducated to work in the nation's most promising fields.

America knows what the rest of the world knows about running great schools. There are thousands of amazing American schools that are public and private, neighborhood and choice. Great schools implement what we know works in education unencumbered by the effects that such reforms will have on grown people.

Indeed, America's best schools have the most effective teachers and school leaders in education. These teachers are available at all hours. Their years and days are often longer. Students are assigned an advisor or in some way are connected to a caring adult. Income, family structure and their students' race are never even considered. Excuses are just that and are not tolerated. These great schools are laboratories where administrators and teachers collaborate to devise strategies to inspire students.

Successful schools just feel successful. The focus on their students is obvious. There is a palpable joy in the halls, classrooms and even in the greeting you receive from the secretary when you call. As soon as one walks in, you're inundated with the feeling that something great can happen and therefore it usually does. Both the students and teachers feel like they belong. Most importantly, in these institutions everyone knows that the purpose of a great school is to educate children even if that means that some adults might become uncomfortable in the process.

NOTES

[1] Sam Dillon, "Large Urban Surburban Gap Seen in Graduation Rates," *The New York Times*, April 22, 2009 (see at *http://www.nytimes.com/2009/04/22/education/22dropout.html*) (Accessed January 2011)

[2] Organisation for Economic Co-operation and Development (OECD), P"resentation of the PISA 2010 Results: Remarks by Angel Gurria," December 7, 2010 (see *http://www.oecd.org/document/7/0,3746, en_21571361_44315115_46635719_1_1_1,00.html*) (Accessed January 2012)

[3] U.S. Department of Education, Secretary Arne Duncan, Dream Act Testimony, June 28, 2011 (see *http://www.ed.gov/news/speeches/dream-act-testimony*) (Accessed January 2012)

COLLEGE FOR ALL?

AMARA C. ENYIA, PH.D., J.D.

The notion that playing by the rules and making all of the "right" decisions will inevitably bring success stands as one of the hallmarks of what it means to achieve the American dream. But what happens when you've made all of the "right" moves and the reward remains elusive?

For the last few decades, Americans have been inundated with the mantra "go to college". The 'college for all' premise dominated educational discourse and, I would argue, created a culture in which a bachelor's degree was viewed as the only viable entry point into the economy and thus the only path to upward social mobility.

The value of a traditional college education is especially keen to those groups, like African Americans, that were historically denied this powerful tool for social and societal advancement. Access to a college degree meant access to a broader array of jobs and a higher level of income than one's high-school diploma-toting colleagues. However, during the midst of the recent recession, as job opportunities were slow to materialize (if at all), another, more subtle question began to tug at the conscious of newly-minted graduates—"college for what end?" More specifically, as the six-month loan repayment grace period deadline swiftly approached with no new interviews, and no call-backs, bewildered graduates began to re-think the practical sense of becoming indebted to the tune of tens of thousands of dollars for their bachelor's degree, only to now have to accept entry level jobs that pay a mere fraction of what they spent on their education. Suddenly, it seemed that the treasure waiting at the end of the higher education rainbow was actually fool's gold.

So perhaps the question that should be foremost in our minds is not, "Should I go to college?," but instead "What kind of education will allow me to thrive in society?" Degrees are evidence of expertise in a particular field. The price tag for higher education is an investment in a future in which one utilizes their subject matter expertise by way of a career. Trends usually determine the "hot" majors although there are a few stalwarts that seem to thrive regardless of the economy: pre-medicine, engineering, pre-law, and accounting, to name a few.

But the truth of the matter is that there exist several entry points to becoming productive members of society and a traditional college

degree is only one of those entry points. We can no longer afford to narrowly define that. Indeed, for far too long, we've mostly focused on steering high school students onto the traditional four-year higher education track and failed to fully develop and advocate for viable alternatives for those who a traditional four year college education does not fit. Those alternatives include certification programs, community colleges, and sector-specific training programs.

What's happening in Chicago, led by the Center for Labor and Community Research (CLCR) and the Chicago Manufacturing Renaissance Council (CMRC), illustrates such an alternative. In 2001, CLCR conducted a labor market study in Chicago which found that thousands of jobs in advanced manufacturing were going unfilled simply because there were not enough qualified individuals to take those jobs.[1] Advanced manufacturing is the development and production of high-tech, complex products particularly in emerging industries of the future such as renewable energy, nanotechnology, and biotechnology. It is argued that an economy based on advanced manufacturing holds the greatest potential to create sustainable, long-term economic growth; rebuild the American middle class; and solve the global environmental crisis. While much of what Americans popularly understand as "manufacturing" has indeed gone off-shore, the U.S. maintains a competitive advantage in the type of cutting edge production that drives technological development and economic growth.

In response to their finding of an unqualified workforce and realizing that the best way to address the issues in the economy was through public education, CLCR and the CMRC started a public high school—Austin Polytechnical Academy. Located on the West Side of Chicago, Austin Polytech offers high school students a rigorous Science, Technology, Engineering and Mathematics (S.T.E.M.) based education focused on advanced manufacturing and engineering principles. Students are afforded job-shadowing opportunities and internships with one of the school's 67 company partners. Most importantly, students utilize a state-of-the-art facility where they earn National Institute for Metalworking Skills (NIMS) credentials that equip them with the high-demand skills needed to thrive in the advanced manufacturing sector.

Upon graduation, Austin Polytech students have the option of working directly for a company partner, going to college, or both. Therefore, as we lament a national unemployment rate of 8.5% for the general population, 11% for Latinos and 15.8% for African Americans in December 2011[2], and decry the astronomical costs of higher education, we should look to examples like Austin Polytech, which gives students a type of affordable education that allows them to maximize their options by providing them with marketable high-demand skill sets in a forward-moving sector starved for talented employees.

A good education is one that allows individuals to sustain themselves by finding employment in a field of their interest with opportunities for advancement. Consequently, it is critical, especially during this recession, that we turn away from asking the oversimplified question "Should I go to college?" and instead, shift our national focus to areas in the economy where tangible opportunities exist. We must work to develop educational systems that offer a continuum of options for students with practical implications for both their lives and the reinvigoration of our competitive economy.

NOTES

[1] Chicago Federation of Labor and the Center for Labor and Community Research, "Creating a Manufacturing Career Path System in Cook County," December 2001 (see at http://www.clcr.org/publications/pdf/final%20MWDP%20report030802.pdf) (Accessed January 27, 2012)

[2] U.S. Department of Labor, Bureau of Labor Statistics, "The Employment Situation—December 2011," January 6, 2012 (see at http://www.bls.gov/news.release/pdf/empsit.pdf) (Accessed January 27, 2012)

THE SHOW ME CAMPAIGN

A CONVERSATION WITH JOHN LEGEND

① You have used the Show Me Campaign to highlight education as the civil rights issue of our time. At the National Urban League we have called economic empowerment today's civil rights issue. We agree—education is the path to economic independence. How do we make this message have real meaning for today's students?

We are very much in agreement here—the overarching mission of the Show Me Campaign is to break the cycle of poverty using solutions that have been proven to improve people's lives. Show Me concentrates on education reform in the U.S. because it is a high-leverage, critically important tool in helping people achieve economic success. The best thing we can do to help students understand this is to give them the facts. Without an education, you are much less likely to earn a living wage. We need to spread this message to youth, especially in low-income areas—that doing well in school and going to college is far and away your best shot at having options for a better life.

② According to a study from Harvard's Kennedy School of Government, U.S. students lag behind many other countries in math and reading skills.[1] African-American and Latino students, in particular, are falling way behind. Tell us how you use the Show Me Campaign to address the achievement gap.

Show Me partners with leading organizations across the country proving that even the most disadvantaged students can achieve when given the right opportunities. One of these partners is Harlem Village Academies (HVA), a group of charter schools in NY that serves an overwhelmingly low-income, minority student base. In a neighborhood with alarmingly high dropout rates, HVA is getting results—100% of HVA high school students passed the NY Regents Algebra and History exams in 2010.[2] Together, we are working to disarm the lie that demography is destiny and to promote solutions which enable all kids to get a great education. We are urging the public and politicians to make transforming low-performing schools a national priority.

③ Why do you think black youth are dissuaded from completing their education? How do we create a passion for learning in the earlier grades all the way through high school to ensure students graduate from high school ready for college, career and life?

Black youth disproportionately attend low-performing schools that provide little encouragement or opportunity for success. While personal motivation is a key factor in academic achievement, good schools are an essential pre-requisite. Even the smartest, most motivated student will arrive at college unprepared if he or she attended a substandard high school. We need to drastically improve the schools serving black youth if we want to cultivate a passion for

learning and keep them on track to succeed in high school and beyond. Creating a culture of high expectations for all students and putting excellent teachers in every classroom would bring us closer to this goal.

④ The Show Me Campaign has highlighted and celebrated innovation and experimentation in teaching and learning. What are the barriers in today's education system keeping us from being innovative and discovering new ways to keep the attention of students?

Our education system in the U.S. is outdated—the status quo simply isn't working. We desperately need innovation, but certain long-standing policies leave teachers, principals, and superintendents with their hands tied. One major issue that has received a lot of press is the restrictive nature of teachers' union contracts. Many of these contracts limit the length of the school day and prevent principals from rewarding good teachers and firing bad ones, among other things. Now let me state this clearly—I am not anti-union; however, I am pro-meritocracy and doing what's best for kids. If longer school days improve student outcomes—which they do—we shouldn't let old contract provisions stand in the way of change. If an innovative new teacher is performing better than a veteran, he or she should not be laid off under a "last in, first out" provision that privileges tenure over performance. He or she should be paid more and supported. By lifting restrictive policies, we can give schools the latitude to put students first and maintain a culture of innovation and excellence.

⑤ Do you think lending your voice to better educational opportunities for all students helps to inspire students? What do you say to students who may want to pursue a career in the entertainment industry?

I spend a lot of time speaking to students so I certainly hope so! My main goal is to encourage them to follow their passions and make serving the community a part of their lives. I do talk about the education crisis in this country quite a bit and I believe that resonates with students in particular, but I'm also a firm believer that you should focus on whatever speaks to you. That applies to your job as well—I have a passion for music and that's why I make my living as an artist. At the same time though, I always stress the importance of education in helping you reach any goal. Before I launched my music career, I graduated from the University of Pennsylvania. My education has been critical to my success and I make sure students know that.

NOTES

[1] Paul Peterson, Ludger Woessman, Eric Hanushek, Carlos Lastra-Anadon, "Globally Challenged: Are US Students Ready to Compete? The Latest on Each State's International Standing in Math and Reading," Harvard Kennedy School Program on Education Policy and Governance & Education, August 2011. *http://www.hks.harvard.edu/pepg/PDF/Papers/PEPG11-03_GloballyChallenged.pdf* (Accessed January 2012)

[2] New York State Test Results—All NYS Charter Schools 2005-06 through 2010–11. Prepared by the SUNY Charter Schools Institute. August 2011. *http://www.newyorkcharters.org/parentPerformance.htm* (Accessed January 2012)

ARTS, CULTURE AND COMMUNITIES: DO OUR NEIGHBORHOODS INSPIRE OUR CHILDREN TO REACH HIGHER?

MARIA ROSARIO JACKSON, PH.D.

Many years ago, when I started investigating the role of cultural activity and the arts in low and moderate-income communities of color around the United States, I talked with people all around the country about the qualities of their neighborhoods.

I would ask them what they liked about their communities. What did they miss about their neighborhoods when they were away? Did their communities have art—expressions of creativity that inspired, moved and challenged them? I encouraged them to think broadly about not only those creative and aesthetic expressions that are found typically in museums, art centers and other explicit art spaces, but to also consider aesthetic and creative expressions that might be part of their everyday experiences. These conversations were always interesting, vivid and often passionate. In the best case scenarios, respondents recognized community assets that they almost always took for granted—community traditions, celebrations and rituals involving music, dance, stories and food, notable and sometimes unique architectural features of buildings, landscaping often done by their neighbors and bold visual statements like murals and sculptures. In the worst-case scenarios, respondents saw only bleakness, abandonment, stagnation and decline. However, a common thread throughout these discussions was that a person's environment mattered significantly. How places look, feel, sound and smell are important factors that contribute to our well-being. Additionally, the extent to which neighborhoods have defined meaningful places and spaces that are historic, sacred, special and somehow evident of the community's aspirations and ability to innovate also is important.

This research suggested that this all potentially impacted people's sense of belonging, their sense of safety and even their sense of self-worth. Especially in my conversations with young people, I often was struck by how the physical and sensory qualities of a neighborhood shaped their daily experiences and their interpretations of whether or not their community provided them with a nurturing environment where they felt supported and could thrive. In particular, I recall one conversation with a group of young people on the West Coast where we were talking about cultural assets in their community. A group consensus arose that the landscaping that some neighbors did in their yards was significant. They took note of it. I asked them why they thought this was important and one child said, "That's how we know the good streets—the streets where people care."

Not so long ago the James S. and James L. Knight Foundation published Knight Soul of the Community 2010: Why People Love Where They Live and Why It Matters: A National Perspective. This report was based on a three-year Gallup study of 26 U.S. cities and it concluded that social offerings, openness, and beauty do, in fact, matter and are even more important than peoples' perceptions of the economy, jobs, or basic services in creating lasting emotional bonds between people and their community. Nurturing spaces matter.

As we think about increasing the odds that our children will aspire to high purpose, to higher education and to their individual and our collective uplift, I can't help but think that we miss an enormously important opportunity, if we do not tend to the qualities of our physical and social environment that so crucially impact us on a daily basis. These are not concerns about frivolous or only cosmetic things. These are concerns about the environmental cues that signal to our children on a daily basis whether or not we, and they, are worthy of dignity and capable of human expression at its highest level.

If we expect our children to consider their options related to higher education, we must ask, do our communities offer our children the physical and social environments that can help to propel them forward and upward? Do we have places where our children can exercise their creativity and imagination in constructive and productive ways? Do our communities physically and socially affirm our history and help our children feel rooted, consequential and part of an important legacy? Does the look and feel of our neighborhoods encourage stewardship and excellence? Do we have spaces and places in our communities that are special and inspire awe?

Our children deserve nothing less.

ABOUT
THE AUTHORS

JACQUELINE AYERS

Jacqueline Ayers serves as the Legislative Director of Health & Education Policy at the National Urban League Policy Institute (NULPI), where she is responsible for the development and implementation of the National Urban League's Education and Health goals. Prior to joining NULPI, Jacqueline served as a lobbyist for Planned Parenthood Federation of America (PPFA), directing their advocacy efforts on a variety of legislative issues, including budget and appropriations, Medicaid expansions, and a range of women's reproductive and maternal health matters. Jacqueline began her career as the Associate Director for the American Civil Liberties Union (ACLU) of Indiana, where she advanced the organization's state legislative agenda and developed public education campaigns on racial profiling and the importance of civic participation. Jacqueline earned her Bachelor of Arts degree with a dual concentration in mass communications and government from Western Kentucky University and her Juris Doctorate from the Indiana School of Law in Indianapolis, Indiana.

LLOYD C. BLANKFEIN

Lloyd Blankfein is the Chairman and Chief Executive Officer of Goldman Sachs since June 2006, and a director since April 2003.

Previously, he was the President and Chief Operating Officer since January 2004. Prior to that, from April 2002 until January 2004, he was a Vice Chairman of Goldman Sachs, with management responsibility for Goldman Sachs' Fixed Income, Currency and Commodities Division (FICC) and Equities Division (Equities). Prior to becoming a Vice Chairman, he served as co-head of FICC since its formation in 1997. From 1994 to 1997, he headed or co-headed the Currency and Commodities Division. Lloyd Blankfein is not currently on the board of any public company other than Goldman Sachs. He is affiliated with certain non-profit organizations, including as a member of the Dean's Advisory Board at Harvard Law School, the Dean's Council at Harvard University and the Advisory Board of the Tsinghua University School of Economics and Management, an overseer of the Weill Medical College of Cornell University, and a member of the Board of Directors of the Partnership for New York City.

ALLIE L. BRASWELL, JR.

Allie Braswell is President and CEO, Central Florida Urban League. Mr. Braswell currently serves as a Member of the Executive Advisory Board for *MyRegion.org*, Member of the Quest, Inc. board, and remains active in the community through his membership in the

★ ★ ★ ★ ★ ★ ★ ★ ★ ★ ★ ★ ★ ★ ★

Leadership Orlando Alumni organization. In May of 2009, Allie was welcomed into General Daniel "Chappie" James Chapter of the Tuskegee Airmen, Inc. in recognition of his commitment and service to the Central Florida community. He is also a proud military veteran, having served 13 years in the United States Marine Corps in various regions of the world to include: Southwest Asia, Europe, Asia as well as numerous locations throughout the domestic United States. He continues his service to the country, and his region as a US Army Reserve Ambassador, and most recently was appointed to the Advisory Committee for the Center for Minority Veterans by the Honorable Eric K. Shinseki, Secretary of Veteran Affairs. His support and endorsement of many civic and charitable endeavors has earned him additional recognition from community leaders and organizations nationwide. Mr. Braswell currently leads the Central Florida Urban League's efforts to serve Central Floridians and is responsible for leading the efforts to maintain and grow the extensive network of educational, cultural and community partners and alliances that embrace and articulate the organization's goals publicly. He is also an expert technology leader, inspirational speaker and author. Mr. Braswell is married to Rosemary Harris-Braswell with whom he has six children.

GREGORY E. CARR, PH.D., J.D.

Dr. Gregory "Greg" E. Carr is Associate Professor of Africana Studies and Chair of the Department of Afro-American Studies at Howard University. A teacher/scholar with academic specialties in Africana Studies normative theory, Africana intellectual history, classical African history and historiography and African-American nationalism, Dr. Carr is Howard's only faculty member with a Ph.D. in the academic discipline of Africana Studies. Dr. Carr is a former member of the board of the National Council for Black Studies and is the Second Vice President of the Association for the Study of Classical African Civilizations. A grantee of Howard's Fund for Academic Excellence, invited lecturer on pedagogy from the Center for Excellence in Teaching and Assessment and a twice-named Professor of the Year by the Howard University Student Association, the College of Arts and Sciences Student Council and the College of Arts and Sciences Honors Association, Dr. Carr, Dr. Dana Williams, Howard staff and sixty undergraduate students inaugurated Howard's historic Summer Study Abroad in Egypt in 2008. Dr. Carr has also represented Howard University as a spokesman in a wide range of print and electronic media, including *The New York Times*, *Le Monde*, *USA Today*, *MSNBC*, *National Public Radio*, *WHUR*, *WHUT* and *CNN*, as well as a range of local radio, television and internet media outlets. Dr. Carr received a Bachelor of Science in Speech Communication in Theater from Tennessee State University, a Juris Doctorate from The Ohio State University College of Law, and a Master of Arts in African and African-American Studies from The Ohio State University. His 1998 Temple University Ph.D. was the first scholarly attempt to investigate the long-view intellectual genealogy of the Afrocentric Idea.

ANNA MARIE CHÁVEZ

Anna Maria Chávez is the current Chief Executive Officer of Girl Scouts of the USA. Ms. Chávez has also served as Chief Executive Officer of Girl Scouts of Southwest Texas (GSSWT). Prior to her roles with Girl Scouts, Ms. Chávez served as Deputy Chief of Staff for Urban Relations and Community Development for the former Governor of Arizona and current U.S. Secretary of Homeland Security, Janet Napolitano and the Governor's Policy Advisor to the Arizona Department of Housing. Ms. Chávez entered state service after serving as Senior Policy Advisor to U.S. Secretary of Transportation, Rodney E. Slater. Prior to this appointment, she served as Chief of Staff to the Deputy Administrator at the U.S. Small Business Administration (SBA) in Washington, D.C. From 1996 to 1998, Ms. Chávez served as Legal Counsel for the Federal Highway Administration in Washington, D.C. She also served as an attorney advisor in the Office of the Counsel to the President. Ms. Chávez is a recipient of The Adjutant General's Medal and the Diversity Champion Leadership Award present by the Arizona National Guard. She was presented with the Exemplary Leadership Award by Valle del Sol in 2008 and was named Woman of the Year at the Latina Excellence Awards in 2007. Ms. Chávez has also received the inaugural ATHENA Organizational Leadership Award in 2010 and was inducted into the San Antonio Women's Hall of Fame in March 2011. She received her Juris Doctorate from the University of Arizona, College of Law and a B.A. in American History from Yale University.

GARRICK T. DAVIS

Garrick T. Davis serves as Legislative Director of Economic and Financial Policy at the National Urban League Policy Institute, where he has helped to craft the National Urban League 'Rebuild America Now' 12 Point Jobs Plan, while also actively serving on a host of joint initiatives within the civil rights community and the private sector. Most notably, his efforts focused upon the reform of government sponsored enterprises such as Fannie Mae and Freddie Mac, the revitalization of advanced manufacturing in America's cities, and other aspects of job creation and community development. Prior to joining the National Urban League in 2010, Garrick served as a Presidential Apointee in the Obama White House and worked as a Policy Analyst in the Office of the Vice President, assigned with the tactical implementation of the American Recovery and Reinvestment Act of 2009. Before serving in the Obama Administration, Garrick worked in the financial services industry over the course of a career spanning 16 years. Garrick serves on a host of non-profit boards and committees, including: the Center for Labor and Community Research, US House Minority Whip Steny Hoyer's 'Make It In America' Advisory Board, the National Institute of Metalworking Skills, the National Manufacturing Renaissance Campaign, the Augustus F. Hawkins Foundation, and the Washington Jesuit Academy. Garrick received his Master of Public Administration from the University of Pennsylvania, and a Bachelor of Science from the Edmund A. Walsh School of Foreign Service at Georgetown University.

AMARA C. ENYIA, PH.D., J.D.

Dr. Amara C. Enyia serves as Policy Director for the Center for Labor and Community Research (CLCR) where her role centers on rebuilding advanced manufacturing in the economy as well as education reform that links economics with educational experiences by providing multiple pathways for high school students to succeed after high school. Her work is based upon equity model of community and economic development. She also directs CLCR's education research. Dr. Enyia is also the Executive Director of Austin Coming Together (ACT) a collaborative community and economic development organization based in Chicago. Dr. Enyia received her Bachelor degree with honors from the University of Illinois-Urbana in Broadcast Journalism, Political Science and News/Editorial with concentrations in History and Philosophy. She also received her Master's degree in Education and a Law degree. She completed her Doctoral degree in Educational Policy Studies with a research expertise in evaluation.

TATIANA GARCIA-GRANADOS

Tatiana Garcia-Granados is a Philadelphia-based social entrepreneur who works to improve the vitality of rural and urban communities through food system connectivity and policy change. She is a Co-Founder and Executive Director of the Common Market, a local foods distribution center that connects 170 schools, hospitals, grocers and workplaces to sustainable farms in New Jersey, Pennsylvania and Delaware. She is a graduate of the University of Pennsylvania's Wharton School of Business.

HONORABLE KIRSTEN E. GILLIBRAND

Kirsten E. Gillibrand was sworn in as United States Senator from New York in January 2009, filling the seat of the current Secretary of State, Hillary Rodham Clinton. In November 2010, Gillibrand won election to the seat with 63 percent of the vote. Prior to her service in the Senate, Gillibrand served in the United States House of Representatives, representing New York's 20th Congressional District, which spans across ten counties in upstate New York. Senator Gillibrand's number one priority is to rebuild the American economy, by creating good-paying jobs, helping small businesses get loans, and partnering with the private sector to foster innovation and entrepreneurship. Her steadfast commitment to and strong leadership on behalf of urban youth has led to her introduction and active promotion of the Urban Jobs Act (S.922). She sits on the Environment and Public Works Committee, working to increase investment in infrastructure, including drinking water and sewer systems, rural broadband, health care information technology, and renewable energy. She is also the first New York Senator to sit on the Agriculture Committee in nearly 40 years, taking a leading role to improve child nutrition and combat child obesity by giving children and families more access to fresh fruits and vegetables grown in New York. Senator Gillibrand also serves on the Senate Armed Services and the Aging Committee. Senator Gillibrand graduated from Emma Willard School in Troy, New York, the first all women's high school in the United States. She received her Bachelor degree magna cum laude from Dartmouth College and her Juris Doctorate from UCLA School of Law in 1991.

CHANELLE P. HARDY, ESQ.

Chanelle P. Hardy is the National Urban League Senior Vice President for Policy and Executive Director of the National Urban League Policy Institute, with primary responsibility for developing the League's policy, research and advocacy agenda and expanding its impact and influence inside the beltway. She is Editor in Chief of the annual State of Black America report and is devoted to the League's mission to empower communities through education and economic development. She is the former Chief of Staff and Counsel to former US Representative Artur Davis, who represented the Seventh Congressional District of Alabama and served on the powerful House Ways and Means Committee and the Committee on House Administration. Prior to coming to the Hill, Ms. Hardy was a Staff Attorney at the Federal Trade Commission, a Policy Fellow and Legislative Counsel at Consumers Union, and a Teach for America Corps member, teaching fifth graders in Washington, D.C. She received her Juris Doctorate from the Howard University School of Law, where she finished fifth in her class, and was a member of the Huver I. Brown Trial Advocacy Moot Court Team. Ms. Hardy is a member of the board of Excel Academy Public Charter School, the first all-girls public school in Washington, DC; the board of the Congressional Black Caucus Institute board and a member of Alfred Street Baptist Church in Alexandria, Va.

MARIA ROSARIO JACKSON, PH.D.

Dr. Maria Rosario Jackson is a senior research associate in the Metropolitan Housing and Communities Center at the Urban Institute (UI) and director of UI's Culture, Creativity and Communities Program. Her research expertise includes neighborhood revitalization and comprehensive community planning, the politics of race, ethnicity and gender in urban settings, and the role of arts and culture in communities. Her projects in cities throughout the United States have explored the role of intermediaries in comprehensive community planning, the characteristics of place that lead to cultural vitality, the measurement of arts and cultural vitality and the integration of new topics into policies and programs concerned with quality of life. Dr. Jackson's work has appeared in academic and professional journals as well as edited volumes in the fields of urban planning, sociology, community development and the arts. She has been a speaker at numerous national and international conferences focusing on quality of life, changing demographics, communities and cities of the future, and arts and society. She currently serves on the boards of the Association of Performing Arts Presenters, the National Performance Network and the Alliance for California Traditional Artists. Formerly, she was on the board of the Mid-Atlantic Arts Foundation and the Fund for Folk Culture. Dr. Jackson earned a doctorate in Urban Planning from the University of California, Los Angeles and an MPA from the University of Southern California.

HAILE JOHNSTON

Haile Johnston is the Pennsylvania State Director for the Center for Progressive Leadership, the Board Co-Chair, Co-Founder and Co-Executive Director of Common Market. He is passionate about providing access to healthy local foods to residents of low-income communities in Philadelphia. Mr. Johnston has formerly worked as the Environmental Interventions Coordinator for the Philadelphia Department of Public Health's Division of Chronic Disease Prevention. In this capacity, he was instrumental in crafting the Health Department's testimony on the dangers of trans-fat consumption before City Council, which ultimately banned their use in Philadelphia restaurants. Mr. Johnston is a graduate of the Wharton School with a concentration in Entrepreneurial Management.

JOHN MICHAEL LEE, JR.

John Michael Lee, Jr. is policy director for the Advocacy and Policy Center in the Advocacy, Government Relations and Development unit at the College Board. John works on a variety of projects that include the College Completion Agenda Progress Report, Hispanic Supplement to the College Completion Agenda, the 1st Annual Counselor Survey, and the Educational Experience of Young Men of Color. John's research interests include student access and participation in higher education, student preparation, and higher education policy. Prior to joining the College Board, John served as a policy analyst for the Georgia Department of Economic Development. John is a member of several professional associations including the American Educational Research Association (AERA), the National Council on Measurement in Education (NCME), the Association for Institutional Research (AIR), and the Association

for the Study of Higher Education (ASHE). John earned his Ph.D. in higher education administration from New York University and his MPA with a concentration in economic development from the Andrew Young School at Georgia State University.

JOHN LEGEND

John Legend is a recording artist, concert performer and philanthropist who has won nine Grammy awards and was named one of *Time* magazine's 100 most influential people. He launched his career as a session player and vocalist, contributing to best-selling recordings by Lauryn Hill, Alicia Keys, Jay-Z and Kanye West before recording his own unbroken chain of Top 10 albums—*Get Lifted* (2004), *Once Again* (2006), and *Evolver* (2008)—each of them reaching #1 on the *Billboard* R&B/Hip Hop charts. Throughout his career, Mr. Legend has worked to make a difference in the lives of others. In 2007, he launched the Show Me Campaign (*ShowMeCampaign.org*), an initiative that uses education to break the cycle of poverty. In 2007, he was named spokesman for *GQ Magazine's* "Gentlemen's Fund," an initiative to raise support and awareness for five cornerstones essential to men: opportunity, health, education, environment, and justice. He was awarded the 2010 *BET* Humanitarian of the Year award, the CARE Humanitarian Award for Global Change in June 2009 and received the 2009 Bishop John T. Walker Distinguished Humanitarian Service Award from Africare. He sits on the Boards of The Education Equality Project, Teach for America,

Stand for Children and the Harlem Village Academies and co-chairs the Harlem Village Academies' National Leadership Board. He is also the national spokesperson for Management Leadership for Tomorrow, a non-profit organization that assists the next generation of minority business leaders; a member of the Board of Directors of PopTech and stars in The People Speak, a film about social change in the U.S.

DESIREÉ LUCKEY

Desireé Luckey is a senior sociology major and political science minor at Howard University from Peoria, IL. Throughout her high school career, she was an active participant in the Peoria Tri-County Urban League Tomorrow's Scientists, Technicians, and Managers program, serving on the executive board for three years. As an undergraduate student, she participated in the fall 2009 White House internship program, studied abroad in Melbourne, Australia, and was inducted into Phi Beta Kappa Honor Society this past fall. In the future, she looks forward to pursuing a career in law or food-related policy.

DARLENE H. MARLIN

Darlene H. Marlin is the Senior Director, Education & Youth Development at the National Urban League. Darlene directs the Education Division's portfolio of keystone programs that are designed to help us reach our goal that every American child will be ready for college, work and life by 2025. These programs serve the needs of urban youth from kindergarten through college. Darlene's job has a wide range

of responsibilities that span the educational continuum, from finding funding and directing early childhood education programs, adolescent literacy and youth development, to high-school-to-college transition programs. With a drive and dedication that exemplify our Quest for Excellence, Darlene developed the groundbreaking Project Ready program that prepares teenagers for life after high school by offering academic support and training in life skills that are useful regardless of whether the next step is college, career, or technical training. This Urban League-branded program has more than 1,700 students enrolled in 29 Urban League affiliate sites in 19 states. In addition, Darlene is responsible for research and development, creating training curricula, and identifying best practices relating to African-American urban youth. Darlene serves as an expert technical advisor to our affiliates across the United States, providing leading-edge information and resources on education trends and topics. Previously she was Director of Community Development for the New York Urban League, Staten Island Branch. Darlene received a master's degree in Childhood Education, and a bachelor's degree in Business Management from City University of New York.

JAMES T. MCLAWHORN

James T. McLawhorn has been president and chief executive officer of the Columbia Urban League since 1979. Under Mr. McLawhorn's leadership, the Columbia Urban League has been recognized locally and nationally as a pacesetter for its advocacy and programmatic expertise in promoting youth leadership development for disadvantaged and foster care youths, along with its advocacy and leadership efforts in the area of equal opportunity and social justice. He initiated the acclaimed Columbia Urban League's publication, *The State of Black South Carolina: An Action Agenda for the Future*. During the 2010 National Urban League Centennial Conference, the Columbia Urban League received the Whitney M. Young, Jr. Leadership Award for Advancing Racial Relations along with the President's Award for public policy advocacy. Additionally, Mr. McLawhorn is a 2011 recipient of the FBI National Director's Community Leadership Award. Mr. McLawhorn serves on several boards, including chair of the United States Department of Veterans Affairs Advisory Committee for Minority Veterans, Greater Columbia Chamber of Commerce, South Carolina Medicaid Advisory Board, Fort Jackson Equal Opportunity Committee, Keenan School Improvement Council, and others. He is the recipient of numerous awards, including the prestigious Order of the Palmetto, the highest award given to a citizen in the state of South Carolina. Additionally, Mr. McLawhorn is an eagle scout and an inductee in the South Carolina Black Hall of Fame. Mr. McLawhorn received his Bachelor of Science degree in Political Science from North Carolina A&T University, Master's degree in City and Regional Planning from the University of North Carolina at Chapel Hill, and Master's degree in Business Administration from the University of Miami at Coral Gables.

MARC H. MORIAL

As President of the National Urban League since 2003, Marc H. Morial has been the primary catalyst for a transformation for the century-old civil rights organization. His energetic and skilled leadership is redefining civil rights in the 21st century with a renewed emphasis on closing the economic gaps between Whites and Blacks as well as rich and poor Americans.

Under his stewardship the League has had record fundraising success towards a 250MM, five-year fundraising goal and he has secured the BBB nonprofit certification, which has established the N.U.L. as a leading national nonprofit.

A graduate of the prestigious University of Pennsylvania with a degree in Economics and African American Studies, he also holds a law degree from the Georgetown University Law Center in Washington, D.C.

Morial was elected Mayor of New Orleans in 1994, serving two terms as popular chief executive with a broad multi-racial coalition who led New Orleans' 1990's renaissance, and left office with a 70% approval rating.

Elected by his peers as President of the bi-partisan U.S. Conference of Mayors, he served during the 9/11 Crisis and championed the creation of the Department of Homeland Security, and the Federalization of airport security screeners.

He serves as an Executive Committee member of the Leadership Conference on Civil Rights, the Black Leadership Forum, and Leadership 18, and is a Board Member of the Muhammad Ali Center, and the New Jersey Performing Arts Center.

Morial, a history, arts, music and sports enthusiast, has an adult daughter, and is married to broadcast journalist Michelle Miller. Together they have two young children.

MAYOR MICHAEL A. NUTTER

The Honorable Michael A. Nutter is the Mayor of Philadelphia, Pennsylvania. Since taking office in January 2008, Mayor Michael A. Nutter has set an aggressive agenda for America's sixth largest city, implementing a crime fighting plan that has sharply reduced the homicide rate, an education strategy to increase the high school graduation rate by 50 percent and a sustainability plan that will reduce the city's energy consumption in the years to come. He has vigorously managed city government through a deep recession, taken advantage of federal recovery funding to create new green-collar jobs and established a customer friendly 311 system. He served almost 15 years on the Philadelphia City Council, earning the reputation of a reformer, before his election as Mayor of Philadelphia. Born in Philadelphia and educated at the Wharton School at the University of Pennsylvania, Michael Nutter has been committed to public service since his youth in West Philadelphia.

STEVE PERRY, PH.D.

Dr. Steve Perry is the Founder and Principal of Capital Prep Magnet School in Hartford, Connecticut, a paradigm-busting success story that has been praised by education experts across America. Dr. Perry is the chief *CNN*

contributor on issues relating to education and can be seen regularly on Anderson Cooper 360 and American Morning. Dr. Perry's latest book Push Has Come to Shove presents his provocative and potentially transformative ideas on how to restore America's schools to greatness. He is also the author of a bestselling self-published book *Man Up!*, a columnist at *Essence* magazine, a frequent radio and television commentator, and a sought-after speaker at colleges and education forums around the country.

KEVIN POWELL

Kevin Powell is an activist, writer, public speaker, and entrepreneur and, in 2008 and 2010, was a Democratic candidate for Congress in Brooklyn, New York. A product of extreme poverty, welfare, fatherlessness, and a single mother-led household, he is a native of Jersey City, New Jersey. Mr. Powell is a longtime resident of Brooklyn, New York, and it is from his base in New York City that he has published eleven books, including his newest collection of political and pop culture writings, Barack Obama, Ronald Reagan, and *The Ghost of Dr. King: Blogs and Essays* (www.lulu.com). Mr. Powell was a cast member on the first season of *MTV's* "The Real World"; has hosted and produced programming for *HBO* and *BET*; written a screenplay; hosted and wrote an award-winning *MTV* documentary about post-riot Los Angeles ("Straight From The 'Hood"); and was the Guest Curator of the Brooklyn Museum of Art's "Hip-Hop Nation: Roots, Rhymes, and Rage"—which originated at the Rock and Roll Hall of Fame and Museum in

Cleveland, Ohio, and of which Kevin was the exhibition consultant—the first major exhibit in America on the history of hip-hop. In 2012, Mr. Powell, with other American leaders of his generation, will launch a new organization, BK Nation. BK Nation will be both a strong online advocate for civic engagement and social change, and also offline with chapters in American communities nationwide, working on issues like education and the creation of jobs and small businesses. Mr. Powell received his Bachelors from Rutgers University.

TAFAYA RANSOM

Tafaya Ransom is a Doctoral Student in Higher Education and Pre-Doctoral Fellow at the Institute of Education Sciences (IES) at the University of Pennsylvania, Graduate School of Education. Her research interests center on increasing the participation of students of color in science, technology, engineering and math (STEM) fields and the role of minority-serving institutions toward this end. Ms. Ransom is currently working on a longitudinal study examining the post-college outcomes of students who participated in the International Baccalaureate program. Prior to enrolling at Penn, she served as a volunteer helping to establish an engineering school at an Ethiopian university, worked in the Detroit and DC Public Schools and worked as a chemical engineer in the food and pharmaceutical industries.

NOLAN V. ROLLINS

Nolan V. Rollins is the President and CEO of the Urban League of Greater New Orleans.

Mr. Rollins has spearheaded the revitalization of the Urban League by balancing tradition with the need to innovate. In September 2007, he streamlined the direct services model of the Urban League to produce programming that is more sustainable and impactful. Rollins increased the agency's staff from 12 to 32 employees and increased its budget for $1 million to over $6 million. Within his first one hundred days on the job, he secured $4.1 million to provide critical support to more than 3,000 Katrina-affected families. Mr. Rollins secured a donation of land valued at $1.1 million from the Housing Authority of New Orleans to build a Head start and Community Development Facility in the 9th Ward and facilitated a New Markets Tax Credit transaction that yielded over $2 million for its construction. He is the architect of the agency's Economic Inclusion efforts, which help to ensure the usage of minority, local and disadvantaged businesses. Currently through this effort the agency is contracted to monitoring over $2 billion in public sector spending. Rollins led the founding of the Urban League Young Professionals Chapter. In its inaugural event, Rollins drew more than 500 young professionals committed to public and community service.

SHARI E. RUNNER

Shari E. Runner has been the Senior Vice President for Strategy and Community Development at the Chicago Urban League since December 2010. Runner has more than 25 years in operations and financial management and a strong background in business development and strategic planning. As Senior Vice President for Strategy and Community Development, Runner's duties include: overseeing and managing operations in all programmatic areas, working with the president and CEO and the development team to increase financial support to the Urban League and assisting the president and CEO in developing short and long term strategic objectives for the Urban League. Prior to joining the Chicago Urban League, Runner was the Director of Finance and Operations at ACT Charter School. Runner has also served as the Chief Operating Officer at the Center for Urban School Improvement at The University of Chicago and a Vice President at ABN-AMRO Bank. Runner received her bachelor's degree from Wesleyan University and her MBA from The University of Chicago Booth School of Business.

HONORABLE ROBERT C. "BOBBY" SCOTT

Congressman Robert C. "Bobby" Scott began serving his tenth term as a Member of Congress on January 5, 2011. Prior to serving in the U.S. House of Representatives, Rep. Scott served in the Virginia House of Delegates from 1978 to 1983 and in the Senate of Virginia from 1983 to 1993. In November 1992, Rep. Scott was elected to the U.S. House of Representatives. Through this election, Rep. Scott made history by becoming the first African American elected to Congress from the Commonwealth of Virginia since Reconstruction and only the second African American elected to Congress in Virginia's history. Having a maternal grandfather of

Filipino ancestry also gives Rep. Scott the distinction of being the first American with Filipino ancestry to serve as a voting member of Congress. Rep. Scott currently serves on the Committee on the Judiciary, where he is the Ranking Member of the Subcommittee on Crime, Terrorism and Homeland Security and a member of the Subcommittee on the Constitution. Rep. Scott also serves on the Committee on Education and the Workforce where he is a member of the Subcommittee on Early Childhood, Elementary and Secondary Education and the Subcommittee on Health, Employment, Labor, and Pensions. Rep. Scott received his Bachelors from Harvard College and his Juris Doctorate from Boston College Law School. After graduating from law school, he returned to Newport News and practiced law from 1973 to 1991. He received an honorable discharge for his service in the Massachusetts National Guard and the United States Army Reserve.

LEE SHAW, JR.

Lee Shaw, Jr. is the Business Development Specialist of the Community Alliances Team for the Boy Scouts of America. In this role, Mr. Shaw provides tactical support to local councils in building their capacity to grow and sustain membership. He develops strategies, and implements a comprehensive framework for advancing community and faith based partnerships. He also provides support to diversity and inclusion components of the National BSA, and Local Councils. Mr. Shaw began his professional Scouting career in Columbus, Ohio in 1990 as District

Executive. He held the positions of Senior District Executive, District Director, Field Director and was promoted to Chief Operating Officer in 2001. He served in that capacity until he joined the national organization in Irving Texas, as the Multicultural Markets Business Development Specialist, focusing on organizational diversity in 2008. He has received recognition in the Who's Who in Black Columbus (Ohio) publication for his role in community leadership. He served on the United Way of Central Ohio, Education Committee and has served on numerous other boards. He is also a United States Army Scholar Athlete of the year recipient, a Past Pennsylvania State Commander of the Sons of the American Legion; and is a member of Kappa Alpha Psi Fraternity, Inc. Mr. Shaw received a Bachelor of Arts degree in Political Science and a minor in history from Clarion University of Pennsylvania.

HAL SMITH, ED.D.

Hal Smith is the Vice President for Education & Youth Development, Health & Quality of Life and a Senior Research Fellow with the National Urban League. Prior to joining the National Urban League in 2008, Hal held teaching, administrative, policy and advocacy positions with the New York City Department of Youth and Community Development (DYCD), the Annenberg Institute for School Reform at Brown University, the City College of New York, the College of the Holy Cross, Northern Illinois University, Lesley University and Harvard University. Mr. Smith holds a B.B.A. in Human Resource Administration from Temple University, a M.A. in Africana Studies from the State University of New York at Albany and an Ed.M. and Ed.D. in Community Education and Lifelong Learning from the Harvard Graduate School of Education.

STEVE STOUTE

Steve Stoute is the founder and CEO of the marketing firm, Translation, whose client roster includes diverse brands such as McDonald's, State Farm, Target, Estee Lauder, Budweiser, Wm. Wrigley, Jr. Co, Microsoft, Coca-Cola, and Lady Gaga. Stoute has made a career out of identifying with and activating a new generation of consumers to create extremely successful marketing campaigns. Stoute's latest effort is the release of his book, *The Tanning of America: How Hip-Hop Created a Culture that Rewrote the Rules of the New Economy*, teaching corporate America how to understand today's newest consumer—The Tan Generation. Stoute also worked with beauty brand Carol's Daughter in 2005, taking the brand from a single-store operation to a multi-million dollar beauty empire with over 1,000 points of distribution. Carol's Daughter now lists Will Smith, Jada Pinkett-Smith, Jimmy Iovine, Jay-Z and Mary J. Blige among its leading investors. In 2008, Stoute partnered with Jay-Z to co-found Translation Advertising. In 2009, the American Advertising Federation inducted Stoute into the Advertising Hall of Achievement and in 2010 he was recognized as Innovator of the Year by *ADCOLOR*. Prior to founding Translation, Stoute spent ten years as President of Urban Music at Sony and later Executive Vice President of Interscope Geffen A&M Records.

He also serves as the co-chairman of the New York City Fresh Air Fund in 2003 and played a key role in the development of minority recruitment campaigns for both the FDNY and NYPD for which he received the 2004 Humanitarian Award.

MADURA WIJEWARDENA

Madura Wijewardena is the Director of Research & Policy at the National Urban League Policy Institute (NULPI), where he uses quantitative analysis and research to promote NUL's legislative agenda in economic policy. Madura also assists in the production of the Equality Index and acts as the coordinator of the NUL's role as a Census Information Center. In addition to research, Madura manages NUL's federal policy in telecoms/technology, energy, and transportation. He also handles special partnerships with the Federal Communications Commission (FCC) and the U.S. Census Bureau to promote joint programs like the FCC's public-private broadband adoption programs. Prior to NULPI, Madura worked for a Chicago consulting firm where he used quantitative analysis of complex databases to assist state governments, foundations, and campaigns to micro-target services and messages. Madura has been interviewed on *C-SPAN*, *ABC-TV*, and *Public Radio International*, and his work has been quoted in *The New York Times* and in testimony before the U.S. Congress. For the first eight years of his career, Madura was a corporate attorney in technology and telecommunications, where he structured and negotiated mergers, acquisitions, and joint ventures for global corporations. Madura has

an MA in Public Policy from the University of Chicago (in statistics), and an LLB (equivalent of a Juris Doctorate) and a Bachelor of Economics degree from the University of Sydney, Australia.

VALERIE R. WILSON, PH.D.

Dr. Valerie Rawlston Wilson is an economist and Vice President of Research at the National Urban League Policy Institute in Washington, DC where she is responsible for planning and directing the Policy Institute's Research Agenda. She is also a member of the National Urban League President's Council of Economic Advisors, which assists the League in shaping national economic policy. Her fields of specialization include labor economics, racial and economic inequality, and economics of higher education. She has authored a number of publications on topics related to these areas and has appeared in print, television and radio media, including *C-SPAN's Washington Journal*, *National Public Radio*, *Fox News*, *USA Today*, *Ebony* and *Time* magazine. Dr. Wilson earned a Ph.D. from the Department of Economics at the University of North Carolina at Chapel Hill.

REVEREND LENNOX YEARWOOD, JR.

Rev. Lennox Yearwood, Jr. is the President and CEO of the Hip Hop Caucus. He is a minister, community activist and one of the most influential people in Hip Hop political life. He works tirelessly to encourage the Hip Hop generation to utilize its political and social voice. In 2010 he was named one of the 100 most powerful African Americans by *Ebony*

Magazine, and one of the 10 Game Changers in the Green movement by the *Huffington Post.* In 2008, Rev. Yearwood created the Hip Hop Caucus' "Respect My Vote!" campaign with celebrity spokespeople T.I. and Keyshia Cole, which turned out record numbers of young people on Election Day. After Hurricane Katrina in 2005, Rev. Yearwood became National Director of the award winning Gulf Coast Renewal Campaign where he led a coalition of national and grassroots organizations to advocate for the rights of Katrina survivors. He served as the Political and Grassroots Director of Russell Simmons' Hip Hop Summit Action Network in 2003 and 2004. In 2004 he also was a key architect and implementer of three other voter turnout operations—P. Diddy's Citizen Change organization which created the "Vote Or Die!" campaign; Jay-Z's "Voice Your Choice" campaign; and, "Hip Hop Voices", a project at the AFL-CIO. Rev. Yearwood is a retired U.S. Air Force Reserve Officer. He was born in Shreveport, Louisiana, and currently lives in Washington, DC. He has been seen in such media outlets as *CNN, MSNBC, BET, Huffington Post, Newsweek, The Nation, MTV, AllHipHop. com, The Source Magazine, Ebony* and *Jet, Al Jazeera, BBC, C-Span,* and *Hardball* with Chris Matthews and featured in the *Washington Post, The New York Times* and *VIBE* magazine.

INDEX
OF AUTHORS AND ARTICLES

In 1987, the National Urban League began publishing *The State of Black America* in a smaller, typeset format. By doing so, it became easier to catalog and archive the various essays by author and article.

The 2012 edition of *The State of Black America* is the seventeenth to feature an Index of the Authors and Articles that have appeared since 1987. The articles have been divided by topic and are listed in alphabetical order by authors' names.

Reprints of the articles catalogued herein are available through the National Urban League Policy Institute, 1101 Connecticut Avenue, NW, Suite 810, Washington, DC 20036, (202) 898-1604.

Holzer, Harry J., "Reconnecting Young Black Men: What Policies Would Help," 2007, pp. 75–87.

Johns, David J., "Re-imagining Black Masculine Identity: An Investigation of the 'Problem' Surrounding the Construction of Black Masculinity in America," 2007, pp. 59–73.

Lanier, James R., "The Empowerment Movement and the Black Male," 2004, pp. 143–148.

———, "The National Urban League's Commission on the Black Male: Renewal, Revival and Resurrection Feasibility and Strategic Planning Study," 2005, pp. 107–109.

Morial, Marc H., "Empowering Black Males to Reach Their Full Potential," 2007, pp. 13–15.

Nutter, Michael A. "Black Men Are Killing Black Men. There, I Said It." 2012, pp. 106–109.

Reed, James, and Aaron Thomas, "The National Urban League: The National Urban League: Empowering Black Males to Reach Their Full Potential," 2007, pp. 217–218.

Rodgers III, William, M., "Why Should African Americans Care About Macroeconomic Policy," 2007, pp. 89–103.

Wilson, Valerie Rawlston, "On Equal Ground: Causes and Solutions for Lower College Completion Rates Among Black Males," 2007, pp. 123–135.

BUSINESS

Blankfein, Lloyd. "Creating Jobs and Opportunities Through Minority Owned Businesses," 2012, pp. 70–73.

Cofield, Natalie M. "What's in it for Us? How Federal Business Inclusion Programs and Legislation Affect Minority Entrepreneurs," 2011, pp. 100–109.

Emerson, Melinda F., "Five Things You Must Have to Run a Successful Business," 2004, pp. 153–156.

Glasgow, Douglas G., "The Black Underclass in Perspective," 1987, pp. 129–144.

Henderson, Lenneal J., "Empowerment through Enterprise: African-American Business Development," 1993, pp. 91–108.

Price, Hugh B., "Beacons in a New Millennium: Reflections on 21st-Century Leaders and Leadership," 2000, pp. 13–39.

Tidwell, Billy J., "Black Wealth: Facts and Fiction," 1988, pp. 193–210.

Turner, Mark D., "Escaping the 'Ghetto' of Subcontracting," 2006, pp. 117–131.

Walker, Juliet E.K., "The Future of Black Business in America: Can It Get Out of the Box?," 2000, pp. 199–226.

CASE STUDIES

Cleaver, Emanuel, II, "Green Impact Zone of Kansas City, MO," 2011, pp. 88–93.

Patrick, Deval L., "Growing an Innovative Economy in Massachusetts," 2011, pp. 154–158.

CHILDREN AND YOUTH

Bell, William C., "How are the Children? Foster Care and African-American Boys," 2007, pp. 151–157.

Chávez, Anna Maria "Helping Girls Make Healthy Choices," 2012, pp. 124–126.

Comer, James P., "Leave No Child Behind: Preparing Today's Youth for Tomorrow's World," 2005, pp. 75–84.

Cox, Kenya L. Covington, "The Childcare Imbalance: Impact on Working Opportunities for Poor Mothers," 2003, pp. 197–224.

Dallas Highlight, "Urban Youth Empowerment Program," 2011, pp. 84–86.

Edelman, Marian Wright, "The State of Our Children," 2006, pp. 133–141.

———, "Losing Our Children in America's Cradle to Prison Pipeline," 2007, pp. 219–227.

Fulbright-Anderson, Karen, "Developing Our Youth: What Works," 1996, pp. 127–143.

Hare, Bruce R., "Black Youth at Risk," 1988, pp. 81–93.

Howard, Jeff P., "The Third Movement: Developing Black Children for the 21st Century," 1993, pp. 11–34.

Knaus, Christopher B., "Still Segregated, Still Unequal: Analyzing the Impact of No Child Left Behind on African-American Students," 2007, pp. 105–121.

McMurray, Georgia L. "Those of Broader Vision: An African-American Perspective on Teenage Pregnancy and Parenting," 1990, pp. 195–211.

Moore, Evelyn K., "The Call: Universal Child Care," 1996, pp. 219–244.

Obama, Michelle, "Let's Move Initiative on Healthier Schools," 2011, pp. 138–140.

Shaw, Lee, Jr., "Healthy Boys Stand SCOUTStrong™," 2012, pp. 126–128.

Scott, Kimberly A., "A Case Study: African-American Girls and Their Families," 2003, pp. 181–195.

Special Report. "Partnering to Empower Healthy Kids," 2012, pp. 120–123.

Williams, Terry M., and William Kornblum, "A Portrait of Youth: Coming of Age in Harlem Public Housing," 1991, pp. 187–207.

CIVIC ENGAGEMENT

Alton, Kimberley, "The State of Civil Rights 2008," 2008, pp. 157–161.

Brazile, Donna, "Fallout from the Mid-term Elections: Making the Most of the Next Two Years," 2011, pp. 180–190.

Campbell, Melanie L., "Election Reform: Protecting Our Vote from the Enemy That Never Sleeps," 2008, pp. 149–156.

Chappell, Kevin, "'Realities' of Black America," 2011, pp. 192–195.

Lindsay, Tiffany, "Weaving the Fabric: The Political Activism of Young African-American Women," 2008, pp. 47–50.

Scott, Robert C. "Bobby," "Minority Voter Participation: Reviewing Past and Present Barriers to the Polls," 2012, pp. 44–47.

Wijewardena, Madura and Kirk Clay, "Government with the Consent of All: Redistricting Strategies for Civil Rights Organizations," 2011, pp. 196–201.

Wijewardena, Madura ,"Understanding the Equality Index," 2012, pp. 16–19.

Wilson, Valerie Rawlston, "Introduction to the 2011 Equality Index," 2011, pp. 14–22.

Wilson, Valerie Rawlston, "Introduction to the 2012 Equality Index," 2012, pp. 10–15.

Yearwood, Lennox, Jr.,"The Rise and Fall and Rise Again of Jim Crow Laws," 2012, pp. 48–53.

CIVIL RIGHTS

Alton, Kimberley, "The State of Civil Rights 2008," 2008, pp. 157–161.

Archer, Dennis W., "Security Must Never Trump Liberty," 2004, pp. 139–142.

Burnham, David, "The Fog of War," 2005, pp. 123–127.

Campbell, Melanie L., "Election Reform: Protecting Our Vote from the Enemy That Never Sleeps," 2008, pp. 149–156.

Chappell, Kevin, " 'Realities' of Black America," 2011, pp. 192–195.

Grant, Gwen, "The Fullness of Time for a More Perfect Union: The Movement Continues," 2009, pp. 171–177.

Jones, Nathaniel R., "The State of Civil Rights," 2006, pp. 165–170.

———, "Did I Ever" 2009, pp. 213–219.

Ogletree, Charles J., Jr., "Brown at 50: Considering the Continuing Legal Struggle for Racial Justice," 2004, pp. 81–96.

Shaw, Theodore M., "The State of Civil Rights," 2007, pp. 173–183.

Wijewardena, Madura and Kirk Clay, "Government with the Consent of All: Redistricting Strategies for Civil Rights Organizations," 2011, pp. 196–201.

CRIMINAL JUSTICE

Curry, George E., "Racial Disparities Drive Prison Boom," 2006, pp. 171–187.

Drucker, Ernest M., "The Impact of Mass Incarceration on Public Health in Black Communities," 2003, pp. 151–168.

Edelman, Marian Wright, "Losing Our Children in America's Cradle to Prison Pipeline," 2007, pp. 219–227.

Lanier, James R., "The Harmful Impact of the Criminal Justice System and War on Drugs on the African-American Family," 2003, pp. 169–179.

DIVERSITY

Bell, Derrick, "The Elusive Quest for Racial Justice: The Chronicle of the Constitutional Contradiction," 1991, pp. 9–23.

Cobbs, Price M., "Critical Perspectives on the Psychology of Race," 1988, pp. 61–70.

———, "Valuing Diversity: The Myth and the Challenge," 1989, pp. 151–159.

Darity, William, Jr., "History, Discrimination and Racial Inequality," 1999, pp. 153–166.

Jones, Stephanie J., "Sunday Morning Apartheid: A Diversity Study of the Sunday Morning Talk Shows," 2006, pp. 189–228.

Stoute, Steve, "Tanning of America Makes Growth, Prosperity and Empowerment Easier," 2012, pp. 84–89.

Watson, Bernard C., "The Demographic Revolution: Diversity in 21st-Century America," 1992, pp. 31–59.

Wiley, Maya, "Hurricane Katrina Exposed the Face of Diversity," 2006, pp. 143–153.

DRUG TRADE

Lanier, James R., "The Harmful Impact of the Criminal Justice System and War on Drugs on the African-American Family," 2003, pp.169–179.

ECONOMICS

Alexis, Marcus and Geraldine R. Henderson, "The Economic Base of African-American Communities: A Study of Consumption Patterns," 1994, pp. 51–82.

Anderson, Bernard, "Lessons Learned from the Economic Crisis: Job Creation and Economy Recovery," 2010, pp. 60–65.

___, William M. Rodgers III, Lucy J. Reuben, and Valerie Rawlston Wilson, "The New Normal? Opportunities for Prosperity in a 'Jobless Recovery,'" 2011, pp. 54–63.

Atlanta Highlight, "Economic Empowerment Tour," 2011, pp. 118–120.

Bradford, William, "Black Family Wealth in the United States," 2000, pp. 103–145.

———, "Money Matters: Lending Discrimination in African-American Communities," 1993, pp. 109–134.

Buckner, Marland and Chanelle P. Hardy, "Leveraging the Greening of America to Strengthen the Workforce Development System," 2011, pp. 76–83.

Burbridge, Lynn C., "Toward Economic Self-Sufficiency: Independence Without Poverty," 1993, pp. 71–90.

Cleaver, Emanuel, II, "Green Impact Zone of Kansas City, MO," 2011, pp. 88–93.

Corbett, Keith, "Economic Innovation: Finance and Lending Initiatives Point Paths to Prosperity for Underserved Communities," 2011, pp. 122–129.

Edwards, Harry, "Playoffs and Payoffs: The African-American Athlete as an Institutional Resource," 1994, pp. 85–111.

Graves, Earl, Jr., "Wealth for Life," 2009, pp. 165–170.

Hamilton, Darrick, "The Racial Composition of American Jobs," 2006, pp. 77–115.

Harris, Andrea, "The Subprime Wipeout: Unsustainable Loans Erase Gains Made by African-American Women," 2008, pp. 125–133.

Henderson, Lenneal J., "Blacks, Budgets, and Taxes: Assessing the Impact of Budget Deficit Reduction and Tax Reform on Blacks," 1987, pp. 75–95.

———, "Budget and Tax Strategy: Implications for Blacks," 1990, pp. 53–71.

———, "Public Investment for Public Good: Needs, Benefits, and Financing Options," 1992, pp. 213–229.

Herman, Alexis, "African-American Women and Work: Still a Tale of Two Cities," 2008, pp. 109–113.

Holzer, Harry J., "Reconnecting Young Black Men: What Policies Would Help," 2007, pp. 75–87.

Jeffries, John M., and Richard L. Schaffer, "Changes in Economy and Labor Market Status of Black Americans," 1996, pp. 12–77.

Jones, Stephanie J., "The Subprime Meltdown: Disarming the 'Weapons of Mass Deception,'" 2009, pp. 157–164.

Malveaux, Julianne, "Shouldering the Third Burden: The Status of African-American Women," 2008, pp. 75–81.

———, "The Parity Imperative: Civil Rights, Economic Justice, and the New American Dilemma," 1992, pp. 281–303.

Mensah, Lisa, "Putting Homeownership Back Within Our Reach," 2008, pp. 135–142.

Morial, Marc H. and Marvin Owens, "The National Urban League Economic Empowerment Initiative," 2005, pp. 111–113.

Myers, Samuel L., Jr., "African-American Economic Well-Being During the Boom and Bust," 2004, pp. 53–80.

National Urban League, "The National Urban League's Homebuyer's Bill of Rights," 2008, pp. 143–147.

National Urban League Research Staff, "African Americans in Profile: Selected Demographic, Social and Economic Data," 1992, pp. 309–325.

———, "The Economic Status of African Americans During the Reagan-Bush Era Withered Opportunities, Limited Outcomes, and Uncertain Outlook," 1993, pp. 135–200.

———, "The Economic Status of African Americans: Limited Ownership and Persistent Inequality," 1992, pp. 61–117.

———, "The Economic Status of African Americans: 'Permanent' Poverty and Inequality," 1991, pp. 25–75.

———, "Economic Status of Black Americans During the 1980s: A Decade of Limited Progress," 1990, pp. 25–52.

———, "Economic Status of Black Americans," 1989, pp. 9–39.

———, "Economic Status of Black 1987," 1988, pp. 129–152.

———, "Economic Status of Blacks 1986," 1987, pp. 49–73.

Patrick, Deval L., "Growing an Innovative Economy in Massachusetts," 2011, pp. 154–158.

Reuben, Lucy J., "Make Room for the New 'She'EOs: An Analysis of Businesses Owned by Black Females," 2008, pp. 115–124.

Richardson, Cy, "What Must Be Done: The Case for More Homeownership and Financial Education Counseling," 2009, pp. 145–155.

Rivlin, Alice M., "Pay Now or Pay Later: Jobs, Fiscal Responsibility and the Future of Black America," 2011, pp. 202–206.

Rodgers III, William, M., "Why Should African Americans Care About Macroeconomic Policy," 2007, pp. 89–103.

Shapiro, Thomas M., "The Racial Wealth Gap," 2005, pp. 41–48.

Sharpe, Rhonda, "Preparing a Diverse and Competitive STEM Workforce," 2011, pp. 142–152.

Spriggs, William, "Nothing Trickled Down: Why Reaganomics Failed America," 2009, pp. 123–133.

Stoute, Steve, "Tanning of America Makes Growth, Prosperity and Empowerment Easier," 2012, pp. 84–89.

Taylor, Robert D., "Wealth Creation: The Next Leadership Challenge," 2005, pp. 119–122.

Thompson, J. Phil, "The Coming Green Economy," 2009, pp. 135–142.

Tidwell, Billy J., "Economic Costs of American Racism," 1991, pp. 219–232.

Turner, Mark D., "Escaping the 'Ghetto' of Subcontracting," 2006, pp. 117–131.

Watkins, Celeste, "The Socio-Economic Divide Among Black Americans Under 35," 2001, pp. 67–85.

Webb, Michael B., "Programs for Progress and Empowerment: The Urban League's National Education Initiative," 1993, pp. 203–216.

EDUCATION

Allen, Walter R., "The Struggle Continues: Race, Equity and Affirmative Action in U.S. Higher Education," 2001, pp. 87–100.

Bailey, Deirdre, "School Choice: The Option of Success," 2001, pp. 101–114.

Bradford, William D., "Dollars for Deeds: Prospects and Prescriptions for African-American Financial Institutions," 1994, pp. 31–50.

Carr, Gregory E., "Sacrifice If You Must—The Reward Is Clear," 2012, pp. 137–139.

Cole, Johnnetta Betsch, "The Triumphs and Challenges of Historically Black Colleges and Universities," 2008, pp. 99–107.

Comer, James P., Norris Haynes, and Muriel Hamilton-Leel, "School Power: A Model for Improving Black Student Achievement," 1990, pp. 225–238.

———"Leave No Child Behind: Preparing Today's Youth for Tomorrow's World," 2005, pp. 75–84.

Dilworth, Mary E. "Historically Black Colleges and Universities: Taking Care of Home," 1994, pp. 127–151.

Duncan, Arne, "The Path to Success for African Americans," 2010, pp. 92–96.

Edelman, Marian Wright, "Black Children in America," 1989, pp. 63–76.

Enyia, Amara, C. "College for All?" 2012, pp. 149–151.

Fattah, Chaka, "Needed: Equality in Education," 2009, pp. 57–60.

Freeman, Dr. Kimberly Edelin, "African-American Men and Women in Higher Education: 'Filling the Glass' in the New Millennium," 2000, pp. 61–90.

Gordon, Edmund W., "The State of Education in Black America," 2004, pp. 97–113.

Guinier, Prof. Lani, "Confirmative Action in a Multiracial Democracy," 2000, pp. 333–364.

Hanson, Renee R., "A Pathway to School Readiness: The Impact of Family on Early Childhood Education," 2008, pp. 89–98.

Hardy, Chanelle P., "Introduction: The Value of College," 2012, pp. 132–135.

Jackson, John, "From Miracle to Movement: Mandating a National Opportunity to Learn, 2009, pp. 61–70.

Jackson, Maria Rosario, "Arts, Culture, and Communities: Do Our Neighborhoods Inspire Our Children to Reach Higher?" 2012, pp. 153–154.

Journal of Blacks in Higher Education (reprint), "The 'Acting White' Myth," 2005, pp.115–117.

Knaus, Christopher B., "Still Segregated, Still Unequal: Analyzing the Impact of No Child Left Behind on African American Students," 2007, pp. 105–121.

Legend, John, "The Show Me Campaign: A Conversation with John Legend," 2012, pp. 151–153.

Luckey, Desireé, "Communities, Schools and Families Make the Education-Career Connection," 2012, pp. 139–141.

McBay, Shirley M. "The Condition of African American Education: Changes and Challenges," 1992, pp. 141–156.

McKenzie, Floretta Dukes with Patricia Evans, "Education Strategies for the 90s," 1991, pp. 95–109.

Morial, Marc H. and Hal Smith, "Education is a Jobs Issue," 2011, pp. 130–137.

Patrick, Deval L., "Growing an Innovative Economy in Massachusetts," 2011, pp. 154–158.

Perry, Dr. Steve, "Real Reform is Getting Kids One Step Closer to Quality Schools," 2012, pp. 147–149.

Powell, Kevin, "Why A College Education Matters," 2012, pp. 136–137.

Ransom, Tafaya and John Michael Lee, "College Readiness and Completion for Young Men of Color," 2012, pp. 141–147.

Ribeau, Sidney, "Foreword: A Competitive Foundation for the Future," 2011, pp. 8–9.

Robinson, Sharon P., "Taking Charge: An Approach to Making the Educational Problems of Blacks Comprehensible and Manageable," 1987, pp. 31–47.

Rose, Dr. Stephanie Bell, "African-American High Achievers: Developing Talented Leaders," 2000, pp. 41–60.

Ross, Ronald O., "Gaps, Traps and Lies: African-American Students and Test Scores," 2004, pp. 157–161.

Sharpe, Rhonda, "Preparing a Diverse and Competitive STEM Workforce," 2011, pp. 142–152.

Smith, Hal, "The Questions Before Us: Opportunity, Education and Equity," 2009, pp. 45–55.

Smith, Hal, Jacqueline Ayers, and Darlene Marlin, "Ready to Succeed: The National Urban League Project Ready: Post-Secondary Success Program," 2012, pp. 114–119.

Sudarkasa, Niara, "Black Enrollment in Higher Education: The Unfulfilled led Promise of Equality," 1988, pp. 7–22.

Thornton, Alvin, "The Nation's Higher Education Agenda: The Continuing Role of HBCUs," 2011, pp. 160–167.

Watson, Bernard C., with Fasaha M. Traylor, "Tomorrow's Teachers: Who Will They Be, What Will They Know?" 1988, pp. 23–37.

Willie, Charles V., "The Future of School Desegregation," 1987, pp. 37–47.

Wilson, Reginald, "Black Higher Education: Crisis and Promise," 1989, pp. 121–135.

Wilson, Valerie Rawlston, "On Equal Ground: Causes and Solutions for Lower College Completion Rates Among Black Males," 2007, pp. 123–135.

___, "Introduction to the 2011 Equality Index," 2011, pp. 14–22.

Wirschem, David, "Community Mobilization for Education in Rochester, New York: A Case Study," 1991, pp. 243–248.

EMERGING IDEAS
Huggins, Sheryl, "The Rules of the Game," 2001, pp. 65–66.

EMPLOYMENT
Anderson, Bernard E., "The Black Worker: Continuing Quest for Economic Parity, 2002, pp. 51–67.

___, William M. Rodgers III, Lucy J. Reuben, and Valerie Rawlston Wilson, "The New Normal? Opportunities for Prosperity in a 'Jobless Recovery,'" 2011, pp. 54–63.

Atlanta Highlight, "Economic Empowerment Tour," 2011, pp. 118–120.

Cleaver, Emanuel, II, "Green Impact Zone of Kansas City, MO," 2011, pp. 88–93.

Coulter, Patricia, "Small Business Growth = Job Growth," 2010, pp. 118–124.

Dallas Highlight, "Urban Youth Empowerment Program," 2011, pp. 84–86.

Darity, William M., Jr., and Samuel L. Myers, Jr., "Racial Earnings Inequality into the 21st Century," 1992, pp. 119–139.

Dodd, Christopher, "Infrastructure as a Job Creation Mechanism," 2009, pp. 101–108.

Gillibrand, Kirsten, "A Dream Not Deferred," 2012, pp. 60–63.

Hamilton, Darrick, "The Racial Composition of American Jobs," 2006, pp. 77–115.

Hammond, Theresa A., "African Americans in White-Collar Professions," 2002, pp. 109–121.

Herman, Alexis, "African-American Women and Work: Still a Tale of Two Cities," 2008, pp. 109–113.

Morial, Marc H. and Hal Smith, "Education is a Jobs Issue," 2011, pp.

★ ☆ ★ ☆ ★ ☆ ★ ☆ ★ ☆ ★ ☆ ★ ☆ ★ ☆ ★

130–137.

National Urban League, "12 Point Urban Jobs Plan," 2011, pp. 46–52.

National Urban League Policy Institute, "Where Do We Go From Here? Projected Employment Growth Industries and Occupations," 2011, pp. 64–75.

———, The National Urban League 8-Point Education and Employment Plan: Employment and Education Empower the Nation, 2012, pp. 54–59.

Nightingale, Demetra S., "Intermediaries in the Workforce Development Systsem," 2010, pp. 84–91.

Patrick, Deval L., "Growing an Innovative Economy in Massachusetts," 2011, pp. 154–158.

Reuben, Lucy J., "Make Room for the New 'She'EOs: An Analysis of Businesses Owned by Black Females," 2008, pp. 115–124.

Rivlin, Alice M., "Pay Now or Pay Later: Jobs, Fiscal Responsibility and the Future of Black America," 2011, pp. 202–206.

Rodgers, William, "Why Reduce African-American Male Unemployment?," 2009, pp. 109–121.

Sharpe, Rhonda, "Preparing a Diverse and Competitive STEM Workforce," 2011, pp. 142–152.

Solis, Hilda, "Creating Good Jobs for Everyone," 2010, pp. 66–72.

Taylor, Barton, "Opening New Doors Through Volunteerism," 2010, pp. 126–131.

Thomas, R. Roosevelt, Jr., "Managing Employee Diversity: An Assessment," 1991, pp. 145–154.

Tidwell, Billy, J., "Parity Progress and Prospects: Racial Inequalities in Economic Well-being," 2000, pp. 287–316.

———, "African Americans and the 21st- Century Labor Market: Improving the Fit," 1993, pp. 35–57.

———, "The Unemployment Experience of African Americans: Some Important Correlates and Consequences," 1990, pp. 213–223.

———, "A Profile of the Black Unemployed," 1987, pp. 223–237.

Wilkins, Ray, "Jobs, the Internet, and Our Exciting Future," 2011, pp. 94–99.

Wilson, Valerie Rawlston, "Introduction to the 2011 Equality Index," 2011, pp. 14–22.

ENVIRONMENT
Buckner, Marland and Chanelle P. Hardy, "Leveraging the Greening of America to Strengthen the Workforce Development System," 2011, pp. 76–83.

Cleaver, Emanuel, II, "Green Impact Zone of Kansas City, MO," 2011, pp. 88–93.

EQUALITY
Raines, Franklin D., "What Equality Would Look Like: Reflections on the Past, Present and Future, 2002, pp. 13–27.

EQUALITY INDEX
Global Insight, Inc., The National Urban League Equality Index, 2004, pp. 15–34.

———, The National Urban League Equality Index, 2005, pp. 15–40.

———, The National Urban League Equality Index, 2010, pp. 18–39.

Thompson, Rondel and Sophia Parker of Global Insight, Inc., The National Urban League Equality Index, 2006, pp. 13–60.

Thompson, Rondel and Sophia Parker of Global Insight, Inc., The National Urban League Equality Index, 2007 pp. 17–58.

Wilson, Valerie Rawlston, The National Urban League 2008 Equality Index: Analysis, 2008, pp. 15–24.

Wilson, Valerie Rawlston, The National Urban League 2008 Equality Index, 2009, pp. 15–24.

Global Insights, Inc., The National Urban League 2012 Equality Index, 2012, pp. 20–43.

FAMILIES
Battle, Juan, Cathy J. Cohen, Angelique Harris, and Beth E. Richie, "We Are Family: Embracing Our Lesbian, Gay, Bisexual, and Transgender (LGBT) Family Members," 2003, pp. 93–106.

Billingsley, Andrew, "Black Families in a Changing Society," 1987, pp. 97–111.

———, "Understanding African-American Family Diversity," 1990, pp. 85–108.

Cox, Kenya L. Covington, "The Childcare Imbalance: Impact on Working Opportunities for Poor Mothers," 2003, pp. 197–224d.

Drucker, Ernest M., "The Impact of Mass Incarceration on Public Health in Black Communities," 2003, pp. 151–168.

Dyson, Eric Michael, "Sexual Fault Lines: Robbing the Love Between Us," 2007, pp. 229–237.

Hanson, Renee R., "A Pathway to School Readiness: The Impact of Family on Early Childhood Education," 2008, pp. 89–98.

Hill, Robert B., "Critical Issues for Black Families by the Year 2000," 1989, pp. 41–61.

———, "The Strengths of Black Families' Revisited," 2003, pp. 107–149.

Ivory, Steven, "Universal Fatherhood: Black Men Sharing the Load," 2007, pp. 243–247.

Lorain County Highlight, "Save Our Sons," 2011, pp. 176–178.

Rawlston, Valerie A., "The Impact of Social Security on Child Poverty," 2000, pp. 317–331.

Scott, Kimberly A., "A Case Study: African-American Girls and Their Families," 2003, pp. 181–195.

Shapiro, Thomas M., "The Racial Wealth Gap," 2005, pp. 41–48.

Stafford, Walter, Angela Dews, Melissa Mendez, and Diana Salas, "Race, Gender and Welfare Reform: The Need for Targeted Support," 2003, pp. 41–92.

Stockard, Russell L., Jr., and M. Belinda Tucker, "Young African-American Men and Women: Separate Paths?," 2001, pp. 143–159.

Teele, James E., "E. Franklin Frazier: The Man and His Intellectual Legacy," 2003, pp. 29–40.

Thompson, Dr. Linda S. and Georgene Butler, "The Role of the Black Family in Promoting Healthy Child Development," 2000, pp. 227–241.

West, Carolyn M., "Feminism is a Black Thing"?: Feminist Contribution to Black Family Life, 2003, pp. 13–27.

Willie, Charles V. "The Black Family: Striving Toward Freedom," 1988, pp. 71–80.

FOREWORD
Height, Dorothy I., "Awakenings," 2008, pp. 9–10.

Obama, Barack, Foreword, 2007, pp. 9–12.

King III, Martin Luther, Foreword, 2009, pp. 9–10.

Ribeau, Sidney, "A Competitive Foundation for the Future," 2011, pp. 8–9.

FROM THE PRESIDENT'S DESK
Morial, Marc H., "The State of Black America: The Complexity of Black Progress," 2004, pp. 11–14.

Morial, Marc H., "The State of Black America 2012: Occupy the Vote to Educate, Employ & Empower," 2012, pp. 6–9.

———, "The State of Black America: Prescriptions for Change," 2005, pp. 11–14.

———, "The National Urban League Opportunity Compact," 2006, pp. 9–11.

———, "Empowering Black Males to Reach Their Full Potential," 2007, pp. 13–15.

———, From the President's Desk, 2008, pp. 11–14.

———, From the President's Desk, 2009, pp. 11–13.

———, From the President's Desk, 2010, pp. 6–7.

———, From the President's Desk, 2011, pp. 10–12.

———, From the President's Desk, 2012, pp. 6–9.

HEALTH
Browne, Doris, "The Impact of Health Disparities in African-American Women," 2008, pp. 163–171.

Carnethon, Mercedes R., "Black Male Life Expectancy in the United States: A Multi-level Exploration of Causes," 2007, pp. 137–150.

Chávez, Anna Maria "Helping Girls Make Healthy Choices," 2012, pp. 124–126.

Christmas, June Jackson, "The Health of African Americans: Progress Toward Healthy People 2000," 1996, pp. 95–126.

Cooper, Maudine R., "The Invisibility Blues' of Black Women in America," 2008, pp. 83–87.

Gaskin, Darrell, "Improving African Americans Access to Quality Healthcare," 2009, pp. 73–86.

Hamilton, Darrick, Goldsmith, Arthur H., and Darity, William, "An Alternative 'Public Option'," 2010, pp. 98–110.

Johnston, Haile, and Tatiana Garcia-Granados, "Common Market: The New Black Farmer," 2012, pp. 100–105.

Leffall, LaSalle D., Jr., "Health Status of Black Americans," 1990, pp. 121–142.

Lorain County Highlight, "Save Our Sons," 2011, pp. 176–178.

McAlpine, Robert, "Toward Development of a National Drug Control Strategy," 1991, pp. 233–241.

Morris, Eboni D., "By the Numbers: Uninsured African-American Women," 2008, pp. 173–177.

——— and Lisa Bland Malone, "Healthy Housing," 2009, pp. 87–98.

Nobles, Wade W., and Lawford L. Goddard, "Drugs in the African-American Community: A Clear and Present Danger," 1989, pp. 161–181.

Obama, Michelle, "Let's Move Initiative on Healthier Schools," 2011, pp. 138–140.

Patrick, Deval L., "Growing an Innovative Economy in Massachusetts," 2011, pp. 154–158.

Primm, Annelle and Marisela B. Gomez, "The Impact of Mental Health on Chronic Disease," 2005, pp. 63–73.

Primm, Beny J., "AIDS: A Special Report," 1987, pp. 159–166.

———, "Drug Use: Special Implications for Black America," 1987, pp. 145–158.

Ribeau, Sidney, "Foreword: A Competitive Foundation for the Future," 2011, pp. 8–9.

Shaw, Lee, Jr., "Healthy Boys Stand SCOUTStrong™," 2012, pp. 126–128.

Smedley, Brian D., "In the Wake of National Health Reform: Will the Affordable Care Act Eliminate Health Inequities?" 2011, pp. 168–175.

———, "Race, Poverty, and Healthcare Disparities," 2006, pp. 155–164.

Williams, David R., "Health and the Quality of Life Among African Americans," 2004, pp. 115–138.

Wilson, Valerie Rawlston, "Introduction to the 2011 Equality Index," 2011, pp. 14–22.

Wilson, Valerie Rawlston, "Introduction to the 2012 Equality Index," 2012, pp. 10–15.

Wijewardena, Madura ,"Understanding the Equality Index," 2012, pp. 16–19.

HIGHLIGHTS
Atlanta, "Economic Empowerment Tour," 2011, pp. 118–120.

Braswell, Allie L., and James T. McLawhorn, Jr., "A Call to Advocate for America's Military Veterans," 2012, pp. 94–99.

Dallas, "Urban Youth Empowerment Program," 2011, pp. 84–86.

Obama, Michelle, "Let's Move Initiative on Healthier Schools," 2011, pp. 138–140.

Lorain County, "Save Our Sons," 2011, pp. 176–178.

Rollins, Nolan V., "The Economic Winds of Change: New Markets for an Old Problem," 2012, pp. 90–93.

Runner, Shari, "Inspiring Innovation: The Chiacago Urban League Youth Investor/Entrepreneurs Project (YIEP)," 2012, pp. 110–113.

HOUSING
Calmore, John O., "To Make Wrong Right: The Necessary and Proper Aspirations of Fair Housing," 1989, pp. 77–109.

Clay, Phillip, "Housing Opportunity: A Dream Deferred," 1990, pp. 73–84.

Cooper, Maudine R., "The Invisibility Blues' of Black Women in America," 2008, pp. 83–87.

Corbett, Keith, "Economic Innovation: Finance and Lending Initiatives Point Paths to Prosperity for Underserved Communities," 2011, pp. 122–129.

Freeman, Lance, "Black Homeownership: A Dream No Longer Deferred?," 2006, pp. 63–75.

_____, "Housing in the Post-Bubble Economy," 2010, pp. 74–83.

Harris, Andrea, "The Subprime Wipeout: Unsustainable Loans Erase Gains Made by African-American Women," 2008, pp. 125–133.

James, Angela, "Black Homeownership: Housing and Black Americans Under 35," 2001, pp. 115–129.

Jones, Stephanie J., "The Subprime Meltdown: Disarming the 'Weapons of Mass Deception,'" 2009, pp. 157–164.

Leigh, Wilhelmina A., "U.S. Housing Policy in 1996: The Outlook for Black Americans," 1996, pp. 188–218.

Morris, Eboni and Lisa Bland Malone, "Healthy Housing," 2009, pp. 87–98.

Richardson, Cy, "What Must Be Done: The Case for More Homeownership and Financial Education Counseling," 2009, pp. 145–155.

___ and Garrick Davis, "Rescue: The Case for Keeping Families in Their Homes by Confronting the Foreclosure Crisis," 2011, pp. 110–117.

Spriggs, William, "Nothing Trickled Down: Why Reaganomics Failed America," 2009. pp. 123–133.

Wilson, Valerie Rawlston, "Introduction to the 2011 Equality Index," 2011, pp. 14–22.

IN MEMORIAM
National Urban League, "William A. Bootle, Ray Charles, Margo T. Clarke, Ossie Davis, Herman C. Ewing, James Forman, Joanne Grant, Ann Kheel, Memphis Norman, Max Schmeling," 2005, pp. 139–152.

———, "Renaldo Benson, Shirley Chisholm, Johnnie Cochran, Jr., Shirley Horn, John H. Johnson, Vivian Malone Jones, Brock Peters, Richard Pryor, Bobby Short, C. Delores Tucker, August Wilson, Luther Vandross, and NUL members Clarence Lyle Barney, Jr., Manuel Augustus Romero;" 2006, pp. 279–287.

———, "Ossie Davis: Still Caught in the Dream," 2005, pp. 137–138.

———, "Ed Bradley, James Brown, Bebe Moore Campbell, Katherine Dunham, Mike Evans, Coretta Scott King, Gerald Levert, Gordon Parks, June Pointer, Lou Rawls, and Helen E. Harden," 2007, pp. 249–257.

———, "Effi Barry, Jane Bolin, Daniel A. Collins (NUL Member), Oliver Hill, Yolanda King, Calvin Lockhart, Mahlon Puryear (NUL Member), Max Roach, Eddie Robinson, William Simms (NUL Member), Darryl Stingley, and Ike Turner," 2008, pp. 205–217.

———, In Memoriam, 2009, pp. 225–241.

Jones, Stephanie J., "Rosa Parks: An Ordinary Woman, An Extraordinary Life," 2006, pp. 245–246.

MILITARY AFFAIRS
Braswell, Allie L., and James T. McLawhorn, Jr., "A Call to Advocate for America's Military Veterans," 2012, pp. 94–99.

Butler, John Sibley, "African Americans and the American Military," 2002, pp. 93–107.

MUSIC
Boles, Mark A., "Breaking the 'Hip Hop' Hold: Looking Beyond the Media Hype," 2007, pp. 239–241.

Brown, David W., "Their Characteristic Music: Thoughts on Rap Music and Hip-Hop Culture," 2001, pp. 189–201.

Bynoe, Yvonne, "The Roots of Rap Music and Hip-Hop Culture: One Perspective," 2001, pp. 175–187.

OP-ED/COMMENTARY
Archer, Dennis W., "Security Must Never Trump Liberty," 2004, pp. 139–142.

Bailey, Moya, "Going in Circles: The Struggle to Diversify Popular Images of Black Women," 2008, pp. 193–196.

Bernard, Michelle, "An Ode to Black America," 2009, pp. 203–207.

Boles, Mark A., "Breaking the 'Hip Hop' Hold: Looking Beyond the Media Hype," 2007, pp. 239–241.

Burnham, David, "The Fog of War," 2005, pp. 123–127.

Chappell, Kevin, " 'Realities' of Black America," 2011, pp. 192–195.

Cooke, Cassye, "The Game Changer: Are We Beyond What is Next to What is Now?," 2009, pp. 209–212.

Covington, Kenya L., "The Transformation of the Welfare Caseload," 2004, pp. 149–152.

Dyson, Eric Michael, "Sexual Fault Lines: Robbing the Love Between Us," 2007, pp. 229–237.

Edelman, Marian Wright, "Losing Our Children in America's Cradle to Prison Pipeline," 2007, pp. 219–227.

Emerson, Melinda F., "Five Things You Must Have to Run a Successful Business," 2004, pp. 153–156.

Ivory, Steven, "Universal Fatherhood: Black Men Sharing the Load," 2007, pp. 243–247.

Jones, Nathaniel R., "Did I Ever? Yes I Did," 2009, pp. 213–219.

Journal of Blacks in Higher Education (reprint), "The 'Acting White' Myth," 2005, pp. 115–117.

Lanier, James R., "The Empowerment Movement and the Black Male," 2004, pp. 143–148.

Lee, Barbara, "President Obama and the CBC: Speaking with One Voice," 2009, pp. 193–197.

Lindsay, Tiffany, "Weaving the Fabric: the Political Activism of Young African-American Women," 2008, pp. 187–192.

Malveaux, Julianne, "Black Women's Hands Can Rock the World: Global Involvement and Understanding," 2008, pp. 197–202.

Rivlin, Alice M., "Pay Now or Pay Later: Jobs, Fiscal Responsibility and the Future of Black America," 2011, pp. 202–206.

Ross, Ronald O., "Gaps, Traps and Lies: African-American Students and Test Scores," 2004, pp. 157–161.

Taylor, Susan L., "Black Love Under Siege," 2008 pp. 179–186.

Taylor, Robert D., "Wealth Creation: The Next Leadership Challenge," 2005, pp. 119–122.

West, Cornel, "Democracy Matters," 2005, pp. 129–132.

Wijewardena, Madura and Kirk Clay, "Government with the Consent of All: Redistricting Strategies for Civil Rights Organizations," 2011, pp. 196–201.

Wilkins, Ray, "Jobs, the Internet, and Our Exciting Future," 2011, pp. 94–99.

OVERVIEW

Morial, Marc H., "Black America's Family Matters," 2003, pp. 9–12.

Price, Hugh B., "Still Worth Fighting For: America After 9/11," 2002, pp. 9–11.

POLITICS

Alton, Kimberley, "The State of Civil Rights 2008," 2008, pp. 157–161.

Brazile, Donna, "Fallout from the Mid-term Elections: Making the Most of the Next Two Years," 2011, pp. 180–190.

Campbell, Melanie L., "Election Reform: Protecting Our Vote from the Enemy Who Never Sleeps," 2008, pp. 149–156.

Coleman, Henry A., "Interagency and Intergovernmental Coordination: New Demands for Domestic Policy Initiatives," 1992, pp. 249–263.

Hamilton, Charles V., "On Parity and Political Empowerment," 1989, pp. 111–120.

———, "Promoting Priorities: African-American Political Influence in the 1990s," 1993, pp. 59–69.

Henderson, Lenneal J., "Budgets, Taxes, and Politics: Options for the African-American Community," 1991, pp. 77–93.

Holden, Matthew, Jr., "The Rewards of Daring and the Ambiguity of Power: Perspectives on the Wilder Election of 1989," 1990, pp. 109–120.

Kilson, Martin L., "African Americans and American Politics 2002: The Maturation Phase," 2002, pp. 147–180.

———, "Thinking About the Black Elite's Role: Yesterday and Today," 2005, pp. 85–106.

Lee, Silas, "Who's Going to Take the Weight? African Americans and Civic Engagement in the 21st Century," 2007, pp. 185–192.

Lindsay, Tiffany, "Weaving the Fabric: The Political Activism of Young African-American Women," 2008, pp. 187–192.

McHenry, Donald F., "A Changing World Order: Implications for Black America," 1991, pp. 155–163.

Persons, Georgia A., "Blacks in State and Local Government: Progress and Constraints," 1987, pp. 167–192.

Pinderhughes, Dianne M., "Power and Progress: African-American Politics in the New Era of Diversity," 1992, pp. 265–280.

———, "The Renewal of the Voting Rights Act," 2005, pp. 49–61.

———, "Civil Rights and the Future of the American Presidency," 1988, pp. 39–60.

Price, Hugh B., "Black America's Challenge: The Re-construction of Black Civil Society," 2001, pp. 13–18.

Rivlin, Alice M., "Pay Now or Pay Later: Jobs, Fiscal Responsibility and the Future of Black America," 2011, pp. 202–206.

Scott, Robert C. "Bobby," "Minority Voter Participation: Reviewing Past and Present Barriers to the Polls," 2012, pp. 44–47.

Tidwell, Billy J., "Serving the National Interest: A Marshall Plan for America," 1992, pp. 11–30.

West, Cornel, "Democracy Matters," 2005, pp. 129–132.

Wijewardena, Madura and Kirk Clay, "Government with the Consent of All: Redistricting Strategies for Civil Rights Organizations," 2011, pp. 196–201.

Williams, Eddie N., "The Evolution of Black Political Power", 2000, pp. 91–102.

Yearwood, Lennox, Jr., "The Rise and Fall and Rise Again of Jim Crow Laws," 2012, pp. 48–53.

POVERTY

Cooper, Maudine R., "The Invisibility Blues' of Black Women in America," 2008, pp. 83–87.

Edelman, Marian Wright, "The State of Our Children," 2006, pp. 133–141.

PRESCRIPTIONS FOR CHANGE

National Urban League, "Prescriptions for Change," 2005, pp. 133–135.

RELATIONSHIPS

Taylor, Susan L., "Black Love Under Siege," 2008, pp. 179–186.

RELIGION

Lincoln, C. Eric, "Knowing the Black Church: What It Is and Why," 1989, pp. 137–149.

Richardson, W. Franklyn, "Mission to Mandate: Self-Development through the Black Church," 1994, pp. 113–126.

Smith, Dr. Drew, "The Evolving Political Priorities of African-American Churches: An Empirical View," 2000, pp. 171–197.

Taylor, Mark V.C., "Young Adults and Religion," 2001, pp. 161–174.

REPORTS FROM THE NATIONAL URBAN LEAGUE
Hanson, Renee, Mark McArdle, and Valerie Rawlston Wilson, "Invisible Men: The Urgent Problems of Low-Income African-American Males," 2007, pp. 209–216.

Hardy, Chanelle P., Dr. Valerie Rawlston Wilson, Madura Wijewardena, and Garrick T. Davis, "At Risk: The State of the Black Middle Class," 2012, pp. 74–83.

Lanier, James, "The National Urban League's Commission on the Black Male: Renewal, Revival and Resurrection Feasibility and Strategic Planning Study," 2005, pp. 107–109.

Jones, Stephanie J., "Sunday Morning Apartheid: A Diversity Study of the Sunday Morning Talk Shows" 2006, pp. 189–228.

National Urban League, "12 Point Urban Jobs Plan," 2011, pp. 46–52.

National Urban League Council of Economic Advisors, Bernard E. Anderson, William M. Rodgers III, Lucy J. Reuben, and Valerie Rawlston Wilson, "The New Normal? Opportunities for Prosperity in a 'Jobless Recovery,'" 2011, pp. 54–63.

National Urban League Policy Institute, The Opportunity Compact: A Blueprint for Economic Equality, 2008, pp. 43–74.

———, "Putting Americans Back to Work: The National Urban League's Plan for Creating Jobs" 2010, pp. 40–44.

———, "African Americans and the Green Revolution" 2010, pp. 46–59.

———, "Where Do We Go From Here? Projected Employment Growth Industries and Occupations," 2011, pp. 64–75.

———, "The 2012 National Urban League 8-Point Education and Employment Plan: Employment and Education Empower the Nation" 2012, pp. 54–59.

———, "The National Urban League Introduces New Reports on the State of Urban Business" 2012, pp. 64–69.

REPORTS
Joint Center for Political and Economic Studies, A Way Out: Creating Partners for Our Nation's Prosperity by Expanding Life Paths for Young Men of Color—Final Report of the Dellums Commission, 2007, pp. 193–207.

Reed, James and Aaron Thomas, The National Urban League: Empowering Black Males to Meet Their Full Potential, 2007, pp. 217–218.

Wilson, Valerie Rawlston, "Introduction to the 2011 Equality Index," 2011, pp. 14–22.

SEXUAL IDENTITY
Bailey, Moya, "Going in Circles: The Struggle to Diversify Popular Images of Black Women," 2008 pp.193–196.

Battle, Juan, Cathy J. Cohen, Angelique Harris, and Beth E. Richie, "We Are Family: Embracing Our Lesbian, Gay, Bisexual, and Transgender (LGBT) Family Members," 2003, pp. 93–106.

Taylor, Susan L., "Black Love Under Siege," 2008, pp. 179–186.

SOCIOLOGY
Cooper, Maudine R., "The Invisibility Blues' of Black Women in America," 2008, pp. 83–87.

Taylor, Susan L., "Black Love Under Siege," 2008, pp. 179–186.

Teele, James E., "E. Franklin Frazier: The Man and His Intellectual Legacy," 2003, pp. 29–40.

SPECIAL SECTION: BLACK WOMEN'S HEALTH
Browne, Doris, "The Impact of Health Disparities in African-American Women," 2008, pp. 163–171.

Morris, Eboni D., "By the Numbers: Uninsured African-American Women," 2008, pp. 173–177.

SPECIAL SECTION: KATRINA AND BEYOND
Brazile, Donna L., "New Orleans: Next Steps on the Road to Recovery," 2006, pp. 233–237.

Morial, Marc H., "New Orleans Revisited," 2006, pp. 229–232.

National Urban League, "The National Urban League Katrina Bill of Rights," 2006, pp. 239–243.

SURVEYS
The National Urban League Survey, 2004, pp. 35–51.

Stafford, Walter S., "The National Urban League Survey: Black America's Under-35 Generation," 2001, pp. 19–63.

———, "The New York Urban League Survey: Black New York—On Edge, But Optimistic," 2001, pp. 203–219.

TECHNOLOGY
Dreyfuss, Joel, "Black Americans and the Internet: The Technological Imperative," 2001, pp. 131–141.

Patrick, Deval L., "Growing an Innovative Economy in Massachusetts," 2011, pp. 154–158.

Ramsey, Rey, "Broadband Matters to All of Us," 2010, pp. 112–116.

Ribeau, Sidney, "A Competitive Foundation for the Future," 2011, pp. 8–9.

Wilkins, Ray, "Jobs, the Internet, and Our Exciting Future," 2011, pp. 94–99.

Wilson Ernest J., III, "Technological Convergence, Media Ownership and Content Diversity," 2000, pp. 147–170.

URBAN AFFAIRS

Allen, Antoine, and Leland Ware, "The Geography of Discrimination: Hypersegregation, Isolation and Fragmentation Within the African-American Community," 2002, pp. 69–92.

Bates, Timothy, "The Paradox of Urban Poverty," 1996, pp. 144–163.

Bell, Carl C., with Esther J. Jenkins, "Preventing Black Homicide," 1990, pp. 143–155.

Bryant Solomon, Barbara, "Social Welfare Reform," 1987, pp. 113–127.

Brown, Lee P., "Crime in the Black Community," 1988, pp. 95–113.

Bullard, Robert D. "Urban Infrastructure: Social, Environmental, and Health Risks to African Americans," 1992, pp. 183–196.

Chambers, Julius L., "The Law and Black Americans: Retreat from Civil Rights," 1987, pp. 15–30.

———, "Black Americans and the Courts: Has the Clock Been Turned Back Permanently?" 1990, pp. 9–24.

Edelin, Ramona H., "Toward an African-American Agenda: An Inward Look," 1990, pp. 173–183.

Fair, T. Willard, "Coordinated Community Empowerment: Experiences of the Urban League of Greater Miami," 1993, pp. 217–233.

Gray, Sandra T., "Public-Private Partnerships: Prospects for America… Promise for African Americans," 1992, pp. 231–247.

Harris, David, "'Driving While Black' and Other African-American Crimes: The Continuing Relevance of Race to American Criminal Justice," 2000, pp. 259–285.

Henderson, Lenneal J., "African Americans in the Urban Milieu: Conditions, Trends, and Development Needs," 1994, pp. 11–29.

Hill, Robert B., "Urban Redevelopment: Developing Effective Targeting Strategies," 1992, pp. 197–211.

Johnston, Haile, and Tatiana Garcia-Granados, "Common Market: The New Black Farmer," 2012, pp. 100–105.

Jones, Dionne J., with Greg Harrison of the National Urban League Research Department, "Fast Facts: Comparative Views of African-American Status and Progress," 1994, pp. 213–236.

Jones, Shirley J., "Silent Suffering: The Plight of Rural Black America,"1994, pp. 171–188.

Massey, Walter E. "Science, Technology, and Human Resources: Preparing for the 21st Century," 1992, pp. 157–169.

Mendez, Garry A., Jr., "Crime Is Not a Part of Our Black Heritage: A Theoretical Essay," 1988, pp. 211–216.

Miller, Warren F., Jr., "Developing Untapped Talent: A National Call for African-American Technologists," 1991, pp. 111–127.

Murray, Sylvester, "Clear and Present Danger: The Decay of America's Physical Infrastructure," 1992, pp. 171–182.

Pemberton, Gayle, "It's the Thing That Counts, Or Reflections on the Legacy of W.E.B. Du Bois," 1991, pp. 129–143.

Pinderhughes, Dianne M., "The Case of African-Americans in the Persian Gulf: The Intersection of American Foreign and Military Policy with Domestic Employment Policy in the United States," 1991, pp. 165–186.

Robinson, Gene S. "Television Advertising and Its Impact on Black America," 1990, pp. 157–171.

Sawyers, Dr. Andrew and Dr. Lenneal Henderson, "Race, Space and Justice: Cities and Growth in the 21st Century," 2000, pp. 243–258.

Schneider, Alvin J., "Blacks in the Military: The Victory and the Challenge," 1988, pp. 115–128.

Smedley, Brian, "Race, Poverty, and Healthcare Disparities," 2006, pp. 155–164.

Stafford, Walter, Angela Dews, Melissa Mendez, and Diana Salas, "Race, Gender and Welfare Reform: The Need for Targeted Support," 2003, pp. 41–92.

Stewart, James B., "Developing Black and Latino Survival Strategies: The Future of Urban Areas," 1996, pp. 164–187.

Stone, Christopher E., "Crime and Justice in Black America," 1996, pp. 78–94.

Tidwell, Billy J., with Monica B. Kuumba, Dionne J. Jones, and Betty C. Watson, "Fast Facts: African Americans in the 1990s," 1993, pp. 243–265.

Wallace-Benjamin, Joan, "Organizing African-American Self-Development: The Role of Community-Based Organizations," 1994, pp. 189–205.

Walters, Ronald, "Serving the People: African-American Leadership and the Challenge of Empowerment," 1994, pp. 153–170.

Allen, Antoine, and Leland Ware, "The Geography of Discrimination: Hypersegregation, Isolation and Fragmentation within the African-American Community," 2002, pp. 69–92.

Wiley, Maya, "Hurricane Katrina Exposed the Face of Poverty," 2006, pp. 143–153.

WELFARE

Bergeron, Suzanne, and William E. Spriggs, "Welfare Reform and Black America," 2002, pp. 29–50.

Cooper, Maudine R., "The Invisibility Blues' of Black Women in America," 2008, pp. 83–87.

Covington, Kenya L., "The Transformation of the Welfare Caseload," 2004, pp. 149–152.

Spriggs, William E., and Suzanne Bergeron, "Welfare Reform and Black America," 2002, pp. 29–50.

Stafford, Walter, Angela Dews, Melissa Mendez, and Diana Salas, "Race, Gender and Welfare Reform: The Need for Targeted Support," 2003, pp. 41–92.

WOMEN'S ISSUES

Bailey, Moya, "Going in Circles: The Struggle to Diversify Popular Images of Black Women," 2008, pp. 193–196.

Browne, Doris, "The Impact of Health Disparities in African-American Women," 2008, pp. 163–171.

Cooper, Maudine R., "The Invisibility Blues' of Black Women in America," 2008, pp. 83–87.

★ ★ ★ ★ ★ ★ ★ ★ ★ ★ ★ ★ ★ ★ ★ ★

Harris, Andrea, "The Subprime Wipeout: Unsustainable Loans Erase Gains Made by African-American Women," 2008, pp. 125–133.

Herman, Alexis, "African-American Women and Work: Still a Tale of Two Cities," 2008, pp. 109–113.

Lindsay, Tiffany, "Weaving the Fabric: The Political Activism of Young African-American Women," 2008, pp. 187–192.

Malveaux, Julianne, "Black Women's Hands Can Rock the World: Global Involvement and Understanding," 2008, pp. 197–202.

———, "Shouldering the Third Burden: The Status of African-American Women," 2008, pp. 75–81.

Mensah, Lisa, "Putting Homeownership Back Within Our Reach," 2008, pp. 135–142.

Morris, Eboni D., "By the Numbers: Uninsured African-American Women," 2008, pp. 173–177.

Reuben, Lucy J., "Make Room for the New 'She'EOs: An Analysis of Businesses Owned by Black Females," 2008, pp. 115–124.

Stafford, Walter, Angela Dews, Melissa Mendez, and Diana Salas, "Race, Gender and Welfare Reform: The Need for Targeted Support," 2003, pp. 41–92.

Taylor, Susan L., "Black Love Under Siege," 2008, pp. 179–186.

West, Carolyn M., "Feminism is a Black Thing?": Feminist Contribution to Black Family Life, 2003, pp. 13–27.

WORLD AFFAIRS

Malveaux, Julianne, "Black Women's Hands Can Rock the World: Global Involvement and Understanding," 2008, pp. 197–202.

NATIONAL URBAN LEAGUE

EXECUTIVE STAFF

EXECUTIVE TEAM

President & CEO
Marc H. Morial

Senior Vice President
Marketing & Communications
Rhonda Spears Bell

Senior Vice President
Programs
Donald E. Bowen

Senior Vice President & Executive Director
Policy Institute
Chanelle P. Hardy, Esq.

Senior Vice President & Chief Talent Officer
Human Resources
Wanda H. Jackson

Senior Vice President
Affiliate Services
Herman L. Lessard, Jr.

Senior Vice President
Strategy, Innovation & Technology
Michael E. Miller

Senior Vice President
Development
Dennis Serrette

Senior Vice President
Finance & Operations
Paul Wycisk

POLICY INSTITUTE STAFF

Senior Vice President & Executive Director
Chanelle P. Hardy, Esq.

Vice President, Research
Valerie Rawlston Wilson, Ph.D.

Vice President, Communication & External Relations
Pamela Rucker Springs

Senior Legislative Director,
Workforce, Civil Rights & Social Services
Suzanne M. Bergeron

Legislative Director, Education & Health Policy
Jacqueline Ayers

Legislative Director, Financial & Economic Policy
Garrick T. Davis

Director, Research & Policy
Madura Wijewardena

Senior Director, Operations & Chief of Staff
Cara M. McKinley

Special Assistant to the Executive Director
Sarah Parker

Associate
Iman Aziz

Broadband and Technology Fellow
Patric Taylor

SOBA Project Manager
Hazeen Y. Ashby

Policy Intern
Halima Adenegan

ROSTER OF NATIONAL URBAN LEAGUE
AFFILIATES

AKRON, OHIO
Akron Community Service Center
and Urban League

ALEXANDRIA, VIRGINIA
Northern Virginia Urban League

ANCHORAGE, ALASKA
Urban League of Anchorage-Alaska

ALTON, ILLINOIS
Madison County Urban League

ANDERSON, INDIANA
Urban League of Madison County, Inc.

ATLANTA, GEORGIA
Atlanta Urban League

AURORA, ILLINOIS
Quad County Urban League

AUSTIN, TEXAS
Austin Area Urban League

BALTIMORE, MARYLAND
Greater Baltimore Urban League

BATTLE CREEK, MICHIGAN
Southwestern Michigan Urban League

BINGHAMTON, NEW YORK
Broome County Urban League

BIRMINGHAM, ALABAMA
Birmingham Urban League

BOSTON, MASSACHUSETTS
Urban League of Eastern Massachusetts

BUFFALO, NEW YORK
Buffalo Urban League

CANTON, OHIO
Greater Stark County
Urban League, Inc.

CHARLESTON, SOUTH CAROLINA
Charleston Trident Urban League

CHARLOTTE, NORTH CAROLINA
Urban League of Central Carolinas, Inc.

CHATTANOOGA, TENNESSEE
Urban League Greater
Chattanooga, Inc.

CHICAGO, ILLINOIS
Chicago Urban League

CINCINNATI, OHIO
Urban League of Greater Cincinnati

CLEVELAND, OHIO
Urban League of Greater Cleveland

COLORADO SPRINGS, COLORADO
Urban League of Pikes Peak Region

COLUMBIA, SOUTH CAROLINA
Columbia Urban League

COLUMBUS, GEORGIA
Urban League of Greater Columbus, Inc.

COLUMBUS, OHIO
Columbus Urban League

DALLAS, TEXAS
Urban League of Greater Dallas and
North Central Texas

DAYTON, OHIO
Dayton Urban League

DENVER, COLORADO
Urban League of Metropolitan Denver

DETROIT, MICHIGAN
Urban League of Detroit
and Southeastern Michigan

ELIZABETH, NEW JERSEY
Urban League of Union County

ELYRIA, OHIO
Lorain County Urban League

ENGLEWOOD, NEW JERSEY
Urban League for Bergen County

FARRELL, PENNSYLVANIA
Urban League of Shenango Valley

FLINT, MICHIGAN
Urban League of Flint

FORT LAUDERDALE, FLORIDA
Urban League of Broward County

FORT WAYNE, INDIANA
Fort Wayne Urban League

GARY, INDIANA
Urban League of
Northwest Indiana, Inc.

GRAND RAPIDS, MICHIGAN
Grand Rapids Urban League

GREENVILLE, SOUTH CAROLINA
Urban League of the Upstate, Inc.

HARTFORD, CONNECTICUT
Urban League of Greater Hartford

HOUSTON, TEXAS
Houston Area Urban League

INDIANAPOLIS, INDIANA
Indianapolis Urban League

JACKSON, MISSISSIPPI
Urban League of Greater Jackson

JACKSONVILLE, FLORIDA
Jacksonville Urban League

JERSEY CITY, NEW JERSEY
Urban League of Hudson County

KANSAS CITY, MISSOURI
Urban League of Kansas City

KNOXVILLE, TENNESSEE
Knoxville Area Urban League

LANCASTER, PENNSYLVANIA
Urban League of Lancaster County

LAS VEGAS, NEVADA
Las Vegas-Clark County
Urban League

LEXINGTON, KENTUCKY
Urban League of Lexington-
Fayette County

LONG ISLAND, NEW YORK
Urban League of Long Island

LOS ANGELES, CALIFORNIA
Los Angeles Urban League

LOUISVILLE, KENTUCKY
Louisville Urban League

MADISON, WISCONSIN
Urban League of Greater Madison

MEMPHIS, TENNESSEE
Memphis Urban League

MIAMI, FLORIDA
Urban League of Greater Miami

MILWAUKEE, WISCONSIN
Milwaukee Urban League

MINNEAPOLIS, MINNESOTA
Minneapolis Urban League

MORRISTOWN, NEW JERSEY
Morris County Urban League

MUSKEGON, MICHIGAN
Urban League of Greater Muskegon

NASHVILLE, TENNESSEE
Urban League of Middle Tennessee

NEW ORLEANS, LOUISIANA
Urban League of Greater New Orleans

NEW YORK, NEW YORK
New York Urban League

NEWARK, NEW JERSEY
Urban League of Essex County

NORFOLK, VIRGINIA
Urban League of Hampton Roads

OKLAHOMA CITY,
OKLAHOMA
Urban League of Oklahoma City

OMAHA, NEBRASKA
Urban League of Nebraska, Inc.

ORLANDO, FLORIDA
Central Florida Urban League

PEORIA, ILLINOIS
Tri-County Urban League

PHILADELPHIA,
PENNSYLVANIA
Urban League of Philadelphia

PHOENIX, ARIZONA
Greater Phoenix Urban League

PITTSBURGH, PENNSYLVANIA
Urban League of Greater Pittsburgh

PORTLAND, OREGON
Urban League of Portland

PROVIDENCE, RHODE ISLAND
Urban League of Rhode Island

RACINE, WISCONSIN
Urban League of Racine & Kenosha,Inc.

RICHMOND, VIRGINIA
Urban League of Greater Richmond, Inc.

ROCHESTER, NEW YORK
Urban League of Rochester

SACRAMENTO, CALIFORNIA
Greater Sacramento Urban League

SAINT LOUIS, MISSOURI
Urban League Metropolitan St. Louis

SAINT PAUL, MINNESOTA
St. Paul Urban League

SAINT PETERSBURG, FLORIDA
Pinellas County Urban League

SAN DIEGO, CALIFORNIA
Urban League of San Diego County

SEATTLE, WASHINGTON
Urban League of Metropolitan Seattle

SPRINGFIELD, ILLINOIS
Springfield Urban League, Inc.

SPRINGFIELD,
MASSACHUSETTS
Urban League of Springfield

STAMFORD, CONNECTICUT
Urban League of Southern Connecticut

TACOMA, WASHINGTON
Tacoma Urban League

TALLAHASSEE, FLORDIA
Tallahassee Urban League

TOLEDO, OHIO
Greater Toledo Urban League

TUCSON, ARIZONA
Tucson Urban League

TULSA, OKLAHOMA
Metropolitan Tulsa Urban League

WARREN, OHIO
Greater Warren-Youngstown
Urban League

WASHINGTON, D.C.
Greater Washington Urban League

WEST PALM BEACH, FLORIDA
Urban League of Palm Beach
County, Inc.

WHITE PLAINS, NEW YORK
Urban League of Westchester County

WICHITA, KANSAS
Urban League of Kansas, Inc.

WILMINGTON, DELAWARE
Metropolitan Wilmington Urban League

WINSTON-SALEM,
NORTH CAROLINA
Winston-Salem Urban League

We must fight voter suppression, we must educate citizens so that new laws won't catch them unaware on Election Day, and we must empower them to get to the polls.

~ *Marc H. Morial*

★ ★ ★ ★ ★ ★ ★ ★ ★ ★ ★ ★ ★ ★ ★ ★ ★ ★

OCCUPY

★ THE ★

VOTE

Ⓣⓞ

EDUCATE, EMPLOY & EMPOWER

★ ★ ★ ★ ★ ★ ★ ★ ★ ★ ★ ★ ★ ★ ★ ★ ★

VISIT

IAMEMPOWERED.COM